Everard Hamilton

The Parish of Taney

A History of Dundrum, near Dublin, and its Neighbourhood

Everard Hamilton

The Parish of Taney
A History of Dundrum, near Dublin, and its Neighbourhood

ISBN/EAN: 9783743400771

Manufactured in Europe, USA, Canada, Australia, Japa

Cover: Foto ©Andreas Hilbeck / pixelio.de

Manufactured and distributed by brebook publishing software (www.brebook.com)

Everard Hamilton

The Parish of Taney

THE PARISH OF TANEY:

A HISTORY OF DUNDRUM,

NEAR DUBLIN,

AND ITS NEIGHBOURHOOD.

BY

FRANCIS ELRINGTON BALL

AND

EVERARD HAMILTON, B.A., Univ. of Dub.,

Member Royal Society of Antiquaries of Ireland

DUBLIN:

HODGES, FIGGIS, & CO., Ltd., GRAFTON ST.,

PUBLISHERS TO THE UNIVERSITY.

———

1895.

PREFACE.

In placing this little work before the public, the authors desire to acknowledge the valuable assistance they have received from the following amongst other friends.

The Rev. Canon Stokes, D.D., the learned author of *Ireland and the Celtic Church*, and *Ireland and the Anglo-Norman Church*, &c., &c., has very kindly revised the chapter upon the Antiquities of the Parish, and supplied the materials for interesting notes.

The Rev. William Reynell, B.D., M.R.I.A., placed his ample knowledge of the clergy of the Diocese of Dublin at their disposal, besides furnishing many particulars for the biographical portions of the work.

To John H. Samuels, Esq., the Diocesan Registrar, they desire to return thanks for his unvarying courtesy in affording access to such of the Diocesan Records as remain in his custody.

They are also indebted to J. J. Digges La Touche, Esq., LL.D., Deputy Keeper of the Records, and the other officials in the Record Office, as well as to the officials of the Library and Registrar's Office of Trinity College and of the National Library, Kildare Street.

September, 1895.

CONTENTS.

ABBREVIATIONS.

—•◦•—

T. C.	=	Taney Church.
T. G.	=	Taney Graveyard.
B. L. G.	=	Burke's Landed Gentry.
B. P.	=	Burke's Peerage.
B. E. P.	=	Burke's Extinct Peerage.
T. C. D.	=	Trinity College, Dublin.
H. O.	=	Holy Orders.
a.	=	aged.
b.	=	born.
m.	=	married.
unm.	=	unmarried.
d.	=	died or dead.
d. s. p. *o. s. p.* }	=	died or dead without issue.
bapt.	=	baptized.
dau.	=	daughter.
bur.	=	buried.
c.	=	called.
q. v.	=	whom see or which see.

THE PARISH OF TANEY.

CHAPTER I.

INTRODUCTION.

THE Parish of Taney comprises a district extending from the top of the Three Rock Mountain to near the sea-shore at Merrion ; it is 5½ miles long from N. to S., and 2¼ miles broad from E. to W. It contains seventeen townlands, covering 4,569A. 3R. 14P. Statute measure, of which all but 6A. 0R. 17P. are in the Half Barony of Rathdown.* This small portion, which forms part of the townland of Roebuck, lies in the Barony of Dublin.

The following are the townlands :—

		A.	R.	P.
1. Balally	... ...	834	2	5
2. Ballinteer	... ...	282	1	24
3. Churchtown, Lower	... ...	180	2	0
4. Churchtown, Upper	... ...	221	0	7

* D'Alton (*History of Co. Dublin*, p. 807) states the entire Barony of Rathdown was originally in the County of Dublin ; but when Wicklow was made into a separate county, the Barony was divided into two parts : that part of it lying to the south of Bray River being comprised in the County of Wicklow, and the remainder in the County of Dublin.

B

				A.	R.	P.
5.	Drummartin	...	...	... 188	2	0
6.	Dundrum	...	...	... 317	2	38
7.	Farranboley	...	...	... 150	3	7
8.	Friarland	...	...	... 39	2	9
9.	Kingstown	...	...	... 194	2	1
10.	Mount Anville...	...	...	... 89	0	26
11.	Mountmerrion or Callary	...		... 376	2	27
12.	Mountmerrion, South	...	...	4	2	25
13.	Rathmines, Great	...	...	88	2	15
14.	Rathmines, Little	...	...	68	3	25
15.	Roebuck	...	...	... 822	2	17
16.	Tiknock	...	...	... 634	1	29
17.	Trimleston or Owenstown		...	75	0	39
				4,569	3	14

The parish is bounded on the east by the parishes
of Booterstown, Stillorgan, Kilmacud, Tullow, and
Kilgobbin; on the west by Rathfarnham and Whitechurch; and on the north by St. Peter's and
Donnybrook. A small portion of the parish touched
the sea-shore at Merrion, but was transferred to the
parish of Booterstown in May, 1877.

The following is a statement of the population
and number of houses, taken from the Census
returns :—

YEARS.	1841.	1851.	1861.	1871.	1881.	1891.
Population	3,848	3,929	4,208	4,310	4,491	4,669
No. of Houses	680	722	766	790	809	856

The parish is a Rectory, which from the time of Archbishop Luke of Dublin (1228-1255) was attached to the Archdeaconry of Dublin, in support of that dignity, and the Archdeacon continued Rector down to the year 1851, when, on the death of Archdeacon Torrens, by an order of the Lord Lieutenant in Council,* the parish was separated from the Archdeaconry.

It is not thought necessary in the following pages to give the succession of the Archdeacons of Dublin, which will be found, with full biographical notes, in Mason's *History of St. Patrick's*, and in Cotton's *Fasti Ecclesiæ Hibernicæ*. So far as is possible, the succession of their curates who have had charge of the parish is given; but owing to the diocesan records not being at present accessible, it is very incomplete until the end of the eighteenth century, when the parish records† begin. Before that time the parish only enjoyed the ministrations of curates who had other churches to serve in the Archdeacon's corps.

In the chapter upon the antiquities of the parish will be found an account of the ancient Deanery of Taney; the modern rural deanery is of much smaller extent. In 1802 the latter comprised the parishes of Taney, Kilgobbin, Rathfarnham, Stillorgan, Crumlin, and Tallaght; and its contents are still the same, with the addition of the parishes of Whitechurch, Kilternan, Zion Church Rathgar,

* Appendix A.   † Appendix B.

and Milltown, and including the chapel of ease, Taney, and the chapels of St. Columba's College, of the Mageough Home, and of the Central Asylum, Dundrum.

It will be noticed that the name of the parish is spelled in many different ways in the following pages; the rule which has been observed is, when quoting from any document, to follow the peculiar spelling found in it. This observation also applies to the names of the other places mentioned.

CHAPTER II.

THE Parish of Taney, as an ecclesiastical establishment, has survived the vicissitudes of many centuries; and there seems little room for doubt, although we cannot point to a noble edifice erected by the master-builders of the middle ages, that the worship of God has been conducted in this place since before the English conquest of Ireland in 1172.

But the parish seems not to have been the earliest ecclesiastical establishment to which the name of Taney was attached.

When Cardinal Paparo visited Ireland in 1152, he found, it is said, that Taney was one of the rural sees, or chorepiscopates, which then existed, and which were taken as the extent of the jurisdiction of the Archpresbyters-rural, who supplanted rural bishops, and who were the predecessors of our present Rural Deans.*

There is no doubt that the Rural Deanery of Taney was of great extent in ancient times.

About 1294, there was a new taxation of the Diocese of Dublin for the Pope, and the total sum

---

* Dansey's *Horae Decanicæ Rurales*, vol. ii., pp. 516, 517.

raised in the Diocese was £707 11s., a very large amount in those days.

In this taxation we find the Deanery of "Tanhy" mentioned, and the following places, &c., included in it :—Church of Coulok (Coolock) ; Chapel of Isolde's Town (Chapelizod), where "the Hospitallers are rectors;" the tithes of the monks of Clonschilagh (Clonsilla) ; Church of Leucane (Lucan) ["Monastery of St. Thomas"] ; Church of Balithermot (Ballyfarmot), where "the Hospitallers are rectors;" Church of Kylmahud (Kilmacud) ; Temporality of the Prior of St. Catherine (St. Catherine's, near Leixlip) ; Church of Kylmatalwey (Kilmactalway); Chapel of Kynturk, "Temporality of All Saints' there ; " Temporality of the Monks at Kylmatalwey; the Prioress of Lesmolyn at Clonschilagh (Clonsilla) ; Dunsenk (Dunsink) and Belegrene (Belgree, Co. Meath ?) ; the Prior of St. John of Dublin at Palmerstown ; the Prior of All Saints' at Ballycollay ; the monks at Kylmacodrek (Kilmacudrick) ; Ballykegh, "nothing, on account of the war ;" the monks at Coulmyne (Coolmine, in the Parish of Saggard) and Clonlyff; Cloghranhydryt (Cloghran, near Hiddart), and Aderk. The total sum for the Deanery of "Tanhy" came to £60 13s. 4d.

It is to be observed that neither the Church of Taney, nor its Chapelries of Donnybrook, Rathfarnham, and Kilgobbin, are mentioned ; this may be accounted for by the fact that these formed part of the corps of the Archdeacon of Dublin, and that he paid £10 as the tax upon his dignity as archdeacon. The Vicarage of Tauelaghte (Tallaght), which is still in the Rural Deanery of Taney, was included among " the dignities and prebends of the Church of St. Patrick, Dublin, with their vicarages;" but it paid nothing, " on account of war."[*]

From the learned paper of Mr. James Mills upon *The Norman Settlement in Leinster*,[†] we find that " when King Henry granted Leinster to Strongbow—certainly when King John confirmed it to the Earl Marshal—he excepted from the grant the two cantreds[‡] nearest to Dublin," and that " further west (from Carrickbrenan) was Dundrum, held soon after the Conquest by Hugh de Clahull. Northwards lay Tacheny, now Churchtown. The name is preserved in the parish name Taney. This was held by John de Clahull, who was Marshal of the Lordship of Leinster, and had also extensive lands near Carlow, and subsequently in Kerry, where his family seems to have settled. De Clahull gave all his land of Thacney to the Archbishop of Dublin. (*Liber Niger Alani*, fol. 108.) Rabo (now Roebuck) is north-east of Tacheny. It was held at first by Thomas de St.

---

[*] *Vide* Calendar to Christ Church Deeds, in the 20th Report of the Deputy Keeper of Records in Ireland, pp. 60, 61.

[†] *Journal of Royal Society of Antiquaries of Ireland*, 1894, pp. 161, 167.

[‡] A cantred was a division of a county corresponding to a " hundred " in England.

Michael, and given by John, the king's son, to Thomas's brother, Robert de St. Michael. By the middle of the thirteenth century it had become the property of a branch of the great Norman family of Basset. A charter from David Basset to Fromund le Brun, of the whole manor of Rabo, for ever, is entered on the Pipe Roll of 46 Hen. III. It is printed in *Irish Record Com. Reports*, vol. i., p. 336."

In the period immediately after the Norman Settlement was constructed the barrier, known as the " Pale," separating the lands occupied by the settlers from those remaining in the hands of the Irish. This barrier consisted of a ditch, raised some ten or twelve feet from the ground, with a hedge of thorn on the outer side. It was constructed, not so much to keep out the Irish, as to form an obstacle in their way in their raids on the cattle of the settlers, and thus give time for a rescue.

The Pale began at Dalkey, and followed a south-westerly direction towards Kilternan; then turning northwards passed Kilgobbin, where a castle still stands, and crossed the Parish of Taney to the south of that part of the lands of Balally now called Moreen,* and thence in a westerly direction to Tallaght, and on to Naas in the County of Kildare.† In the wall bounding Moreen is still to

---

* Now the residence of Major Lenox Mac Farlane, and formerly of the M'Kay family. *Vide* M'Kay, chapter vii.

† A portion of the Pale is still to be seen in Kildare between Clane and Clongowes Wood College at Sallins.

be seen a small watch-tower and the remains of a guard-house adjoining it. From this point a beacon-fire would raise the alarm as far as Tallaght, where an important castle stood.*

The earliest mention of the parish is to be found in 1179, when Pope Alexander III. confirmed to Archbishop Laurence O'Toole "the middle place of Tignai with its church." The Papal Bull which deals with Taney, among the other places in the diocese in that year, is preserved for us in the *Liber Niger* of Archbishop Alan; and a note by the Archbishop himself, in the margin of his *Liber Niger*, informs us that "Tanney" is a church appertaining to the prebend of the Archdeacon of Dublin, the meaning of which will appear later.

John Alan occupied the Archiepiscopal throne of Dublin from 1528 to 1534; he was an Englishman, like most of the prelates who preceded and succeeded him in that office, educated at Cambridge, Treasurer of St. Paul's Cathedral, and succeeded to the See of Dublin through the influence of Cardinal Wolsey, to whom he was chaplain. Having incurred the enmity of the Geraldine family, he was murdered by some of their party at Artane, near Dublin, on 28th July, 1534.†

---

* This sketch of the Pale is based on a note supplied by the Rev. G. T. Stokes, D.D.

† Cotton's *Fasti Ecclesiæ Hibernicæ*, vol. ii., p. 18; and in the *Dictionary of National Biography*, vol. i., p. 305, will be found a fuller account of his life by that eminent historian of the reign of Henry VIII., James Gairdner, Esq., of the English Rolls Office.

To his industry and love of antiquities we are indebted for the preservation of the contents of many ancient documents which existed in his day, but which have long since disappeared. He found already compiled a register of ancient documents called the *Crede Mihi*, which was made about 1275, and this he embellished with notes of his own. The original of this register is in the custody of the Archbishop of Dublin, and is the oldest existing record of the state of the parishes in the Diocese of Dublin. Archbishop Alan caused two other registers to be compiled; one called his *Repertorium Viride*, and the other his *Liber Niger*.[*] The original of the *Repertorium Viride* is not now forthcoming, but several copies of it—the latest being of the seventeenth century—and the original of the *Liber Niger* are in the custody of the Archbishop.[†] In the latter are to be found many marginal notes in the handwriting of Alan, such as that quoted above about this parish.[‡]

In addition to being the name of a rural deanery

[*] Sometimes called *Alan's Register*.

[†] For a minute description of the present condition of the *Crede Mihi* and the *Liber Niger*, *vide* Preface (pp. xvi.-xx.) to *Historic and Municipal Documents of Ireland*, 1172-1320, edited by J. T. Gilbert. London, 1870.

[‡] The late Dr. Reeves, the Bishop of Down, Connor, and Dromore, caused a copy of the *Liber Niger* to be made in MS., and he then copied into it, in his own clear writing, all Alan's notes. This copy is in the Library of T.C.D. *Vide Journal of Royal Society of Antiquaries of Ireland*, 1893, p. 303.

and a parish, Taney is also the title of a prebendal
stall in St. Patrick's Cathedral. In 1227 the value
of this prebend was forty marks, or £26 13s. 4d.,
and the name is written "Tathtoin," by which we
would not recognise our parish, were it not for
Alan's note, "*alias* Tawney."*

At this date it was, no doubt, a separate dignity,
although the names of the prebendaries have not
come down to us; but Archbishop Luke (1228-
1255) granted both the church and the prebend to
the Archdeacon of Dublin, in support of his dignity,
reserving thence to the Legate a latere, the
hundredth part, which had been paid by way of
proxy from very remote times.

The Church of Luske had previously been held
by the Archdeacon; but it was then taken away,
and Taney, which was described as a "mother
church," having three chapels subservient to it—
Donabroke (Donnybrook), Kilgoban (Kilgobbin),
and Rathfarnham—was given in exchange.†

Both the church and prebend remained in the
possession of the Archdeacon from that time until
1851; the prebend remained in abeyance for some
years after 1851; but since St. Patrick's became
the National Cathedral, the stall has been revived,
and is now assigned to the Diocese of Limerick.

Except the occasional mention of the parish
among the possessions of the Archdeacon, and in

* Mason's *History of St. Patrick's*, Appendix v.

† Mason's *History of St. Patrick's*, pp. 44, 45; also Alan's
Repertorium Viride

ancient deeds of the period, we have very little information about it during the fourteenth or fifteenth century.

A considerable portion of the Archbishop's temporalities consisted of the Manor of St. Sepulchre, which extended from near St. Patrick's Cathedral into the Parish of Taney beyond Milltown. In a lease from the Archbishop to Thomas Locum, made in 1414, which is preserved in the *Liber Niger*, a description is given of the style of residence suited to the larger tenants of the manor. By this lease, the tenant was to build within four years, at his own expense, a stone house, walled and battlemented, 18 feet in breadth by 26 feet in length, and 40 feet in height—a house of these dimensions would more resemble a tower than a mere dwelling-house—the rent of the land in time of peace was to be 3d. per acre, and in time of war, nothing.*

The only traces which we find in the records of the Church of the stirring events of Henry VIII.'s reign are those connected with the dissolution of St. Patrick's Cathedral.

By an inquisition held on the 27th January, in the thirty-eighth year of Henry VIII. (1546), the extent and value of the archidiaconal possessions in Taney were reported to be as follows :—

"In the town-land of Tanee (*alias* Church-town†) there is of demesne, appertaining to said

* *Vide* Mr. James Mills' paper on *The Manor of St. Sepulchre*, in *Journal of the Royal Historical and Archæological Association of Ireland*, 1889, p. 31, *et seq.*

† *Vide post*, Survey of Half-Barony of Rathdown, 1654.

rectory or prebend, one messuage and ix acres of arable land, one stang (*i.e.*, a pole or perch) of meadow, value, per annum, ixs. The tithes issue from the town-lands of Tanee, Dondrommy (Don-dromarty, in inquisition of 1 Edw. VI., quoted by Mason [Drummartin or Dundrum?]), Balawly, Balayn (Ballinteer), Rebowe (Rabo or Roebuck), "the Chantrell ferme" and Challorighe (Mount-merrion or Callary) value xixl. per annum; the demesne lands, altarages, and oblations of Tanee are assigned to the curate for his stipend."*

The cathedral was dissolved in 1546, and the possessions of the Archdeacon were confiscated; but in 1547 William Power, who had held the Archdeaconry at the suppression, received a pension from Edward VI. as "Prebendary of Tannee and Rathfernane."† During the time of the suppression the parishes of Taney and Rathfarnham were leased to Sir John Allen, Knight.‡ The Archdeaconry was restored in 1555 by Queen Mary, and, no doubt, the Parish of Taney amongst its possessions.

The next notice which we find of the parish is in 1615, when a "Regal Visitation" was carried out by Archbishop Thomas Jones, in obedience to the command of James I.§ This visitation found Robert Pont resident curate, and the church and chancel in good repair, and furnished with service books. It may be remarked, that the chancel was mentioned

---

* Mason's *History of St. Patrick's*, p. 46.

† Cotton's *Fasti Ecclesiæ Hibernicæ*, vol. ii., p. 129.

‡ Mason's *History of St. Patrick's*, p. 45.

§ Latin MS. in the Public Record Office, Dublin.

separately, because, under the old ecclesiastical law, the rector was bound to keep that part of the fabric in repair.

In 1630 Dr. Lancelot Bulkeley, who was Archbishop from 1619 to 1650, prepared an account of the diocese, and presented it to the Privy Council on the 1st June in that year. The following is a translation of his report of Taney:—"The tithes belong to the Archdeacon of Dublin. The church is ruinous: there are only two householders in that parish that come to church. There is one John Cawhell (Cahill), a priest, that commonly says Mass at Dundrum and Ballawly. Mr. Richard Prescott, Master of Arts and Preacher, serves the cure. The Archdeaconry of Dublin is worth per annum a hundred pounds sterling."*

There are still the ruins of a small church to be seen in the townland, Balally (Ballawley†), and

---

* The original Latin document is in the Library of T.C.D., and there is a translation in the *Irish Ecclesiastical Record*, 1869, vol. v., p. 145, *et seq.* (Under the head of "Donnabrooke" it is stated that the tithes of that parish, and of Taney and Rathfarnham, belong to the Archdeacon of Dublin, being worth £100 per annum, and that Mr. Prescott discharges the cures, for which he receives £12.)

† Derivation of Ballawley:—Balamhlaibh or Bally—Amhlaibh, or Olaf, or Olave=the town of Olave, the famous Danish saint, who had a church off Fishamble Street. This corroborates the tradition that there was a colony of Danes at the foot of the "Three Rock Mountain." It is also to be noted that there is a place called "Harold's Grange," near Ballawley, and that the Harold family have held land near Kilgobbin from the twelfth century. (Note supplied by Rev. G. T. Stokes, D.D.)

this is the only mention which we can find of its being used for service.

The plans of Cromwoll for the settlement of Ireland, after he had obtained the mastery of it, are well known to all readers of history. His method, in this instance, was conceived with the same thoroughness of design which always distinguished his courses of action. Before proceeding to hand over the lands upon which he intended to establish his followers and other English settlers, he caused a careful survey to be made of all the lands which had been forfeited. Of the Half-Barony of Rathdown, two of such surveys were made—the first in 1654, by order of Charles Fleetwood, Lord Deputy,* and the second in 1657, by Sir William Petty—the latter being the celebrated *Down Survey.*†

Fleetwood's *Survey* describes the Parish of Taney as containing the townlands of " Bellawly," " Dondrom" and "Ballintry " (Ballinteer), " Rabuck " (Roebuck), Owenstown, Kilmacud ; a moiety of Churchtown, Churchtown *alias* " Tanee," and Tipperstown.‡ The parish is stated to be bounded on the west by Rathfarnham, on the south by the Parish of Kilgobbin, on the east and north by the Parish of " Donnebrook."

---

* Lodge's *Desiderata Curiosa Hibernica,* vol. ii., pp. 529-568.

† Public Record Office, Dublin.

‡ Tipperstown is Tubberstown, the Town of the Well, and is the townland on which Stillorgan station now stands. (Note supplied by Rev. G. T. Stokes, D.D.)

The townland of "Bellawly" is returned as the property of James Walsh* of Ballawley, "Irish Papist," containing 220 acres, having on the premises one castle thatched, and the walls of a chapel; the tithes had belonged to St. Patrick's, Dublin, but then to the College of Dublin.

The townlands of "Dondrom" and "Ballintry" are stated to be the property of Colonel Oliver Fitzwilliam,† of Merrion, "Irish Papist," who acted in the Irish Army as Major-General; the area was 500 acres; there was on the premises one castle slated, and a barn; one garden plot, and a small churchyard; the premises had been a manor, and had kept court-leet and court-baron; the tithes belonged to the College of Dublin.

The townland of "Rabuck" is stated to be the property of "Mathew," Lord Baron Trimblestown,‡

* Brewer, in his *Beauties of Ireland*, p. 216, says that the family of Walsh were of the line of Carrickmaine, and that Kilgobbin Castle was erected by them, but was forfeited in the reign of Charles I., when it passed to the Loftus family.

† Afterwards second Viscount Fitzwilliam. He was a distinguished military officer, and was a Lieutenant-General under the Marquis of Ormonde. He was created Earl of Tyrconnel, *circa* 1661. He *m.*, first, Dorothy Brereton, of Malpas, Cheshire, and secondly, Lady Eleanor Holles, eldest dau. of John, first Earl of Clare. (Creation 1624, *vide* B. E. P., 1866, p. 281.) He *d. s. p.* April 11, 1667, and was *bur.* at Donnybrook. (Blacker's *Sketches of Booterstown*, p. 112.)

‡ Matthias, eighth Baron Trimleston, took his seat in Parliament, March 18, 1639. He *m.* Jane, dau. of Nicholas Viscount Netterville, and *d.* in 1667, leaving issue. *Vide* Trimleston, B. P., 1895.

"Irish Papist," who acted in the Irish Army as Colonel of Horse. It contained 400 acres; there were on the premises one castle, which had been destroyed by the rebels, one garden plot, and one mill; the tithes belonged to the College of Dublin.

The townland of Owenstown is returned as the property of Lord Fitzwilliam, of Merrion,* "Irish Papist;" it contained 68 acres, and the tithes belonged to the College of Dublin.

The townland of Kilmacud is stated to have been the property of Maurice Archbold, of Kilmacud, deceased, a "Papist," who left his interest to Richard Archbold,† of Malpas, in England; the

---

* Thomas, first Baron and Viscount Fitzwilliam (Aug. 5, 1629); knighted, Aug. 23, 1608; Sheriff of Co. Dublin, 1609. He served faithfully under Charles I. in England, with his two sons, Richard, who d. during his father's lifetime, and Oliver, who succeeded to the title. He m. Margaret, eldest dau. of Oliver, fourth Baron Louth. (Blacker's *Sketches of Booterstown*, p. 111.)

In the Records of the Corporation of Dublin, there is an account of the riding of the bounds of the city in 1603, which mentions that the procession "turned northward to the sowth-west corner of the orchard diche of Merryon, through which corner the elder (fathers) of the citty said that of ould tyme they did ryde. And now, that for the same was soe strongly fensed with trees and thornes, which, in favor of the gentleman of the House of Merryon (Sir Thomas Fitzwilliam) being the citty tennant they would loathly breake downe, they rode a lyttell besydes it." (Gilbert's *Records of Dublin*, vol. i., p. 191.)

† He d. June 6, 1678, and in his will, which was proved in 1681, he directs that his body may have "decent and

area was 95 acres, and the tithes belonged to Christ Church (Cathedral).

The townland, described as " a moiety of Church-town," is stated to be the property of Sir William Ussher, Knt.,* " English Protestant ; " it contained 60 acres, and the tithes belonged to the College of Dublin.

The townland of Churchtown *alias* " Tanee," is

Christian buryall in the Parrish Church of Churchtowne." He mentions his wife, mother, brothers, and sisters, and as he was expecting a child, makes provision for it. He appoints as his executors " Gerrald Archbold, of Newtowne, in ye co. Kildare, gent., and Christopher Cauldwell, of the citty of Dublin, gent.," and leaves them " twenty shillings a peece to buy them rings in remembrance of me." *Vide* Tomb-stones I. & II., and notes, chapter iii. In 1741 the will of James Archbold, of Kilmacud, probably Richard's son, who *d.* Feb. 17, 1738-39, was proved. (Consistorial Wills, Public Record Office, Dublin.)

The Archbolds were people of importance. In the *Funeral Entries*, in Ulster's office, it is recorded that Edmond Archbold, of Kilmacud, who *d.* April 12, 1617, and who "had to wife Anne Warrin," was buried with all the pomp of that time. An inquisition of James I., in 1619, shows that Edmond's son, William, and Maurice, son of Patrick Archbold (*d.* Oct. 31, 1616), were in possession ; and in Fleetwood's *Survey* it is mentioned that William, sometime of Cloghran, near Swords, and Maurice, held the premises in 1641.

* Memoirs of Sir Wm. Ussher, sen. (1561-1659), who was Clerk of the Council and M.P. for Co. Wicklow, and of his grandson, Sir Wm. Ussher, jun. (1610-71), who was M.P. for Co. Dublin, will be found in Ball Wright's *Ussher Fami-lies*, pp. 118-145.

returned as the property of John Kemp, of the city of Dublin, tailor, who held it under a lease from the "Bishop" of Dublin; it contained 88 acres, and the tithes belonged to the College of Dublin.

The townland of Tipperstown is returned as the property of Dean Margetson,* "a Protestant," who held it in right of his Deanery, *i.e.*, of Christ Church Cathedral; it contained 76 acres, and the tithes belonged to itself.

It is to be remarked that Kilmacud and Tipperstown are not now in the Parish of Taney, but are in the Parish of Stillorgan; as is also a townland called Mulchanstown, which lies between them, and which is included in the *Down Survey.* The number of acres in the parish belonging to "Irish Papist" proprietors was 1,883; to "English Protestant" proprietors, 60; and to Church lands, 164.

The *Down Survey*, which comprises a map of the parish and of the Barony of Rathdown, gives the boundaries of the parish as follows :—On the north, the parish of "Donabrooke;" on the east, the parishes of Monkstown, Tully, and Kill; on the south, the Parish of Whitechurch, and on the west, the Baronies of Newcastle and Uppercross. The quality of the soil is stated to be arable,

* James Margetson was a native of Yorkshire, and was brought to Ireland by the Earl of Strafford. He was Dean of Christ Church from 1639 to 1660, and subsequently Archbishop of Dublin (1660-63), and Archbishop of Armagh from 1663 until his death in 1678. *Vide* Cotton's *Fasti, &c.*, vol. iii., p. 22, and *Notes and Queries*, 8th S., VII., p. 255.

meadow, and pasture. The townlands comprised in the parish were as follows :—" Dondrom," " Ballintiry," " Rabuck," Owenstown, Kilmacud, Ballawley, " Tyberstown," Moltanstown (Mulchanstown), and Milltown.

It will be noticed that this survey omitted the moiety of Churchtown, and Churchtown *alias* " Tanee," which were included in Fleetwood's *Survey*, but included Mulchanstown and Milltown ; from the fact that Sir William Ussher is stated to be the owner of the moiety of Churchtown, in the one, and of Milltown, in the other, it would seem that they were the same townland.

The following are the owners and area of the townlands as given in it; and, as will be seen, they are substantially the same as in Fleetwood's *Survey :—*

Names of Owners.	Lands.	Acres.
Colonel Oliver Fitzwilliam	{ Dondrom and Ballintery, } ...	562
Lord of Trimlestowne,	... Rabuck, ...	500
Lord of Meryyoung,	... Owenenstowne, ...	100
Morris Archbold,	... Kilmacudd, ...	150
James Walsh, ...	... Ballowley, ...	440
Deane of Christ Church,	... Tyberstowne, ...	87
The same, ...	... Moltanstowne, ...	294
Sir William Ussher, } Protestant,	... Milltowne, ...	—

Total acres ... 2,133

The Church land is returned at 381 acres, and all the owners as " Irish Papists," except Sir William Ussher.

The only road marked on the map of the parish is one from Dundrum towards Milltown, which branches towards the east to a bridge at Clonskeagh, and towards the west to a bridge at Milltown.

It is stated that there stands in "Dondrom" a castle in repair, in "Rabuck" another, and in Ballawley another, and that the river of "Donnabrooke" bounds part of the west of the parish.

Mason* remarks that although in 1649 the Parliament Commissioners had forbidden the public use of the established ritual, it did not appear that they at once deprived the clergy of their temporal possessions. As soon, however, as the usurpers had established themselves, they assigned to certain trustees, to whom were confided all matters concerning the university, the possessions of the Archbishop and of the Dean and Chapter of St. Patrick's Cathedral. Hence it is that in the *Down Survey* we find the College of Dublin noted as proprietors of several tracts of land which belong properly to the Archbishop and others, and that in Fleetwood's *Survey* the College is reported to be proprietor of the tithes of Tanee and Rathmichael, parishes which previously belonged to St. Patrick's.

Mason† also mentions that in 1660 the glebe of nine acres one stang of arable land at Tawney, which

* *History of St. Patrick's*, p. 188, *et seq.*
† *Ibid.*, p. 46.

the Archdeacon possessed at the dissolution of the Cathedral, was reported to be concealed, and adds : " Some portion, however, has been since recovered, for in 1701 six acres of glebe land near the Church of Tannee (*sic*) were demised for twenty-one years to Eliphal Dobson* for £2 6s. per annum; this glebe was surveyed about 1750, and found to contain 6A. 2R. 8P., besides the churchyard, which measured 1 rood 8 perches; it is situated on the east and south-east sides of the Church of Tawney, and is divided into two portions by the road from Dundrum to Dublin."

From the Hearth-money Returns and Subsidy Rolls of 1664, we can gain an estimate of the number of householders in the parish in that year.

* Gilbert, in his *History of Dublin*, vol. i., p. 13, says: "At the 'Stationers' Arms,' in Castle Street, in the reign of James II. was the shop of Eliphal Dobson, the most wealthy Dublin bookseller and publisher of his day. He was attainted in the Parliament of 1689, and returned to his former habitation after the evacuation of Dublin by the Jacobites. 'Eliphal Dobson's wooden leg,' says Dunton, 'startled me with the creaking of it; for I took it for the *crepitus ossium* which I have heard some of our physicians speak of. Mr. Dobson is a great Dissenter; but his pretence to religion does not make him a jot precise. He values no man for his starched looks or supercilious gravity, or for being a Churchman, Presbyterian, Independent, &c., provided he is sound in the main points wherein all good men are agreed.'" This Dunton was a travelling bookseller, and gives very interesting particulars about the Dublin citizens at the end of the seventeenth century, in a curious book called the *Dublin Scuffle*. Amongst the burial entries in

In "Dondrom" Isaac Dobson* was the only inhabitant who paid the tax for three hearths; there were twenty-two others who paid for one each. In "Tengknock" (Tiknock) there were four inhabitants paying for one hearth each. In Ballawley John Burr paid for three hearths, and seven others paid for one each. In "Rawbuck" (Roebuck) William Nally† paid for two hearths, and

Hughes's *St. Werburgh's*, p. 126, appears "Alderman Eliphal Dobson, publisher, in 7 Castle Street, March 17th, 1719-20." He lived at Dundrum, in the old house or castle which still stands in the grounds of the present Dundrum Castle (recently occupied by that distinguished prelate of the Irish Church, the Most Rev. Charles Parsons Reichel, Bishop of Meath); and in his will, which was proved in 1720, he leaves his interest in it and in the town and lands of Dundrum, which he inherited from his father, and which he held under Lord Fitzwilliam, to trustees, and directs that his wife Mary (*alias* Saunders) should have the use of the castle, of the "castle garden lately made by me," and of the pleasure-grounds. He mentions his sons Isaac (Six Clerk, *d.* 1754); Eliphal (Sheriff of Dublin, 1730, *d.* 1732); Joseph (of Dundrum, *d.* 1762), [Hughes's *St. Werburgh's*]; Samuel; his only daughter Hannah, wife of John Davis. To the Library of T.C.D. he bequeathed £10 and "one of the best folio Bibles printed by me." (Prerogative Wills, Public Record Office, Dublin.)

* He was the father of Eliphal Dobson. (*Vide ante.*) His will, which was proved on March 12, 1700-1, is dated October 24, 1700, and describes him as of Dundrum. He mentions in it that he was then eighty years of age. (Prerogative Wills, Public Record Office.)

† Blacker, in his *Sketches of Booterstown*, p. 125, gives the following amongst the earliest tombstone inscriptions in

five others paid for one each. In Churchtown two inhabitants paid for one hearth each.

In the Subsidy Rolls we find Isaac Dobson paying for " Dondrom," William Nally for " Robucke " and Owenstowne, Richard Archbold for Kilmacud, John Borr for Ballawley, Owen Jones for Churchtowne, and " ye tennant" for " part of Merrion."

In the *Act for the Attainder of Divers Rebels*, passed in 1689, after the deposition of James II., the name of " Isaac Dobson, of Dundrum, gentleman," is given as having " gone into England or some other place beyond the seas," and to forfeit all his lands in this kingdom (of Ireland).*

The next fact in the history of the parish which has come to our hands, is recorded upon the older of the two chalices which are used in the celebration of the Holy Communion in the parish church. This chalice was presented by Archdeacon Isaac Mann† in 1760, and the inscription‡ upon it tells us that the church had then been once more rebuilt.

Donnybrook graveyard:—" Hereunder lyeth the body of William Nally, of ———, in the County of Dublin, gent., who departed this life October ye 7th, 1669." He was an ancestor of Leonard M'Nally, well known for his connection with the Revolution of 1798. (*Vide* Blacker, pp. 90, 197, 434.)

* Appendix to King's *State of the Protestants in Ireland under James II.*, p. 241.

† Isaac Mann, D.D., Archdeacon of Dublin, 1757; Bishop of Cork, 1772; *d*. 1789. *Vide* Cotton's *Fasti*, &c., vol. ii., p. 131.

‡ Appendix B. In Erck's *Ecclesiastical Register* (1834), amongst the grants of the Board of First Fruits, there is a gift of £200 to Tawney. The date is not given, but it was *circa* 1745.

This record gives us the date of the old church as we now see it, and there cannot have been much change in its outward appearance since then. The east gable at one time contained two windows, similar in design to those in the side walls, but these have been for many years past built up. The arrangement, which still remains, of Communion table, with reading-desk and pulpit above it, standing against the east wall, no doubt, dates from 1760, when the public sense of correctness in things ecclesiastical had reached, perhaps, its lowest point. Except that the pews have been removed, the interior of the building remains unaltered since it was used as the parish church; and its appearance can best be described by saying that it is barnlike and dismal in the extreme.

CHAPTER III.

THE original graveyard was contained in the plot of ground which adjoins the road leading from Dundrum to Churchtown, and was bounded on the north partly by the old church, and partly by a wall forming a continuation of the north wall of the church, and on the east by a wall running in a curve towards the cottages upon the road above mentioned. About the year 1872, an addition was made to the graveyard, by taking a piece of the field forming part of the glebe land at the north side of the church ; and again, in the year 1887, a further addition was made, by taking another piece of the same field, and extending the graveyard further to the east. On the occasion of the second extension, the old wall bounding the graveyard on the east was removed, and a new wall built enclosing the additional space.

Some idea of the number of interments in this graveyard may be obtained from the fact that during the short period of twenty-one years, from 1814 to 1835, there were 1,044 burials entered in the register.

A table of the fees charged in the parish in 1814 for funerals and other offices is to be found in the vestry book.* The fees for burials in the oldest part of the graveyard are still the same as in 1814 ; but in the new ground somewhat higher fees are charged. In both cases, however, the fees are very low—a fact which probably accounts for the large number of burials of persons belonging to Dublin and elsewhere outside the parish which is recorded in the registers.

A careful examination of the inscribed stones in the graveyard discloses only two of the seventeenth century ; these, with any others which appear to be of interest, are inserted in full, and a list is given of the rest, which may be useful for reference.

A large enclosure, surrounded by an iron railing, near the east end of the church, is known to be the burial-place of the Lighton family.†

I.

Here under lyes the Body of James Nicholson, whose fidelity as clerk hath been sufficiently shown in His Majestie's Treasury Office, in the city of Dublin, for 36 yeares or thereabouts. Aged sixty foure, and was here interred 10 September, Anno Domini 1676.

> Quæstor honestus amans solvi tenui reparavi
> Credita parta meos sponte labore manu
> Funde preces Regi fueram per debita fidus
> Fidus pontifici cætera funde preces.
> Memento mori.‡

---

* Appendix C.
† See Lighton, Sir Thomas, chap. vii.
‡ The will of James Nicholson, of the parish of " St. Michaell in the Citty of Dublin," which was proved in 1676, directs that his body should be " enterred in the Church of Churchtowne." He mentions in it Mary (*als.* Nicholson), wife of Edward Archbold, also his cousin Richard Archbold of Kilmacud (p. 17), and " Gerrard Archbold of Newtowne, in the Co. Kildare." (Prerogative Wills, Public Record Office, Dublin.)

II.

This burial place belong*eth*
*to Gerrard A*rchbold of Eadston .
Here lyeth the body of
. . . . *A*rchbold, *alias* Ball his *wife*
who departed this life January ye
. . . . . . aged 67 years.
*R*equiescant in pace.*

III.

Here lies the body of Selina Elizabeth Atkinson, daughter
of John Atkinson, Esq., Ely Place, Dublin, who, in the
blossom of youth, was untimely cut off, one of Nature's fairest
flowers, leaving her afflicted parents and friends unceasingly
to deplore her loss, and to look forward with anxious hope
to a reunion in that World of Peace, the reward of Innocence
and Virtue. She died 17th September, 1813, aged 13 years
and 4 months. Here also are buried John Atkinson, Esq.,
who died the 30th October, 1823, aged 63 years. Judith
Atkinson, his wife, who died the 14th May, 1821, aged 57
years. Also Anne Atkinson, wife of John Atkinson, junr.,
Esq., who died 7th April, 1824, aged 30 years. John
Atkinson, Esq., died December 13th, 1859, aged 68 years,
deeply regretted by his sorrowing wife and family. Also
Mary Atkinson, widow of the said John Atkinson, and
eldest daughter of the late John Hemphill, Esq., of Cashel,
she died at Ely Place, the 18th July, 1888, beloved and
mourned by her children and relations. Also Ellena Mary
Atkinson, daughter of the said John and Mary Atkinson, who
died 9th December, 1890, loved and regretted by all who
knew her. "Of such is the kingdom of heaven."

IV.

Richard Atkinson died at Gortmore, 18th July, 1871, aged
53 years. "Mark the perfect man, and behold the upright:
for the end of that man is peace."—Ps. xxxvii. 37.

---

* The will of Gerard Archbold of Eadstown, Co. Kildare,
dated 25th March, 1694-5, says : "My body I pray my friends
to see buried in Churchtowne, als. Tanij." He is evidently
the person mentioned as "Gerrald" in Richard Archbold's
will (p. 17), and as "Gerrard" in James Nicholson's will—
Eadstown and Newtown being adjoining townlands in the
North Barony of Naas. He mentions his dau. Joan Archbold
and her son James ; and from this fact it would seem probable that he was the father-in-law of Richard Archbold.
(Consistorial Wills, Public Record Office, Dublin.)

Mary Jane Atkinson died in Dublin, 17th June, 1889, aged 67 years. "If we believe that Jesus died and rose again, even so them also which sleep in Jesus will God bring with him."—1 Thess. iv. 14.

V.

In Loving Memory of Michael Charles Bernard, M.B., T.C.D., & L.R.C.S.I., who for forty years labored as a Physician in this parish. Died 24th April, 1881, in his 71st year. "I know that my Redeemer liveth."

In Loving Memory of Henry Hilton Bernard, Medical Student, who died on the 11th December, 1887, of scarlatina, caught in the path of duty, in his 20th year. "Blessed are the pure in heart: for they shall see God."

In Memory of Joshua Bernard, died 9th February, 1843, aged 1 month. Sarah Maria Leigh, relict of John Leigh, Lymm Cheshire, died 14th October, 1856, aged 74. Adeliza Bernard, died 13th May, 1864, aged 1 year. Anna Mayne, died 7th April, 1870, aged 3 days. Godfrey Bernard, died 16th April, 1870, in his 19th year. Annie Bernard, died 14th March, 1876, aged 10 years. Louisa Bernard, died 6th November, 1887, after a lingering illness.

VI.

Sacred to the Memory of the Barrys of Lislee here interred, viz., James Redmond, late of Glandore, died June 18th, 1879, aged 90; his wife Anne, died 1869, aged 80; his mother, died 1852; his Aunt Johanna, died 1851; his daughter Mary Theresa, died 1860, aged 32. R.I.P.

VII.

Sacred to the Memory of William Ball, Esq.,* who died July 18th, 1824, aged 73 years.

---

* "Counsellor" Ball lived in Churchtown from *circa* 1812 until his death, and his name will be found amongst the original purchasers of pews in the present church. (See Appendix D.) He was a Scholar of T.C.D., and graduated B.A. 1769. He was called to the Bar in 1775. In 1806 the degree of LL.D. *honoris causâ* was conferred on him by his University. Ball Wright, in his *Records of the Families of Ball* (p. 38), mentions that he was commonly known as "Index" Ball, because he edited a book of legal indexes. He was the third son of the Rev. Thomas Ball, a celebrated schoolmaster in Dublin in the eighteenth century, who, Ball Wright says, was descended from a Co. Fermanagh family. He was married twice, and left two daughters.

VIII.

Sacred to the Memory of Elizabeth Ball, who died March 28th, 1838, aged 49 years; also of her husband Major Benjamin Ball, formerly of the 40th Regiment, who died April 10, 1841, aged 52 years; and of their daughter Jane, wife of John Dickinson, who died May 20, 1843, aged 25 years; and of her husband John Dickinson, who died May 26, 1851, aged 38 years; and of Charlotte Elizabeth, widow of Robert Lloyd, M.D., sister of the above Major Ball, who died August 5, 1853; and of the Rev. Ruttledge Ball, son of the above Major Ball, who died March 16, 1858, aged 27 years.

IX.

In Memoriam. Charlotte Beaufort, died November 15th, 1868. She walked with God. Also of her sister Fanny Mary Anne, who died October 20, 1875. " He that believeth on me hath everlasting life."—John vi. 47. " There the weary are at rest."—Job iii. 17.

X.

The Burial Ground of Patrick Bride, Esq., and his posterity. 1798. T. Taylor, *fecit.*

In the firm hope of a blessed immortality, here lies the body of Margaret Bride, wife of Patrick Bride, Esq., and the daughter of Arthur Lamprey, Esq., who departed this life on the 9th May, 1796, in the 69th year of her age, and the — year of her marriage. Here also lieth the body of Eliza Bride, their daughter, who died on the 1st September, 1797, in the 22nd year of her age. She inherited the suavity of manners, kindness of disposition, solid understanding, and true piety, which her dear mother so eminently possessed. *Heu! quanto minus est cum aliis versari quam vestri meminisse.*

In the firm hope and confidence in the goodness and mercy of Almighty God, here lies the body of Patrick Bride, late of Stephen's Green, Esq., who died 29th day of September, 1808, aged 82 years. He had been an eminent druggist, but retired from business in the year 1773. He served the office of High Sheriff of the Honorable City of Dublin in the year 1780; had been elected a Director of the Bank of Ireland in the year 1784; and served the office of Governor of that Honorable Corporation in the years 1805 and 1806. In every station of public and private life his conduct was pure and correct. He has left one son and four grandsons.

XI.

Sacred to the Memory of T. R. Burke, Esq., who departed this life the 25th day of June, 1841, aged 22 years.

XII.

In Loving Memory of James Carnegie, who died 18 March, 1866, aged 75 years. " As in Adam all die, even so in Christ shall all be made alive."—1 Cor. xv. 22. Also of Beatrice Carnegie, his wife, who died the 24th May, 1883, aged 87 years. " I know whom I have believed, and am persuaded that he is able to keep that which I have committed to him against that day."—2 Timothy i. 12. Also of their daughter Jane, who died 15 April, 1891, and their daughter Eliza von der Nahmer, who died 12 March, 1894, aged 57.

XIII.

Sacred to the Memory of Lieut.-Col. Wm. Cowell, c.b., late of the 42nd Royal Highlanders, whose premature death was occasioned by severe campaigns and wounds received in the Peninsula during the war; died 24th September, 1827, aged 45 years.

XIV.

Deposited here lie the mortal remains of what was Frances, the beloved wife of James Crofton, of Roebuck Castle. He, in deep, in sincere affliction, has lived to record her the best of wives, of mothers, and of friends. She ceased her earthly existence on the 8th day of January, 1811, at the early age of thirty-four years, to appear before her God arrayed and conducted to His presence by every virtue. Here also is deposited the body of Eliza, the infant child of the above-named.

XV.

In Loving Memory of Michael Carr, died 21st June, 1876, aged 35 years. Also his daughter, Margaret A. Carr, aged 12 years, and his son, William T. Carr, died 20th July, 1889, aged 19 years. " To be with Christ, which is far better."

XVI.

Erected by Thomas Clarke to the memory of Jane Clarke, his wife, whose many virtues endeared her to every person by whom she was known. She died the 1st of May, 1806, in the 23rd-year of her age, and is here interred with her father, Garrett English, Esq.,* who died on the 5th May,

---

* " A steady friend, and an upright and active magistrate."
—*Anthologia Hibernica*, vol. i., p. 402.

1793, aged 36 years. Here also lyeth the remains of Mary, second daughter of the above-named Garrett English, who departed this life on the 21st of November, 1807, aged 22 years. Here also are deposited the remains of the above-mentioned Thomas Clarke, who departed this life on the 21st of May, 1825, aged 52 years. Here also lieth the remains of the Rev. Geor. D. Crooke, son-in-law of the above-mentioned Thomas Clarke, who departed this life October the 5th, 1836, aged 38 years. There also is interred the remains of John Clarke, Esq., son of the above-named Thomas Clarke, who departed this life November 14th, 1836, aged 30 years. Here also are deposited the remains of Eliza Clarke, daughter of the above-named Thomas Clarke, who departed this life on the 12th day of January, 1844, in the 24th year of her age ; and also the remains of Sarah Tilly, wife of Benjamin Tilly, Esq., another of the daughters of the above-named Thomas Clarke, who departed this life on the 25th July, 1852, in the 34th year of her age.

XVII.

Here lie the remains of Mrs. Jane S. Corry, nat. 1775, ob. Jan., 1820.

XVIII.

To record conjugal affection, parental tenderness, and every virtue that constitutes genuine worth, this stone has been placed over the remains of Nathaniel Creed, Esq., late of the City of Dublin, by his sorrowing widow, Mrs. Rebecca Creed, as a humble testimony of her gratitude to his memory. He departed this life the 17th day of April, 1805, aged 55 years. Here also are interred the remains of their infant son, Nathaniel Creed, who died 17th January, 1805, aged 11 months. Here also are interred the remains of William Nat. Creed, eldest son of the said Nathaniel Creed, who departed this life June 13th, 1815, in the 21st year of his age. He was a young man of unspotted purity, and possessed of every virtue which could endear him to society. Here also are interred the remains of James Joseph Creed, son of the above Nathaniel Creed, who departed this life the 18th of April, 1825, aged 24 years. A young man who lived beloved, and died deeply regretted by his family and friends.

This tomb was erected by James Allen Heyland, Esq., of the City of Dublin, to the memory of Maria, his beloved wife, and eldest daughter of the late Nathaniel Creed, Esq., of Roebuck, County of Dublin. She departed this life in the

38th year of her age on the 8th of December, A.D. 1830. Here also are interred the remains of the above-named James Allen Heyland, Esq., who departed this life on the 11th of December, A.D. 1837, aged 53 years.

XIX.

Sacred to the Memory of Elizabeth Cage, daughter of William Cage, Esq. Born June 19th, 1798, died at Sydenham Road, Dundrum, December 24th, 1876. "Blessed are the dead which die in the Lord."—Rev. xiv. 13. "For God so loved the world, that he gave his only begotten Son, that whosoever believeth in him should not perish, but have everlasting life."—John iii. 16.

XX.

Sacred to the Memory of Louisa Coxe, daughter of Baron Schele, of Osnaburg, in Westphalia, and wife of Daniel Coxe, junr., Esq. She died January 30th, 1819, aged 48 years. Her father-in-law, D. Coxe, hath placed this monument. Also Sacred to the Memory of Daniel Coxe, junr., Esq., who died 5th June, 1819, aged 47 years.

XXI.

In Loving Memory of Elizabeth Frances Darlington, who fell asleep in Jesus 27th April, 1875, aged 18 years. Also her sister Margaret, died December 16th, 1850, aged 10 months.

Here lieth the body of Francis Darlington, who departed this life the 9th day of September, 1804, aged 47 years; also his daughter Susanna, who departed this life the 14th day of November, 1802, aged 22 years.

XXII.

In Loving Memory of Arthur, only son of the late W. D. Dickie, Cedarmount, Dundrum, died 15th January, 1891, aged 21 years. "I will arise, and go to my Father."

XXIII.

This stone was erected by Thomas Dillon, Esq., of Mount Dillon, Roebuck, and Marcella, his wife, in memory of their sons Cornelius and Thomas, who died in their infancy.

D

XXIV.

Underneath are deposited the mortal remains of Mr. Peter Depoe,* of Leinster Street, in the City of Dublin, who departed this life the 16th of November, 1826, aged 68 years. A man very generally known, and as generally esteemed and respected for all the Qualities that constitute a valuable Member of Society. Here also lie interred the Remains of his Son James Mark Depoe, who died the 25th February, 1826, in the 26th year of his age. This stone is dedicated to their memory by Mrs. Elizabeth Depoe, widow of the above-named Peter, tho' imperfectly can such a testimonial convey a sense of her grief or of her lasting affliction. Also the remains of Mrs. Depoe, who departed this life the 1st January, 1848, aged 81 years.

XXV.

Sacred to the Memory of Capt. James Espinasse, late 1st Royal Regt., who died at Dundrum, Co. Dublin, 1st March, 1874, aged 70 years. Erected by his sorrowing widow. "Precious in the sight of the Lord is the death of His saints."—Ps. cxvi. 15. Also Julia, his wife, died 19th June, 1877, and their daughter Mary, died 29th December, 1879.

XXVI.

Sir John Franks, died 10th January, 1852, aged 83 years. Also his attached wife Sarah Franks, who died 22nd February, 1874, aged 78 years.

XXVII.

Edward, infant son of Edward and Amy Fitzgerald, born August 21st, 1890, and died on the 23rd.

XXVIII.

Sacred to the Memory of William John Freke, who died 17 November, 1879, aged 71 years; and of Frances May, his wife, who died 3 June, 1880, aged 64 years.

XXIX.

1868. To the Memory of three dear sisters, who are interred here, Eliza Findlay, died 16th December, 1847, aged 83 years. Charlotte Findlay, died 17th May, 1849, in her

---

* Manager of Daly's Club-house in College Green.— Gilbert's *History of Dublin*, vol. iii., p. 40.

81st year. Annie Findlay, died the 3rd June, 1858, in her 85th year. "They shall be mine, saith the Lord of hosts, in that day when I make up my jewels; and I will spare them, as a man spareth his own son that serveth him."—Mal. iii. 17. Erected by their affectionate grandniece A. H. Church. Here also are interred the remains of their beloved grand-nephew, Mark Bloxham, Esq., County Inspector, R.I.C., who departed this life on the 13th May, 1876, aged 53 years. "I know that my Redeemer liveth."

XXX.

The persons here interred are Mrs. George, the wife of Baron George, A.D. 1814.* Master Richard George, their fifth son, 1806.

XXXI.

Charles Samuel Grey, born January 22nd, 1811, died June 12th, 1860. "Blessed are the poor in spirit : for theirs is the kingdom of heaven." Also Henry Charles Martin Grey, his son, born April 15th, 1851, died May 3rd, 1851. "Of such is the kingdom of heaven."

XXXII.

In Memory of Frances Camac Hutchins, wife of Samuel Hutchins, of Ardnacashel, Co. Cork, who died 16th Sep-tember, 1839, aged 44, and lieth at Monkstown. Also of Ellen Elizabeth Hutchins, who lieth here, having died 18th June, 1838, aged 28. "So he giveth unto his beloved sleep."

XXXIII.

In loving memory of Emma Hudson, died 3rd July, 1894. "With Christ, which is far better."

XXXIV.

Sacred to the memory of Alexander Henry, M.D., born 17th March, 1805, died 6th May, 1888 ; and of Caroline, his wife, born July, 1814, died January, 1873. Mary, daughter of Alexander Henry and Caroline, his wife, born May, 1853, died June, 1878, aged 25 years.

XXXV.

Died on 24th May, 1853, aged 52, Mary, wife of W. R. Hopkins, Esq., h.p., 5th Fusiliers, and daughter of the late Henry Baldwin, Esq., of Mount Pleasant, Bandon, Co. Cork.

---

* Dorothea George, *bur.* June 1, 1814.

XXXVI.

In Loving Memory of William Andrew Hayes, B.A., T.C.D., of Summerville, Dundrum, died 12th May, 1889, aged 61 years. " I will arise."

XXXVII.

Beneath this stone are deposited the remains of William Haliday, Junior, cut off by a lingering disease in the early bloom of life. He anticipated the progress of years in the maturity of understanding, in the acquisition of knowledge, and the successful cultivation of a mind gifted by providence with endowments of the highest order.

At a period of life when the severe studies have scarcely commenced, he had acquired an accurate knowledge of most of the European languages, of Latin, Greek, Hebrew, and Arabic. But of his own, the Hiberno-Celtic, so little, Oh ! shame to the youth of this once lettered Island, an object of attainment and study, he had fathomed all the depths, explored the beauties, and unravelled the intricacies. He possessed whatever was calculated to exalt, to ennoble, to endear: great talents, social virtues, sincere religion, a good son, and an affectionate husband, a steadfast friend. Carried off in the 24th year of his age, his worth will be long remembered, and his death lamented. Obiit 26th October, A.D. 1812. Requiescat in Pace.

Danielis Haliday, Edinburgensis Parisiensisque, Medicinæ Facultatum Socius ; Academiæ Regiæ Hiberniæ Sodalis. Natus Dublinii, 19 October, 1798, Obiit Die nono Maii, 1836, Ætatis 38. Requiescat in Pace.*

XXXVIII.

Beneath this stone are deposited the mortal remains of the late Lieut.-Colonel George Hart, formerly of His Majesty's 26th Regiment; he served for upwards of 28 years. He departed this life at his house on Rathmines Road on Thursday, the 7th day of April, 1811, in the 78th year of his age, and is buried here at his own desire. Here also lieth buried the remains of John Hart, Esq., Barrister, who died on the 5th February, 1833, aged 27 years. He was the eldest son of W. S. Hart, Esq., of Fitzwilliam Square.

---

* See *The Scandinavian Kingdom of Dublin*, by Charles Haliday (Dublin, 1882), which contains a notice of the Author's life, by John P. Prendergast, who gives much interesting information about William and Daniel Haliday ; also see biographical notices in the *Dictionary of National Biography* and in Webb's *Compendium of Irish Biography*.

XXXIX.

In memory of William Richard Hamilton, M.D., of Urlar, Co. Sligo, died January 1st, 1882, aged 80 years. " Until the day dawn."—2 Pet. i. 19. Also of Gertrude, who died 29 March, 1890, aged 31 years, eldest daughter of the above William R. Hamilton. "Blessed are the pure in heart : for they shall see God."—Matt. v. 8. Anita Hamilton, daughter of Alex. Hamilton, B.L., J.P., died 26th August, 1885, aged 7 days.

XL.

Sacred to the memory of Catherine Mary James, the dearly beloved wife of Charles Henry James, of Rockmount House, in this parish, born November 25, 1835, died June 21, 1875. " He giveth his beloved sleep." Also to the loving memory of Katherine Caroline, third daughter of the above, who died at Clifton, Bristol, on the 18th July, 1886, in her twentieth year. " Heaven is my home."

XLI.

Here are interred the bodies of Mrs. Susan Johnston, wife of Richard Johnston, of the City of Dublin, Architect, who departed this life on the 8th September, 1799, aged 33 years. Also the remains of the above-named Richard Johnston, who departed this life on the 20th of March, 1806, aged 47 years.

XLII.

In memory of Julia Leslie, wife of Robert Grove Leslie, of the City of Dublin, Esq., Barrister-at-law, who died in the Parish of Taney, on the 28th day of June, 1806, in the 29th year of her age. Her afflicted husband has placed this stone, imposing that his mortal remains shall rest here with those of her whose loss he now deplores, and humbly hoping, through the Redeemer of mankind, that the souls of both shall meet in heaven to be blessed for ever.

XLIII.

Sacred to the memory of Maria Mary Lloyd, who departed this life March 21, 1881, aged 63 years.

XLIV.

Sacred to the memory of Fanny, the beloved wife of the Rev. Dr. Chas. MacDonnell, who died in the Lord July 17th, 1838. To record her devoted love and affection as a wife and mother this monument is erected by her affectionate and sorrowing husband. Also his son Richard, died January 8th, 1837, aged 19 years.

XLV.

This tomb and burial-place belongeth to the family of the Merritts of the City of Dublin. Here lieth the remains of Mr. Math. Merritt, who departed this life the 3rd December, 1775, aged 63 years. Here also lieth the remains of his wife, Mrs. Eliza Merritt, who departed this life 21 June, 1778, aged 60 years. Here also lieth the remains of Mr. Barth. Merritt, who departed this life 15th November, 1790, aged 30 years. Here also lieth the remains of his wife, Mrs. Mary Merritt, who departed this life 3rd June, 1801, aged 42 years. Here also lieth the remains of Mr. John Merritt, who departed this life 29th April, 1804, aged 54 years.

XLVI.

Beneath lie the remains of Frances Maria M'Naghten, relict of the late Henry M'Naghten, of Coleraine, in the County of Londonderry, Esq., who departed this life at Dundrum, on the 16th of April, 1839, aged 65 years.

XLVII.

This monument, erected by Mark Monsarrat, of North Great George's Street, as a token of his devoted attachment to his beloved child, George Darley Cranfield Monsarrat, born 19th December, 1830, died 23rd May, 1834. " The Lord gave, and the Lord hath taken away : blessed be the name of the Lord."

XLVIII.

Sacred to the memory of Adolphina, youngest daughter of the late Capt. Nicholas Malassey, Deputy Commissary General, died 24th February, 1875.

XLIX.

Here lie the remains, by her own desire, of Maria Rose White Mulville, otherwise Tuite, sister of the late Sir George Tuite, Bart. She departed this life on the 18th January, 1860, in the 79th year of her age, esteemed and beloved by all who had the happiness of her acquaintance. This monument is erected by her affectionate and only surviving child, W. O'Grady. They that have seen thy look in death, no more may fear to die.

> Happy soul, thy days are ended,
> All thy mourning days below,
> Go, by angel guards attended,
> To the sight of Jesus go.

L.

This tomb was erected by William M'Caskey, of Roebuck, Esq., in respect and memory of his much lamented and beloved wife, Frances Louisa M'Caskey, who departed this life the 3rd day of December, 1830, aged 55 years, sincerely and affectionately esteemed by all who knew her.

Thou art gone to the grave, but we will not deplore thee,
Whose God was thy Ransom, thy Guardian, and Guide.
He gave thee, He took thee, and He will restore thee;
And death has no sting, for the Saviour has died.

Here lieth the remains of the late William M'Caskey, of Roebuck, in the County of Dublin, who departed this life on the 9th day of June, 1834, aged 62.

LI.

Cyril Morphy died 6th March, 1879, aged 15 years. Alexander Morphy died 30th September, 1889, aged 63 years. Kate Morphy died 5th January, 1894, aged 65. R.I.P.

LII.

Frances M'Causland departed this life the 14th April, 1820, aged 30 years; and to the memory of Elizabeth Gerrard, departed this life the 27th October, 1848, aged 70 years; and to the memory of Mary Gerrard, departed this life on the 18th day of May, 1862, aged 89 years; also Hannah M'Causland, who died February 16th, 1865, aged 81 years.

LIII.

Here lieth the remains of Anne Minchin, daughter of William Augustus Minchin, late of Woodville, in the County of Wexford, who departed this life September the 5th, 1819, aged 16 years. She now inherits the fulfilment of that promise, Because I live, ye shall live also. Adjoining this tomb on the left lies the body of William Minchin, son of the above William Augt. Minchin, who departed this life 22nd April, 1825, aged 18 years. Also the remains of William Augt. Minchin, who departed this life the 3rd January, 1841, aged 73 years.

LIV.

In memory of Catherine Lucinda, wife of John Maunsell, Esq., who died 3rd February, 1862, aged 34 years. " I know that my Redeemer liveth."—Job, 19 chap., 25 verse. Also in loving memory of Edmund Robert Lloyd Maunsell, eldest so of John and Catherine Lucinda Maunsell, born 18th October, 1852, died 2nd November, 1886. "Blessed are the pure in heart: for they shall see God."—Matt. v. 8.

LV.

Sacred to the memory of Daniel Neill, who died on the 23rd day of April, 1877, aged 57 years ; and of Harriet Haughton, his wife, who died on the 27th day of May, 1872, aged 50 years ; also of their son, Daniel Arthur Neill, who died on 12th July, 1885, aged 35 years. "I am the resurrection and the life ; he that believeth on me, though he were dead, yet shall he live."—John xi., verse 25.

LVI.

The Family Vault of Michael O'Brien, Esq., of the City of Dublin, who died the 2nd February, 1783, aged 68 years, leaving issue one daughter and two sons, Richard and Michael. Christiana, wife of Nicholas Mulligan, and only daughter of Michael O'Brien, died the 25th April, 1800, aged 42 years. Her husband died the 28th December, 1808, aged 62 years. Richard O'Brien, eldest son of Michael O'Brien, died the 4th of May, 1807, unmarried, aged 48 years. Here also lieth the remains of Catherine Lyons, daughter of James Lyons, Esq., formerly of Newcastle, in the County of Dublin, and maternal aunt of Mary O'Brien. She died on the 5th April, 1852, aged 96 years. Mary, wife of Michael O'Brien, jun., died the 26th of January, 1819, aged 55 years. Her beloved husband died the 27th of February, 1829, aged 60 years. Kate Mary O'Brien, daughter of Michael and Mary O'Brien, died the 30th July, 1834, aged 24 years. Maria Anne O'Brien, a twin daughter of Michael and Mary O'Brien, died the 16th of April, 1847, aged 28 years. Brigid Mary O'Brien, died on the 15th November, 1876. R.I.P.

LVII.

Here lieth interred the mortal remains of Mrs. Mary O'Neill, daughter of the late James Kenney, Esq., of Milltown, and wife of Patrick O'Neill, of Harcourt Street, Dublin, by whom this monument has been erected as an affectionate tribute to her worth. She departed this life the 10th May, 1819, aged 43 years. Here also are deposited the remains of the above Patrick O'Neill, Esq., for many years an eminent merchant in the City of Dublin. He departed this life July 16th, 1828, aged 58 years. Here lieth the remains of James Kenney, Esq., of Milltown, County Dublin, who died the 10th September,

1809, aged 73 years. " The noblest work of God an honest man." Here also is interred the remains of his wife, Mary Kenney, who died the 16th November, 1815.*

LVIII.

Sacred to the memory of Alphonsine Maria Pellegrini, eldest daughter of Doctor Pellegrini, of Trinity College, born in Berne, Switzerland, the 13th March, 1789, died July 6, 1822.

LIX.

Henrietta Ponsonby, daughter of C. B. Ponsonby, Esq., ob. April 12th, 1815, aged 16 years. She pleased God, and was beloved of Him, so that living among sinners she was translated.

LX.

Christina, wife of David Richard Pigot, died 8th April, 1387, aged 65 years.

LXI.

Frances Phillips, infant daughter of George and Mary Phillips, born 2nd May, died 17th May, 1858. Also Alix Maud Phillips, born January the 25th, died December 24th, 1863.

LXII.

To the beloved memory of my husband George Laurence Gardiner Ross, who died November 3, 1891, aged 29 years. "At evening time it shall be light."

LXIII.

In memory of Emily Radcliffe, widow of J. Radcliffe, loving, loved, and only sister of Davenport Crosthwaite, LL.D. She was called home 25 July, 1885, aged 57 years. At rest.

LXIV.

Annie Rossiter, died 18th January, 1886, aged 43 years. Grace, her daughter, died 8th October, 1885, aged 14 years.

LXV.

This Stone was erected by Bernard Reilly, Esq., in Memory of his beloved wife, Hannah Reilly, who departed this life

---

* D'Alton (*History of Co. Dublin*, p. 813) describes this tomb as a "very handsome sarcophagus." One of the tablets has been injured, apparently by a bullet, reported to have been in an affray with " resurrectionists."

3rd May, 1817, aged 45 years. Here also are deposited the remains of the above-named Bernard Reilly, Esq., late Paymaster of the 18th or Royal Irish Regt. of Foot, who died on the 20th January, 1841, aged 63 years. Universally regretted by those who knew him.

LXVI.

Job. xix. 23, 26. In loving memory of two dear children taken home, Devonsher Jackson Rowan, on March 17th, 1889, aged 7 years; and Eliza Villiers Rowan, on April 10th, 1889, aged 21 years. " From the bondage of corruption into the liberty of the glory of the children of God."—Rom. viii. 21.

LXVII.

Here lieth the body of William Reynolds, of Ash Street, in the City of Dublin, who died the . . . of February, 1736. Also the body of his wife Joanna Reynolds, alias Fagan, who died the . . . of April, 1739, anno Ætatis 68. Also the bodies of their daughters, Margaret and Catherine and Elioner; and of their son Patrick, and of eight more of their children. Filius eorum Gulielmus . . . . et . . . . Minimis Obiit in . . . Nube (?) pacem meridionali . . . mo Novembris 1771, Anno Vero Suo . . . et sepultus fuit ibidem in locatione cathedrali.

Here lyeth the body of Alice Reynolds, who died 10th Oct., 177 . . aged 31, to whose memory this Stone was placed by her husband, Edward Reynolds, of St. James St., Dublin. Here also are buried two of their children, Patrick and Edward.

LXVIII.

Sacred to the memory of Catherine Rowley, widow of the Revd. John Rowley, LL.D., Rector of Lurgan, County Cavan, and of St. Michan's, Dublin, died 10th April, 1879, aged 72 years. "Whether we live therefore or die, we are the Lord's."—Romans, 14 Chapt., 8th verse. Also in loving memory of Josias, Commander, R.N., their eldest son, who died 15th Feb., 1887, aged 57 years, late of Mt. Campbell, Co. Leitrim, J.P. and D.L.

LXIX.

This tomb was erected by John Roe, of North Frederick Street, in the City of Dublin, Esq., in respect and memory of his lamented and beloved wife, Eliza Roe (otherwise Campbell, only daughter of the Rev. Matthew Campbell, late of

Barn Elm, in this county) ; she departed this life on the
15th day of October, A.D. 1826, in the 24th year of her age,
sincerely esteemed and regretted by all who knew her. Here
also lieth the remains of Eliza Campbell, relict of the late
Rev. Matthew Campbell, of Barn Elm, County Dublin, who
departed this life June the 1st, 1835, in the 74th year of her
age. Here also are deposited the remains of Frederick
Campbell, Esq., only son of the above-named Rev. Matthew
Campbell, late of Barn Elm, Co. Dublin, who departed this
life on the 15th day of February, 1861, in the 61st year of
his age. Here also are interred the remains of Maria Campbell (otherwise Murray), relict of the above-named Frederick
Campbell, who departed this life on the 22nd day of November, 1885, aged 82 years.

LXX.

Here lieth the body of Philip Roe, who departed this life
December the 11th, 1817, aged 53 years. May he rest in
peace. Amen.

LXXI.

In Memory of Robert Sherlock, fourth son of Major.
William Joshua Compton, and Isabella, his wife, who died at
Belfield, December 26th, 1852, aged 5 months.

LXXII.

Sacred to the memory of Dr. Whitley Stokes, ex-F.T.C.D., of
16 Harcourt Street, Dublin, who departed this life in the
peace of Christ on the 13th April, 1845, aged 82; and of
Mary Anne, his wife, only daughter of William Picknoll,
Esq., of Seatown House, Swords, who departed this life on the
13th July, 1844, aged 68. They were lovely in their lives.
This stone is placed here by their youngest daughter, Ellen
Honoria Stokes, May, 1863. Also of Ellen Honoria Stokes,
died Augt. 6th, 1880.

Beneath this stone are interred the Mortal Remains of
Harriet Stokes, who died on the 10th June, 1825, aged 27
years. And of her sister Mary Anne, who died on the 14th
October, 1838, aged 39 years. "I heard a voice from heaven
saying unto me, Write, From henceforth blessed are the dead
which die in the Lord: Even so, saith the Spirit, for they rest
from their labours." "Gather my saints together unto me,
those that have made a covenant with me with sacrifice."

LXXIII.

In fraternal remembrance of Edward Alma Stanley, died
12th November, 1881, aged 36 years. This stone was erected

as a tribute to his memory by his brethren and friends. He was a loving husband, fond father, faithful brother, and true friend. " And they laid him in his own grave, and mourned over him, saying, Alas! our brother." Also his beloved wife Catherine, who died 26th November, 1890, aged 46 years; and their eldest son Charles, died 6th December, 1890, aged 22 years.

LXXIV.

Margaret Sophia, second daughter of Robert Johnstone Stoney, Esq., of Parsonstown, and for nine years the wife of George Johnstone Stoney, M.D., F.R.S., died October 13th, 1872, aged 29 years.

"Some men a forward motion love,
But I by backward steps would move."
"For time, that gave, doth now his gift confound."

In loving remembrance of Anne, third daughter of Bindon Blood, D.L., of Granaher and Rockforest, County Clare, and widow of George Stoney, of Oakley Park, King's County, born June 4th, 1801, died October 29, 1883, aged 82 years. " Thy Word is very pure; therefore thy servant loved it." —Psalm cxix. v. 140.

In loving remembrance of Katharine Harriet Stoney, second daughter of George and Anne Stoney, of Oakley Park, King's County, born February 5, 1824, died February 24, 1887, aged 63 years.

LXXV.

TURBETT. Sacred to the memory of Robert Turbett, Esq., of Greenmount, who departed this life the 21st January, 1830, aged 70 years. A sincere and exalted Christian, he fulfilled the relative duties of husband, parent, and friend with unaffected piety and exemplary affection. His virtues could only be duly appreciated by those who knew him, whilst the sorrowing recollection of so much departed worth affords the most convincing assurance that he lived respected and esteemed, and died lamented by all who knew him.

LXXVI.

Emma Usher, daughter of Lieut. Usher, R.N., died Dec. 8, 1889, aged 62 years.

LXXVII.

Family burial-place of J. L. Verschoyle, eldest son of the Rev. Joseph and Catherine Verschoyle, Captain, H.M. 66th Regiment, Douro, Talavera, Albuhera, Vittoria, Pyrenees,

Nivelle, Nive, Orthes, Peninsula. He departed this life the 28th Sept., 1875. Erected by his wife and three sons. " The Lord gave, and the Lord hath taken away: blessed be the name of the Lord."

LXXVIII.

Thé family vault of Patrick Waldron, Rathgar House. Mary, wife of Patrick Waldron, born 21st Augt., 1787, died 19th Dec., 1824. R.I.P. Laurence Waldron, elder brother of Patrick Waldron, born . . 1763, died 20th May, 1833. R.I.P. James S. Murphy, son of Jeremiah Murphy of Cork, born . . 1817, died . . 1825. R.I.P. Patrick Waldron, who caused this tomb to be erected, was born 5th September, 1772, died 31st Dec., 1851. R.I.P. John Waldron, second son of Patrick and Mary Waldron, born 13th April, 1815, died 8th December, 1847. R.I.P. Patrick Edward Waldron, fourth son of Patrick and Mary Waldron, born 11th January, 1824, died 22nd May, 1846. R.I.P.

LXXIX.

This Stone was erected by Maria to the memory of her husband William White, of the 61st Regiment, who departed this life the 30th April, 1828.

LXXX.

In memory of John L. White, Esq., Surgeon, who departed this life on the 25th day of June, 1870, aged 65 years. This monument was erected by a few personal friends and in-habitants of Dundrum, in remembrance of his many social qualities, his care and kindness as a physician, and especially his attention to the poor of the village and surrounding district.

Lieutenant Henry White, died December, 1870. Mary Wright, died October, 1871. Frances Dorothea, wife of Dr. J. L. White, died July 8th, 1874.

LIST OF BURIALS

From Inscriptions not printed in full.

Bridget, wife of John Anderson, of Dundrum, *d.* June 10, 1881, *a.* 69.

Mary Elizabeth Addy, *d.* Sept. 10, 1859, *a.* 4.

William Ashton, of Clonskeagh, *d.* Oct. 28, 1879, *a.* 24.

William Burke, Woollen Manufacturer, of Milltown Mills, *d.* Aug. 19, 1823, *a.* 43 ; also his son, Christopher, *d.* an infant.

Garret Byrne, of Milltown, *d.* Oct. 5, 1882, *a.* 72 ; also his
wife Esther, *d.* Jan. 31, 1886, *a.* 66; their dau., Elizabeth, *d.* June 12, 1863, *a.* 3½ ; and their dau., Ellen,
d. March 17, 1870, *a.* 14 ; also Michael Butler, brother
of Esther Byrne, *d.* April 24, 1881, *a.* 42.

Henry Byrne, *d.* Oct. 21, 1877, *a.* 12.

John Byrne, *d.* Dec. 22, 1880, *a.* 18 ; also three children, at
an early age.

James Burke, *d.* March 16. 1889, *a.* 69; also his wife,
Catherine, *d.* Nov. 4, 1870, *a.* 41.

Anne, wife of Francis Burke, of Fleet St., *d.* Feb. 28, 1789,
a. 34 ; also nine of her children.

John Byrne, *d.* March 9, 1862 ; and his son, Edward, *d.* Jan.
21, 1889, *a.* 18.

James Barrett, of Churchtown, *d.* Oct. 18, 1818, *a.* 78 ; also
his wife, Mary, *d.* March 18, 1820, *a.* 54 ; their dau.,
Margaret, *d.* July 10, 1829, *a.* 24 ; and their son, Luke,
d. July 2, 1850, *a.* 48.

Clare, wife of John Byrne, of Townsend Street, *d.* April 8,
1821, *a* 38 ; also three children, Margaret, Teresa, and
Eliza.

Robert Barnes, *d.* Aug. 8, 1820, *a.* 87; also his dau.,
Charlotte Dillon, *d.* March 4, 1800, *a.* 33 ; and her son,
George Barnes Loughlin, *d.* July 2, 1830, *a.* 32.

William Browne, *d.* April, 20, 1892, *a.* 50; also his dau.,
Kate, *d.* May 10, 1879, *a.* 1½ ; his son, Thomas F., *d.*
Aug. 26, 1893, *a.* 9½ ; and his son, Ephraim J., *d.* Aug.
28, 1893, *a.* 8½.

Richard Beasley, of Ballinteer, *d.* April 12, 1870, *a.* 45.

Larence Byrne, *d.* May 15, 1773.

Julia, wife of Patrick Cumiskey, *d.* Dec. 8, 1861, *a.* 28 ; and
his father, Terence, *d.* May 10, 1863, *a.* 74.

Arthur Carton, *d.* Feb. 20, 1871, *a.* 74; his wife, Catherine,
d. May 7, 1857, *a.* 58 ; and their three grand-children,
who *d.* young.

Edward Connor, *d.* . . . . . 15, 1775, *a.* 57.

Margaret, wife of John Canna, of Harold's Cross, *d.* May 28,
1816, *a.* 60.

Stephen Connor, of Dundrum, *d.* April 2, 1886, *a.* 30 ; and
his wife, Esther (who *m.* 2ndly Albert Gate), *d.* Aug. 5,
1890.

John Carroll, *d.* Nov. 19, 1887, *a.* 56; also his wife, Catherine, *d.* Oct. 26, 1867, *a.* 40 ; and their grandchild, Catherine, *d.* May 28, 1880, *a.* 1½ ; also Ellen Billings, mother of Catherine Byrne, *d.* Sept. 21, 1885, *a.* 87.

Patrick Cantwell, of South King St., *d.* June 8, 1810, *a.* 60 ; also two of his children, who *d.* young.

Thomas Coyle, of South Earl St., *d.* March 29, 1793, *a.* 41.

Timothy Cahill, of Exchequer St., *d.* Jan. 11, 1825, *a.* 80.

Richard Carr, of Park St., *d.* June 24, 1788, *a.* 49 ; and his wife, Mary, *d.* April 15, 1788, *a.* 46.

Henry Curran, *d.* July 28, 1856, *a.* 57; also his wife, Elizabeth, *d.* Jan. 29, 1883, *a.* 76 ; their eldest son, Thomas, who *d.* in New Zealand, Jan. 26, 1868, *a.* 34 ; and four children, who *d.* young ; also dau., Caroline, *d.* Nov. 2, 1891, *a.* 50.

John Cannon, *d.* April 21, 1888, *a.* 17.

Margaret, wife of Thomas Clarke, *d.* July 10, 1892, *a.* 42.

Anna Coombs, *d.* Dec. 9, 1890.

Martha Costello, *d.* Dec. 23, 1891, *a.* 20.

Bridget Craven, of Montague Lane, *d.* November 14, 1891, *a.* 48.

Mary, wife of Edward Courtney, of Dundrum, *d.* August 11, 1890, *a.* 50; and their son, Edward James, *d.* June 1, 1884, *a.* 4½.

Catherine, wife of John Donnellan, of Milltown, *d.* April 16, 1792, *a.* 46 ; also three of their children, who *d.* young.

Five children of Bryan Duffy, of Clarendon Market ; and his brother, Miles, *d.* January 29, 1739, *a.* 18.

Ellen, wife of Timothy Duggan, *d.* February 1, 1887, *a.* 72.

Sarah, wife of Charles Dickenson, *d.* March 22, 1883, *a.* 35.

Bridget, wife of Christopher Dromgoole, of Weaver's Square, *d.* March 7, 1805, *a.* 32 ; also three of their children, who *d.* young.

William Dromgoole, of Rathfarnham, *d.* February 3, 1809, *a.* 79 ; his wife, Catherine, and his son, Edward.

John D'Arcy, *d.* March 4, 1842, *a.* 46 ; and his wife, Mary, *d.* March 18, 1858, *a.* 60.

Mary Delaney, *d.* Aug. 23, 1882, *a.* 1½.

John and Catherine Doyle ; and their dau., Jane, *d.* July 15, 1889, *a.* 35.

Patrick Duras, *d.* November 28, 1766, *a.* 44.

William Duff, of Golding Lane, *d.* November 26, 1776, *a.* 76.

Anne, wife of William Dunne, of Beaver Row, *d.* October 7, 1885, *a.* 58.

Kate, sister of James Egan, of Newtown-le-Willows, *d.* March 6, 1877, *a.* 27.

James Elverd, *d.* February 6, 1892, *a.* 70.

William Ennis. of Kingston, *d.* December 11, 1826, *a.* 68; also his wife, Alicia, *d.* March 23, 1808, *a.* 49; and their son, Andrew, *d.* January 1, 1815, *a.* 21.

William Flannagan, of Rathfarnham, *d.* November 15, 1759, *a.* 91; also seven of his children.

Charles, father of Patrick Farrel, "chaneman," of New St., *d.* April 21, 1735, *a.* 55; also his dau., Catrein, Hugh Farrel, and his wife, Catrein.

Eliza Avice, wife of Henry Edward Flynn, *d.* March 8, 1855.

Anne M. Fox, of Milltown; also her daus., Kate, Avice, Monica, Josephine, and her son, Thomas J. Fox, M.D., of Cottage Park, Kilgobbin, and his wife, Julia Maria, and their children.

Patrick Fleming, Inspector, D.M.P., *d.* April 22, 1892, *a.* 46; also his wife, Elizabeth, *d.* January 17, 1890, *a.* 40; and their dau., Mary, *d.* May 1, 1880, *a.* 5½.

Bridget Anne, dau. of Patrick Field, of Ranelagh, *d.* Feb. 20, 1888, *a.* 21; also Patrick, jun., *d.* November 12, 1891, *a.* 24.

Mrs. Maria Fox, a faithful servant of R. W. Hillas, Esq., of Farm Hill, *d.* February 11, 1889.

Daniel Finn, of Patrick Street, *d.* October 6, 1808, *a.* 31.

Henry Fullerton, *d.* Feb. 20, 1863, *a.* 52; and his son, Thomas, *d.* March 16, 1859, *a.* 7.

Patrick and Hannah Farrell; also their son, John, *d.* December 16, 1879; and their dau.-in-law, Mary, wife of Patrick Farrell, *d.* May 6, 1884.

William Finn, *d.* January 9, 1891, *a.* 74.

David Goold, of Clare Street, *d.* Jan. 27, 1790, *a.* 74; and his brother, Patrick, *d.* Aug. 1, 1781, *a.* 57.

Amos Godsell, *d.* April 22, 1883, *a.* 62; and his wife, Mary, *d.* December 5, 1886, *a.* 66.

Michael Garvey, *d.* Dec. 8, 1890, *a.* 72, and his wife Catherine, *d.* May 8, 1894, *a.* 69.

Robert, youngest son of Wm. Hall, of Aberdeen, *d.* May 4, 1883, *a.* 5.

Paul Ham, *d.* November 15, 1816, *a.* 54; and his dau., *d.* July 26, 1815, *a.* 19.

John, son of Daniel Hayes, of Portobello, *d.* March 24, 1817, *a.* 19.

Mary, wife of Matthew Hart, of Churchtown, *d.* May 9, 1893, *a.* 45.

Ann, wife of Thomas Hughes, *d.* Aug. 26, 1769, *a.* 34.

Edmund Jones, *d.* October 20, 1766, *a.* 45.

James Jackson, *d.* October 4, 1806, *a.* 67.

James Kearney, of . . . Hill, *d.* October 17, 1758, *a.* 46; also two of his children.

Mrs. Mary Kearney, *d.* September 10, 1811.

Elizabeth Mary Kinlen, *d.* March 26, 1880, *a.* 14½.

Daniel Kane, *d.* June 22, 1824, *a.* 60.

Mrs. Elnoir Kelly, *d.* Feb. 9, 1773, *a.* 40; also five of her children, and Michael Kelly, sen., *d.* November 23, 1785.

Simon, son of Terence Kane, of Cullenswood, *d.* Oct. 4, 1803.

Mary Elizabeth, wife of John F. Knott, l.r.c.s.i., *d.* March 26, 1879, *a.* 28.

Mary, wife of James Kennedy, of Dublin, merchant, *d.* Jan. 7, 1779, *a.* 60.

John Kelly, *d.* May 20, 1884, *a.* 61.

Thomas Kinsella, *d.* Dec. 25, 1804, *a.* 39.

Ambrose Langan, of Windy Arbour, *d.* October 14, 1887, *a.* 55.

Marian Letheby, *d.* March 1, 1891, *a.* 68.

John Lee, of Wall's Lane, *d.* Jan. 20, 1822, *a.* 58.

Jos. Lennon, *d.* Jan. 4, 1891, *a.* 85.

Marcella Leonard, *d.* Oct. 21, 1882, *a.* 10.

Mary Jane Meates, *d.* April 17, 1853; and her brother, Abraham, *d.* May 26, 1882.

Catherine, wife of Wm. M'Kee, of Haddington Road, *d.* May 24, 1873, *a.* 61; and their daughter, Catherine, *d.* Sept. 19, 1872, *a.* 30.

Thomas Messett, of Dundrum, *a.* 86; also his wife, Sarah, *a.* 102; their son, Solomon, *d.* May 22, 1808, *a.* 66; and several more of their family; also their son, Thomas, *d.* March 5, 1827, *a.* 76, and his wife, Margaret, *d.* 1826, *a.* 56; and their son, Solomon, *d.* Aug. 9, 1859, *a.* 57.

E

Anne, dau. of Bryan McGarry, of Pill Lane, *d.* May 1, 1772.

Agnes, wife of Timothy Maguire, *d.* June 10, 1779, *a.* 33; also two of her children.

James M'Kenna, *d.* March 2, 1883, *a.* 34; also his child, Catherine, *d.* young; and parents, Christopher and Ellen, *a.* 74 and 68; and his sisters, Catherine, *a.* 16, and Anne, *a.* 12.

John, son of John M'Loughlin, of Milltown, *d.* July 4, 1880, *a.* 9 months; also his sons, Patrick and Thomas, *a.* 14½ and 13½, who were accidentally drowned on Dec. 19, 1886.

Annie, wife of Christopher Mulligan, *d.* March 17, 1756.

Mrs. Frances Newton, *d.* June 30, 1814, *a.* 80.

Elizabeth, wife of Thomas Moran, of Winetavern Street, *d.* Aug. 23, 1810, *a.* 75.

Edward Mullins, *d.* Dec. 11, 1817, *a.* 37.

Anne, youngest dau. of D'Arcy Mahon, *d.* March 2, 1824, *a.* 5.

James Murphy, *d.* June 25, 1882, *a.* 76; also his wife, Mary, *d.* March 13, 1882, *a.* 75.

William M'Arthur, *d.* July 28, 1880, *a.* 11.

William, brother of John M'Cabe, *d.* Aug. 16, 1865, *a.* 20; also his infant sister, Kate; his grandfather, Michael O'Neill, *d.* March 14, 1857, *a.* 71; and his grandmother, Jane O'Neill, *d.* Sept. 16, 1861, *a.* 60.

Thomas Murphy, *d.* Jan. 31, 1867, *a.* 47; also Ellen Murphy, *d.* July 26, 1868, *a.* 44; and John M'Donnell, *d.* July 19, 1884, *a.* 40.

M. Jane, dau. of Patrick Murphy, Milltown, *d.* Oct. 21, 1881, *a.* 5½; also his wife, Ellen, *d.* Dec. 22, 1883, *a.* 43; his son, Joseph, *d.* June 4, 1889, *a.* 4½; his dau., Esther, *d.* May 21, 1891, *a.* 14; seven other children, *d.* young; and his son, John, *d.* March 8, 1871, *a.* 4½.

Elizabeth English, dau. of John O'Neill, of Frederick Street, *d.* Dec. 3, 1780, *a.* 27.

Mary Dora, dau. of Thomas and Sarah O'Neill, of Dunlavin, *d.* July 30, 1878, *a.* ½; also their dau., Bridget Mary, *d.* Jan. 13, 1888, *a.* 1½.

Laurence O'Rorke, *d.* June 11, 1891, *a.* 64.

Mary O'Connor, *d.* April 26, 1853, *a.* 63; also Patrick, *d.* Jan. 21, 1869, *a.* 88; and Christopher, *d.* June 30, 1890, *a.* 56.

Anthony O'Brien, *d.* Jan. 19, 1795, *a.* 62; his wife, Julian, *d.* Nov. 17, ... *a.* 42; and five of their children.

Cecilia Russell Patterson, wife of William Mitchel of Londonderry, *d*. April 9, 1881.

Anne Panton, *d*. June, 1872, *a*. 4½ ; and her brother, John, *d*. Jan., 1873, *a*. ½.

Edward Purcell, of Windy Arbour, *d*. Feb. 1, 1868, *a*. 82 ; also nine of his children, who *d*. young.

Thomas Godfrey Power, *d*. May 27, 1881, *a*. 52.

Two children of John James Quinn, Oct. 6, 1759.

George Quinn, Weaver, of Ash Street, *d*. Jan. 30, 1758, *a*. 45 ; also four of his children; and Jane, his wife, who *d*. Feb. 23, 1774, *a*. 63 ; with six of their grandchildren.

The Mother and four Children of Patrick Reynolds, of Plunket Street.

Edward Ryan, *d*. Feb. 17, 1771, *a*. 56 ; also his wife, Jane, *d*. Sept. 27, 1788, *a*. 49.

Mary Redmond, of Ballypierce, Co. Carlow, *d*. Jan. 9, 1872, *a*. 72; and two grandchildren, Johanna, *a*. 7 ; and Bridget, *a*. 5.

Sarah Jane, dau. of Wm. and Mary Richardson, *d*. Aug. 9, 1882, *a*. 15; and Wm. Richardson, *d*. Sept. 9, 1894, *a*. 61.

Samuel Ranson, *d*. Nov. 17, 1860, *a*. 32; and his wife, Maria, *d*. May 28, 1888, *a*. 70; also their child, Maria Louisa, *d*. May 3, 1859, *a*. 2½.

William Sutton, *d*. June 4, 1893, *a*. 78 ; and his wife, Anne, *d*. Jan. 7, 1890, *a*. 60.

Maria, wife of William Sproule, *d*. May 18, 1880, *a*. 50.

Elizabeth, wife of John Sheridan, and dau. of Robert Taylor of Ballymascanlon, Co. Louth, *d*. May 15, 1881, *a*. 44.

George Henry Searle, formerly of Louth, Lincolnshire, *d*. April 12, 1890, *a*. 70.

Rosie, dau. of Joseph and Georgina Smith, *d*. Jan. 31, 1891, *a*. 10½.

Anne, wife of John Seth, *d*. Aug. 7, 1875, *a*. 31.

Mrs. Anne Sharman, *d*. June 16, 1838, *a*. 72.

Nine children of John Scott, 1774.

William Sheedy, *d*. March 14, 1886, *a*. 55 ; and his dau., Ellie, *d*. Feb. 17, 1894.

Mary J. Thompson, *d*. July 6, 1886, *a*. 46.

Jane, wife of Peter Tobin (alias Johnston), *d*. Nov. 21, 1778, *a*. 27.

Richard Turner, *d.* March 31, 1841, *a.* 45 ; also his wife, Jane, *d.* May 5, 1833, *a.* 36 ; and the following children of their son, Joseph Turner of Newtown Park:—Richard, *d.* Sept. 1, 1853, *a.* 3½ ; Sarah, *d.* March 25, 1855, *a.* 3¼ ; Joseph, *d.* Dec. 27, 1858, *a.* 1¼ ; John, Feb. 8, 1861, *a.* 1 day ; Esther, *d.* Nov. 23, 1867, *a.* 1½ ; also Mrs. Sarah Turner, *d.* Sept. 15, 1864, *a.* 68.

Walter Blake Kirwan Tyner, *d.* Oct. 26, 1891, *a.* 32.

Carolina Elizabeth, dau. of Arthur W. Webb and Catherine Elinor Webb, *d.* May 1, 1851, *a.* 17.

Catherine, wife of John Wright, of Ormond Street, *d.* Aug. 23, 1770, *a.* 42.

James Whittey, of Rathfarnham, *d.* Nov. 8, 1756, *a.* 36 ; and three of his children, who *d.* young.

The Husband of Mrs. Bridget Walsh, *d.* June 17, 1793, *a.* 36.

Emily Walsh, *d.* Oct. 9, 1891, *a.* 62.

John Wade of Terenure, Farmer, *d.* April 12, 1761, *a.* 88.

Lorance, son of Nicholas Whitty, of Dublin, Throster, *d.* April 17, 1755, *a.* 20 ; also his grandfather, Lorance Byrne, *d.* Oct. 12, 1748, *a.* 94.

CHAPTER IV.

CHRIST CHURCH.

A BOUT the year 1809, it was found that the old parish church was no longer large enough for the congregation attending it, and at a Vestry held on June 13th in that year, it was resolved that a new church should be built, on a site then approved of, near the old church, that the expense should not exceed £2,000, and that the private property in the seats of the old church should be preserved.

Nothing came of this resolution ; for in 1812, at a Vestry held on October 22nd, it was rescinded, and it was decided that the new church should be built upon ground at Drumartane, then thought to belong to Mr. John Giffard,* but afterwards found to be owned partly by Alderman Hone,† and that an application should be made to Lord Fitzwilliam for a grant of the fee.

A year afterwards, the consent of Lord Fitzwilliam to grant the fee having been obtained, a petition to the Lord Lieutenant and Privy Council for leave to change the site of the parish church was prepared, and an application made to

---

* See Giffard, John, chapter vii.
† See Hone, Nathaniel, chapter vii.

the Board of First Fruits for a loan of funds to build the new church.

Subsequently the plans of the new building, which had been prepared by Mr. William Farrell, Architect, of Kildare Street, Dublin, were approved of, and ordered to be forwarded to the Board of First Fruits, with a memorial for the loan.

This memorial appears upon the minutes of the Board of First Fruits,* under date of 28th October, 1813, and states that the parish church was too small for the congregation attending it; that it was intended to build a large and handsome church in a more convenient situation; that several of the parishioners supported themselves and their families by farms upon the mountains, and that they were unable to pay any considerable cess. The memorial resulted in a grant of £4,300, as a loan in aid of the building of the church.

In 1844 the Vestry was still in doubt as to what plans it would adopt. In that year a committee was appointed to view Monkstown Church, and it reported that the plan of that church was more eligible than the one drawn by Mr. Farrell. Accordingly, in May 1814, the Vestry adopted the design of Monkstown Church, with what would now seem to have been considerable alterations, and directed the plans to be laid before the Archbishop and the Board of First Fruits.

This Vestry also determined that the loan of £4,300 should be assessed on the parish, to be re-

* Public Record Office, Dublin.

paid by instalments in seventeen years, and should be applotted at the rate of 2s. 3d. per acre per annum, under 48 Geo. III., Chap. 65, and 49 Geo. III., Chap. 103.

No reply appears to have been given by the Archbishop until April, 1815, when a communication was received from the Archbishop of Cashel (then acting as coadjutor for Dr. Euseby Cleaver, Archbishop of Dublin, whose mind had become impaired some years before his death in 1819), to the effect that the plans were approved of, subject to the church being duly placed having regard to the orientation of the chancel.*

At length, without waiting for the order of the Privy Council allowing the site of the parish church to be changed—which order was not made until the 31st August, 1815—all other preliminaries having been arranged, the building of the church was commenced in June, 1815.

The different classes of the work were contracted for separately ; and it appears from the Vestry book that the contractor for the masonry work was Mr. Williams ; for the stone-cutting, Alderman Darley ; for the plaistering, Mr. Luke Storey ; and for the painting and glazing, Mr. Veto.

As the work proceeded, it was found that the

---

* In rebuilding the Church of St. Michael the Archangel in Dublin in 1814, the Archbishop of Cashel (the Most Rev. and Hon. Charles Brodrick) required similar alteration in the original plans, to secure proper orientation. *Vide Irish Builder*, vol. xxxiii., p. 164.

cost of the church would considerably exceed the
loan obtained from the Board of First Fruits; and
in September, 1816, it was decided to sell the sites
of the pews by auction, the purchasers to pay for
the carpenters' work of fitting the pews, as well as
for the sites themselves, and to be allowed either
to attach the pews to their houses in perpetuity, or
to retain them in their own name, in which case
they were given power to assign them to anyone
resident in the parish.

The Vestry presented the site of a pew to Lord
Chief Justice Downes,* who was then resident in
the parish, " as a small but grateful acknowledg-
ment of his unremitting attention to the interests
of the parish, and particularly of his having pro-
cured the means of building the church at a com-
paratively trifling expense."† A similar benefit
was conferred upon Alderman Hone and upon Mr.
Giffard, " as an act of proper respect" for having
granted a moiety of the ground on which the church
was built.

The auction was held on Thursday, the 24th
October, 1816, at the house of Mr. Curran, in Dundrum, " commonly called the Olympus Boarding
House," and the sites of twenty-six pews were sold,
realizing £384 10s.‡

* See Right Hon. William, Baron Downes, chapter viii.

† Vestry book, from which all the quotations in this
chapter are taken, except where another authority is mentioned.

‡ Appendix D.

The funds raised by the sale of the pew sites were not, however, sufficient to complete the building, and in February, 1817, a petition to the Board of First Fruits for an additional loan was prepared. It is not clear whether the petition was actually presented to the Board or not ; at all events, it was not successful. We learn from this petition, which was accompanied by an estimate of the expense,* that the plans of the church included the erection of a spire, with a clock and two bells.

At length, in June, 1818, the church was so far finished as to admit of its being used for Divine Service; and the Archbishop of Cashel having granted the necessary license for its use previous to consecration, the Vestry resolved that the church should be opened on Sunday, the 21st June.

It is evident, however, from subsequent proceedings of the Vestry, that the church was then far from completed. In June, 1820, the churchwardens were directed to procure spouts to carry off the water from the roof, which caused " so much damp inside the church;" and in April, 1821, they were ordered to obtain estimates for roofing the tower. At the Easter Vestry in 1824, Mr. James Crofton,† the outgoing churchwarden, presented his account, amounting to £90, for building the sexton's lodge, and finishing the vestry-room. In the same year the churchwardens were directed to purchase

---

* Appendix E.

† See Crofton, James, chapter vii.

a bell, which was to weigh about five cwt., and to cost £60. In April, 1825, the Vestry accepted an estimate, amounting to £167 17s. 3d., from Wm. Moyers, of Rathfarnham, for cementing the outside of the church, and putting up metal pipes, and in 1832 it was found necessary to expend £95 on re-roofing the church—which does not speak well for the manner in which the work was done in the first instance.

The loan from the Board of First Fruits was never fully repaid. At a Vestry held in 1833 the tenth instalment was ordered to be applotted; but it was not levied, in consequence of the passing of the Church Temporalities Act, which exonerated the parishioners from repayment of all sums of money due to the Board.

About 1833 the south gallery was erected, partly by private subscriptions,* and partly by a grant from the Ecclesiastical Commissioners.

The building, which is now used as an infant school and teacher's residence, appears to have been built about 1836 for a Sunday school.

In 1844 a small organ was purchased for the church at an expense of £47 19s. 6d., and was placed in the south gallery.

In 1853 the church was broken into by robbers, who stole the brass branches from the pulpit and reading-desk, the sconces in the body of the church, and brass fittings from the organ loft.

* See Appendix D.

There are persons still residing in the parish who remember the appearance of the church interior at this time; and plans of the alterations subsequently made, which are in the possession of the Representative Church Body, afford additional assistance in correctly describing it. It consisted of the rectangular space now forming the body of the church, with a shallow recess in the eastern wall, in which there was an east window, with a small side-light to the north. In this recess the communion table stood, having in front of the rails, and standing out into the church, the pulpit raised above two reading-desks, one of which stood on either side. The pews were the high square erections in which our ancestors concealed themselves from the gaze of their neighbours. A desk for the clerk stood under the south gallery near the large window; the stairs to that gallery being near the clerk's desk. By the door which now leads into the south porch, the clergymen retired into the "robing-room," as the vestry-room is called in one of the old plans. The north and south galleries were different in design from the present galleries; the front panelling, which was made of solid oak, was higher, and obstructed the view more, than the present panelling; the front was curvilinear, instead of being straight; and the pews were all on nearly the same level, so that persons sitting in the back seats could not see down into the body of the church. Part of the oak panelling was placed in the hall of the rectory, where it forms a dado.

In the year 1858 the congregation had increased so much, that it was found necessary to afford more accommodation, as we find from a resolution passed by a meeting of the parishioners in that year ; but it was not until 1861 or 1862 that anything was actually done. About that time, the nave was built, the west gallery erected, and the stairs removed from under the south gallery, and placed in the south porch, which was then built. The communion table rails were placed upon a platform, and the pulpit and reading-desk erected behind the communion table according to the arrangement not inappropriately called " three-decker."

These improvements were carried out at a cost of £1,200, which was raised partly by private subscriptions, and partly by a grant from the Ecclesiastical Commissioners.

When the present Rector came into office, in 1867, he found the church arranged as we have now described it; and within two years of his institution, he had effected the first of the long series of improvements which have been carried out through his instrumentality. The old square pews were then remodelled, and the " three-decker " arrangement removed, the pulpit being placed at the north, and the reading-desk at the south, side of the communion table.

In 1871 Mr. Henry Roe* presented to the church a very fine organ, made by Forster and

---

* See Roe, Henry, chapter vii.

Andrews, of Hull, which was placed in the west gallery.*

The erection of the new chancel, with its painted windows, by Mr. Roe, in 1872, completed the transformation of the church, as erected in 1818, into the vastly different building which we are accustomed to see now.

This portion of the church is built in the decorated style, of limestone in broken ashlar masonry, with chiselled limestone dressings and mouldings to the windows, and with coigns of the same material. It contains a large east window, with a five-light decorated tracery. The subjects depicted on the window are seven. In the first section, commencing to the left, we have the Finding of Moses in the ark of bulrushes, and the Building of Solomon's Temple; in the second, the Brazen Serpent raised upon a well-defined Latin cross; in the third, the Translation of Elijah; in the fourth, Abraham's Sacrifice; and in the fifth, Moses descending from Mount Sinai, with the Tables of the Law, and King Solomon worshipping in the Temple. The legend upon the glass is as follows:

" The gift of Mr. and Mrs. Roe, of Mount Anville, 1872 ;"

---

* It was built at a cost of £600, and was first used at Divine Service on Sunday, March 26, 1871. The Archbishop of Dublin (the Most Rev. Richard Chenevix Trench, D.D.) preached a suitable sermon on the occasion, and Dr. Stewart, afterwards so well known as Sir Robert Prescott Stewart, played the instrument "with his wonted skill and taste, displaying to perfection the various and charming combinations of which the organ is capable." *Vide Daily Express*, March 27, 1871.

and below the window there is a brass plate inscribed thus :—

"This chancel presented to Taney Parish by Henry Roe,
Esq., Mount Anville, Dundrum, 1872."

The small single-light windows in the sanctuary, to the north and south of the east window, illustrate the texts—"I was in prison, and ye came unto me," and " I was sick, and ye visited me ; " which are also inscribed upon the glass, one being " the gift of Florence Roe," and the other " the gift of George Roe." There are also two windows in the north wall of the chancel, each with two-light tracery, one illustrating the texts : " I was an hungered, and ye gave me meat," and " I was thirsty, and ye gave me drink ; " and the other illustrating " I was a stranger, and ye took me in," and " naked, and ye clothed me ; " all of which are also inscribed upon the glass, being " the gift of Charlotte Roe," " the gift of Elizabeth Roe," " the gift of Richard Roe, " and " the gift of Maude Roe," respectively. Mr. Roe furnished the chancel with two handsome brass candelabra, and gave elaborate wrought-iron communion rails, and a handsome tessellated pavement in the sanctuary and chancel aisle.

Mr. Roe also supplied funds to pay off the old debt remaining upon the church, thus enabling it to be fully consecrated.

By the act of consecration, which took place on the 10th June, 1872, it was " ordained and constituted the Parochial Church of the Parish of

Tawney," and consecrated "to the Honor of God and to Holy Uses," by the name of " Christ Church, Tawney."*

Since then the church has been further adorned by many gifts, including a handsome carved stone pulpit, erected by Mr. George Kinahan,† of Roebuck Park. Upon the six panels of the pulpit are inscribed the following :—

"In my Father's house are many mansions." "Feed my lambs." "The Spirit and the Bride say, Come. And let him that heareth say, Come." "Feed my sheep." "I am the Resurrection and the Life." "In memory of a beloved child, George D. Kinahan, born Sept. 21, 1865, died March 13, 1878; and of a dear brother, Charles H. Kinahan, born Sept. 29, 1836, died April 13, 1878.—1 Thes. iv. 14."

Upon a fillet below the panels are the words :

"Give unto the Lord the glory due unto His name."

Mr. Charles H. James has given a handsome carved stone prayer-desk, inscribed as follows :

"O Thou that hearest prayer, unto Thee shall all flesh come." "In loving memory of Catherine Mary James ;"

and a brass plate records that it was

"Erected to the revered memory of a beloved wife, by her husband, Charles Henry James, of Rockmount House, in this Parish, April, 1879."‡

* The consecrating prelate, and also the preacher, was the Most Rev. Richard Chenevix Trench, D.D., Archbishop of Dublin. See account of the ceremony in the *Daily Express*, *Irish Times*, and *Saunders' News Letter*, June 11, 1872.

† See Kinahan, George, chapter vii.

‡ See Tombstone No. XL., chapter iii.

Mr. R. Henry A. M'Comas,* of Homestead, presented a reredos, upon which are inscribed the words :—

"Come unto me, all that travail and are heavy laden, and I will refresh you." "This do in remembrance of me." "So God loved the world, that He gave His only begotten Son."

Mr. J. F. Fuller, F.S.A., gave a carved wood lectern.

Mr. W. J. Goulding, of Roebuck Hill, has erected a beautiful painted window in the north gallery, representing "the Good Shepherd," after the well-known picture by Plöckhorst :—

"In loving memory of William Goulding, D.L., formerly M.P. for Cork, born 1817, died 1884."

A mural tablet under the south gallery was—

"Erected by a few friends in memory of Michael Charles Bernard, M.B., T.C.D., L.R.C.S.I., who for forty years laboured as a physician in this parish; died 24th April, 1881, aged 71 years. 'I know that my Redeemer liveth.'—Job xix. 25."†

The church was also much improved by the remodelling of the north and south galleries in 1885.

In 1875 the extension of the church grounds to the east of the church was completed, and a lease of the additional ground was obtained from the

* See M'Comas, Richard Henry Archibald, chapter vii.

† See Bernard, Michael Charles, chapter vii., and Tombstone No. V., chapter iii.

Earl of Pembroke for 150 years, at a rent of 1s. per year. To the expense of the new entrance gates and walls of the extension, as well as to the cost of erecting the new front entrance gates in 1884, and to many other objects connected with the parish, Lord Pembroke* subscribed liberally.

* George Robert Charles Herbert, thirteenth Earl of Pembroke, and tenth Earl of Montgomery, whose premature death in his forty-fifth year took place on May 3, 1895, while this chapter was in the press.

F'

CHAPTER V.

ROBERT PONT, *circa* 1615,

is mentioned in the *Regal Visitation* of 1615 as serving the churches of Taney, Rathfarnham, and Donnybrook. On Feb. 26, in the thirteenth year of the reign of James I. (*i.e.*, 1617-18), he was presented to "Silva Salvatoris, otherwise Rathdrum, Vicarage, Dublin Diocese, vacant by lapse or otherwise, and in the King's gift of full right." Probably he went afterwards to the Diocese of Raphoe, for it appears from a correspondence between Archbishop Laud and Lord Strafford that a clergyman of the same surname—the Christian name is not given—was beneficed there *circa* 1638. He "made a wild sermon" against the Bishop's jurisdiction, and had to leave the diocese. On May 22, 1640, as appears from the *Dublin Titles Book*, a licence was issued to Robert Pont, B.A., who possibly was a son of the Curate of Taney, to serve the cure of Kilpipe, Diocese of Ferns; and on May 31 in the same year he was admitted a Deacon at "Tawlaght." (*Earl Strafford's Letters*, Dublin, 1740, ed. by Dr. Wm. Knowles, vol. ii., pp. 245, 270, 337; Bishop Mant's *History of the Church of Ireland*, p. 544; *Diocesan Register; Patent Rolls*, James I., p. 299.)

* See chapter i., p. 3.

RICHARD PRESCOTT, *circa* 1630,
graduated in T.C.D., B.A., 1620, and M.A., 1623 ; his
entrance is not recorded. He is mentioned in Archbishop Bulkeley's report (see p. 14) as serving the
churches of Taney, Donnybrook, and Rathfarnham.

JOHN SANKEY, 1679,
was licensed on May 8, 1679, to serve the churches
of "Rathfarnam, Donnabrook, Kilgobban, Tawney,
Cruagh, and Whitechurch." (*Dublin Titles Book.*)

MERVYN ARCHDALL, 1753,
son of William Archdall, Goldsmith and Assay
Master, of Skinner Row, Dublin (who was a member
of the family of the Archdalls of Fermanagh), by
his wife, Henrietta, dau. of Rev. Henry Gonne, was
b. in Dublin, on April 22, 1723, and *bapt.* in St.
Werburgh's, on May 9. He entered T.C.D. on Oct.
10, 1739, and graduated B.A., 1744, and M.A., 1747.
He was licensed on Jan. 24, 1750, as Curate Assistant of the Parishes of Howth and Kilbarrack, and
on Oct. 2, 1753, on the nomination of Archdeacon
Pococke, as Curate of "Kilgobban and Tawnee" at
a stipend of £35 and "book money." He was also
the non-resident Rector of Nathlash and Kildorrery,
in the Diocese of Cloyne, from 1749 to 1758. In
the year 1761 Dr. Pococke, who had become Bishop
of Ossory, gave him the living of Agharney and
Attannagh in that diocese, which he held until
1786, with the Prebend of Cloneamery, and subsequently of Mayne. He resigned Agharney on

being appointed Rector of Slane, Diocese of Meath,
where he continued to reside until his death, on
Aug. 6, 1791. He was *bur.* in Slane Churchyard,
and a monument was erected to his memory there.
He *m.*, firstly, *circa* 1748, Miss Sarah Collis, of a
Kilkenny family, who *d.* May 28, 1782, having
had issue—1. Thomas Prior, *bur.* in St. Werburgh's,
1750; 2. Mervyn, a lawyer, *m.*, and *d.* 1809,
leaving issue; 8. Henrietta, *m.* Rev. John Dalton
Harwood; he *m.*, secondly, in St. Mary's Church,
Dublin, on Nov. 25, 1782, Miss Abigail Young.
He was the well-known antiquary, author of the
Monasticon Hibernicum, and of an enlarged edition
of *Lodge's Peerage.* (Brady's *Records of Cork*, vol. ii..
p. 863; vol. iii., p. 143; *Dictionary of National
Biography*, vol. ii., p. 67; Webb's *Compendium of
Irish Biography*, p. 5; *Dublin Titles Book;* Hughes's
St. Werburgh's, pp. 99, 131.)*

JEREMY WALSH, 1758,

son of Rev. Philip Walsh, was *b.* at Dublin in 1702,
educated by his father in the Co. Wicklow, and
entered T.C.D., May 11, 1719. He graduated B.A.,
1724, and M.A., 1727. He was instituted on Feb.
23, 1729, to the Rectories of Kilweilagh and Kil-
loah, in the Diocese of Meath, on the presentation
of the Earl of Drogheda. On the nomination

* The following authorities have been consulted, in addition
to those mentioned under the several notices :—Todd's *List of
Graduates of T.C.D.*, *Matriculation Books of T.C.D.*, *Registers
of Taney Parish*, and *Dublin Directories and Newspapers.*

of Archdeacon Mann, he was licensed on Sept. 1,
1758, Curate of "Kilgobbin and Tawney," at a
stipend of "£35 and book-money." He *m.* at
Whitehall, Sept., 1778, Mrs. Eyre, widow of the
late Thomas Eyre, M.P. for the borough of Fore, Co.
Westmeath. (*Meath and Dublin Titles Books;*
Walker's *Hibernian Magazine*, Sept., 1778, p. 536.)

WILLIAM DWYER, 1787,

son of Mr. Darby Dwyer, of Tipperary, was *b.* 1753,
and entered T.C.D. as a sizar on June 13, 1775.
He took a Scholarship in 1777, and graduated B.A.,
1780. He was ordained on July 25, 1780, in
St. Mark's Church, Dublin, by the Bishop of Dromore. He was licensed Jan. 10, 1787, on the
nomination of Archdeacon Hastings to the Curacy
of Taney, but only held it until October in the same
year, when he was appointed Curate of St. John's,
Dublin. He was subsequently, from March to
June, 1789, Rector of Clonmult, and from the
latter date to 1813 Rector of Templeroan, both in
the Diocese of Cloyne. He also held the Curacy
of Nohoval, Diocese of Cork, to which he was
licensed Sept. 18, 1802. (Brady's *Records of Cork*,
vol. i., p. 225, vol. ii., pp. 153, 397 ; *Dublin License
for Ordination;* Hughes's *St. John's*, p. 75.)

MATTHEW CAMPBELL, 1787-1814,

son of Mr. Robert Campbell, of Monaghan, was *b.*
1758. He was educated at Mr. Allen's School, and
entered T.C.D., Nov. 4, 1776. He graduated B.A.,

1781. On the nomination of Archdeacon Hastings, he was licensed to the Curacy of Taney on Nov. 9, 1787, and was appointed subsequently Rural Dean of Taney on Aug. 17, 1802. On June 10, 1813, he was appointed Perpetual Curate of Kilgobbin, on the nomination of Archdeacon Fowler, but seems to have continued to discharge the duty of Taney until the following year, when his successor, Mr. Ryan, was appointed. At a Vestry held on April 12, 1814, it was resolved to present him with an address "for his faithful conduct in the discharge of his duty during a period of twenty-five years." He retained the Curacy of Kilgobbin until his death, which occurred *circa* 1817. He *m.* June 17, 1795, Elizabeth (*d.* June 1, 1835), widow of Garret English, Esq. (whom she *m.* 1780, her maiden name being White), and had issue one son, Frederick, *b.* 1800, who *m.*, 1826, Miss Maria Murray (*d.* Nov. 22, 1885), and *d.* Feb. 15, 1861, and one daughter, Eliza, *b.* 1802, who *m.* in T. C., Sept. 18, 1824, John Roe, Esq., and *d.* Oct. 15, 1826. (See Tombstones XVI. and LXIX., chapter iii.) (*Dublin Titles Book.*)

RICHARD RYAN, 1814-20,

was a son of the Rev. William Ryan, of Tipperary, and was *b.* 1787. He was educated at Mr. White's school in Dublin, and entered T.C.D. May 5, 1806. He graduated B.A., 1811, and M.A., 1832. He was nominated on March 24, 1814, by Archdeacon Saurin to the Curacy of Taney, and was licensed on

April 15 following. He held this cure until 1820, when he was appointed to the Vicarage of Rathconnell, Diocese of Meath. He resigned it in 1825 on being nominated to the Vicarage of Rathcore, in the same diocese, to which he was admitted on Jan. 19, 1826. He continued to reside there until his death on July 8, 1837, and was *bur.* in Rathcore churchyard. He *m.*, in T. C., Aug. 3, 1814, Mary Lees, second dau. of John Giffard, Esq.,* and had issue, *bapt.* in T. C.—1. William, called to the bar 1839, q.c., 1867, j.p. Wexford, Wicklow, and Dublin ; 2. Sarah ; 3. Ellen. (*Dublin Titles Book ; Ecclesiastical Commissioners' Report,* 1836, p. 224.)

HENRY HUNT, 1820-21,

son of Mr. James Hunt, State Apothecary, of Sackville Street, Dublin, was *b.* 1792, and having been educated at Dr. Dowdall's school, entered T.C.D. as a pensioner on Sept. 3, 1810, taking second place at entrance. He graduated b.a., 1815, and m.a., 1818. He took Holy Orders in 1815, and on Dec. 26 of that year was licensed to the Curacy of Banbridge (Seapatrick), in the Diocese of Dromore. In 1818 he became Vicar of Ballynafeagh, in the Diocese of Kildare; and in 1820, on the nomination of the Marquis of Drogheda, Vicar of Rathconnell, in the Diocese of Meath. In March, 1820, when he assumed the duties, he was nominated Curate of Taney by Archdeacon Torrens, although not licensed until July 21. He held the Curacy until

* See Giffard, John, chapter vii.

June in the following year, when his successor, Mr. Vance, took charge of the parish. At a Vestry held on Sept. 18, 1821, a resolution was proposed by Mr. Wadden,* seconded by Chief Justice Downes,† and unanimously adopted, requesting the Archdeacon to convey to Mr. Hunt "the thanks of the congregation, and their sense of the pure zeal which influenced him in the discharge of his clerical duties." He was subsequently appointed in 1822 Vicar of Kiltoom and Camma, in the Diocese of Elphin, on the nomination of Dr. John Leslie, then Bishop of that see; on Aug. 23, 1827, a Minor Canon of St. Patrick's Cathedral, Dublin; and on March 7, 1829, Rector of Ahascragh, also in Elphin, of which diocese he had been nominated Vicar-General. On March 8, 1845, Dr. Leslie, who had become Bishop of Kilmore and Ardagh, as well as of Elphin, collated him to the Rectory of Lurgan (Virginia), Diocese of Kilmore, which he held with his minor canonry and vicar-generalship until his death, which occurred on May 22, 1861, at Donnybrook. His remains were interred at Shercock, Co. Cavan. He *m.*, 1823, Miss Rose Anne Adair, and had issue. (*Ecclesiastical Commissioners' Report*, 1836, p. 564 ; *Kilmore Register ;* Cotton's *Fasti*, &c., vol. ii., p. 200.)

WILLIAM FORDE VANCE, 1821, son of the Rev. Patrick Vance, of Antrim, was *b.* 1796, educated at Armagh School, under Dr. Miller,

---

* See Wadden, Barret, chapter vii.
† See Right Hon. William, Baron Downes, chapter viii.

and entered T.C.D. as a pensioner, Nov. 1, 1818.
The date of his B.A. degree is not recorded. He
took out his M.A. in 1822. He acted as Curate of
Taney from June to December, 1821; but no
license for him appears in the *Titles Book.* It
was resolved, at a Vestry on Jan. 1, 1822, that an
address expressing regret at his departure, and the
parishioners' wishes for his future welfare, should
be drawn up and presented to him. He *m.* in
Crumlin Church on March 1, 1823, Miss Anna-
bella Oakley.

JAMES BULWER, 1821-24,

was the only son of James Bulwer, Esq., of Ayl-
sham, Norfolk, by his wife Mary, dau. of John
Seaman, Esq., of Felmingham Hall, Norfolk. He
entered Jesus College, Cambridge, and graduated
B.A., 1818, and M.A., 1823. He was ordained Deacon
by the Bishop of Norwich, 1818, and Priest by the
Bishop of Kilmore, June 23, 1822. He served as
Curate of Taney from December, 1821, to 1824, but
does not appear to have been licensed. A vote of
thanks was accorded to him by the Vestry on April
20, 1824, "for his indefatigable zeal." He resigned, on being appointed (May 16, 1824) to the
Perpetual Curacy of Booterstown, which he held
only a short time, resigning it in the following year
(1825). The years 1825 and 1826 he spent in
Madeira and Portugal, and from 1827 to 1833 resided at Clifton, and served as Curate of St. Paul's,
Bristol. He was present at the memorable Bristol

riots in 1831, when he was assaulted by the mob;
and he afterwards gave evidence for the defence at
the trial, in Oct., 1832, of Charles Pinney, Esq.,
the Mayor of Bristol, for having neglected his duty
on that occasion. He was Minister of York Chapel,
and Curate of St. James', Westminster, from 1833
to 1840, and Curate of Blickling and South Er-
pingham, in Norfolk, until 1848, when he was
appointed by the Dowager Lady Suffield, of Blickling, Rector of Stody with Hunworth, in the Diocese
of Norwich. He held this cure until his death. He
d. on June 11, 1879, aged 84, and was *bur.* at Hunworth. He *m.* Eliza, only dau. of Archibald Redford,
Esq., of the Irish Bar, and had issue: 1. James
Benjamin Redford, of the English Bar, Q.C., formerly
M.P. for Ipswich, from Feb., 1874, to March, 1880,
and for Cambridgeshire, from Sept., 1881, to Nov.,
1885, and now Chairman of the Norfolk Quarter
Sessions, Recorder of Cambridge, and Master in
Lunacy; 2. Archibald Redford, of Tomard, Co.
Kildare, *m.*, 1856, Jean Hamilton, sister of Sir
Alexander Gibson Maitland, third Baronet, of Clif-
ton Hall, Co. Midlothian, and has issue two daus.,
Agnes and Dora Eleanor; 3. Walter John Redford,
of Barrowford, Co. Kildare, *m.*, 1851, Helena Sarah,
third dau. of Rev. Henry Moore, Rector of Ferns,
Co. Wexford, and has issue one son, Henry Alan,
b. 1854, *m.*, 1886, Mary, third dau. of Richard
Robert Wingfield, of Fairy Hall, Co. Wicklow, and
has issue one dau., Dorothy; 4. Dorothea Maria
Redford, *m.*, 1840, Rev. Humphrey Lloyd, D.D.,
late Provost of Trinity College, Dublin.

Mr. Bulwer was author of *Views of Madeira*, 1825-26 ; *Views of Cintra in Portugal ;* and *Views in the West of England.* For upwards of twenty years from 1840, he had charge of the Library of rare and valuable books at Blickling Hall, collected by Maittaire, early in the eighteenth century, and was a frequent contributor to the *Norfolk Archæo-logical Journal.* He was learned in botany and mineralogy, and possessed a complete collection of British shells, most of which are now in the British Museum. He was an accomplished artist in water colours, and made two beautiful collections of draw-ings and engravings, one illustrating Blomefield's *History of Norfolk*, the other Collinson's *History of Somersetshire*, which together fill upwards of seventy large folios, and are now in the possession of his eldest son. (Blacker's *Sketches of Booterstown, &c.,* p. 8; *Trial of Charles Pinney, Esq.* Blackwood, 1833.)

HENRY HAMILTON, 1824-25,

son of Henry Hamilton, Esq., of Dublin, *b.* 1796, was educated privately, and entered T.C.D., April 6, 1812, as a Fellow-Commoner. He graduated B.A., 1819, and M.A., 1832. He was ordained Deacon at Kilmore, July 5, 1822. He was instituted as Incum-bent of the Union of Thomastown, Pollardstown, and Dunmurry, in the Diocese of Kildare, on June 8, 1822, on the presentation of the Duke of Leinster; he was at first non-resident, and though not li-censed, acted as Curate of Taney from May, 1824, to May, 1825. In the latter year a Glebe House was built at Thomastown, and he went to reside there. He held the living until his death, which occurred *circa* 1854. (*Ecclesiastical Commissioners' Report*, 1837, p. 138.)

ALEXANDER BURROWES CAMPBELL, 1825-28,

son of Burrowes Campbell, Esq., Barrister-at-Law, was educated by Mr. White, and having entered T.C.D., won a Scholarship, 1819, and graduated B.A., 1820, and M.A., 1828. He was ordained a Deacon, and subsequently admitted to Priest's Orders at Kilmore, on June 23, 1823. He acted as Curate of Taney from May, 1825, but was not licensed until Feb. 24 in the following year. His nomination by Archdeacon Torrens is dated Aug. 23, 1825. He held the curacy until 1828. He was Perpetual Curate of Great Reddisham, Suffolk, from 1849 to 1858, and Chaplain to the Earl of Cowley from 1858 to 1886. He had a son, John, by his wife, Caroline, *bapt.* in T. C. (Crockford's *Clerical Directory*, 1879-86.)

JOHN PRIOR, 1828-1834,

eldest son of Dr. Thomas Prior, Vice-Provost of T.C.D., was *b.* May 25, 1803 ; and having been educated by Mr. Jones, entered T.C.D., and graduated B.A., 1826, and M.A., 1829. Having taken Holy Orders, he was licensed March 1, 1828, on the nomination of Archdeacon Torrens, Curate Assistant of Donnybrook, and on March 8, 1830, Curate of Taney. The license mentions that he had for some months previously discharged the duties. He held this cure until Aug., 1834, when he was obliged to resign on account of ill-health. At a meeting of the parishioners, held on Oct. 27, 1834, a resolution was adopted expressive of regret at the cause of his resignation, and "recording the sense entertained of his activity, benevolence, and Christian charity." It was also decided that a piece of plate should be subscribed for and presented to him. On July 13, 1851, he was appointed Rector of Rathcormack, Diocese of Cloyne, and was subsequently Rector of Kirklington, Diocese of Ripon, and Rural Dean of East Catterick, Yorkshire. He *d.* Dec. 21, 1867. He *m.*, firstly, 1833, Sophia, second dau. of John Odell, Esq., of Carriglea, Co. Waterford, by whom he had no issue surviving; and secondly, Sept. 13, 1836, Sarah, only surviving dau. of the Hon. Charles Butler, and had issue by her—1. Charles Butler, J.P., *m.* Dora, dau. of Richard Phillips, Esq., D.L., *d.* Jan. 7, 1875, leaving a son Richard Henry, and other issue ; 2. Henry Wallis, *m.* Mary Anne, dau. of Richard Phillips, Esq., and has issue; 3. Alice Maria, *d. unm.;* 4. Sophia Elizabeth, *m.* Major-Gen. Henry Frederick Winchilse Ely. On the death of her nephew, Mrs. Prior succeeded to her paternal estates of Castlecomer, Co. Kilkenny, Kirklington, Hipswell, and Hudswell, Co. York ; and on Aug. 30, 1882, assumed, by royal license, the surname of Wandesforde. She *d.* Dec. 21, 1892, and was succeeded by her grandson, Richard Henry Prior Wandesforde. (Brady's *Records of*

Cork, vol. ii., p. 373; *Titles Book; Wandesforde of Castlecomer and Kirklington*, B.L.G., 1894.)

SAMUEL HENRY MASON, 1834-36,

son of William Mason, Esq., *b.* 1809, was educated at Mr. Flinn's school, and entered T.C.D., Oct. 18, 1824. He graduated B.A., 1831, and took out a LL.B. degree 1851, and a LL.D., 1852. He acted as Curate of Taney from August, 1834, to March, 1836, but was not licensed. He was one of the officials in the Ecclesiastical Commissioners' office from 1849 to 1863. He *d.* April 15, 1865.

CLEMENT ARCHER SCHOALES, 1836-37,

son of John Schoales, Esq., Q.C., Assistant Barrister, Co. Kildare, by his wife Clementina, dau. of Clement Archer, Esq., M.D., was *b.* 1807. He was educated at Mr. White's school, in Dublin, and having entered T.C.D. on July 7, 1823, graduated B.A., 1829, and M.A., 1832. He was ordained Deacon in Ferns Cathedral, Oct. 18, 1832, and subsequently Priest. He acted as Curate of Taney from March, 1836, to October, 1837. He was afterwards Curate of Ballyshannon, in the Diocese of Raphoe, for some years. Owing to ill-health, he did not seek further preferment, and *d.* in Dublin in March, 1864.

WILLIAM HENRY STANFORD, 1836-51,

was a son of William Stanford, Esq., of Cavan, a descendant of Bishop Bedell, by his wife Sarah, dau.

of John M'Mullen, Esq., K.C. He entered T.C.D., and graduated B.A., 1827, and M.A., 1839. He was ordained Deacon by the Bishop of Kildare, Feb. 25, 1827, and Priest by the Bishop of Meath, June 10, 1827. He was Curate of Slane until Nov., 1829, and Curate of Maynooth from that date until May, 1832. He then went to England, and was Curate at Birmingham and of St. Mary's, Lancaster. He returned to Ireland, and was appointed Curate of Bray by the Hon. and Rev. William Plunket, then Rector of that parish. He again went to England, and was Curate of Stottesdon, in the Diocese of Hereford, for a short time. In 1836, on the nomination of Archdeacon Torrens, he was appointed second Curate of Taney with Mr. Schoales, and after the resignation of the latter in the following year had sole charge of the parish. He was appointed first chaplain to the Criminal Lunatic Asylum by the Lord Lieutenant on Nov. 26, 1850. He held Taney until it was disunited from the corps of the Archdeaconry in 1851, and on Mr. Bredin being nominated as the first Rector, it was arranged that he should succeed him as Rector of Rincurran, in the Diocese of Cork. An address and purse of sovereigns was presented to him on leaving the parish ; the address, which is entered in the vestry minute book, mentions that the feeling of regret at his departure was sincere and general, as he had laboured amongst the parishioners for fifteen years with steady and indefatigable zeal, and speaks in high terms of his

character as a Christian minister. He held Rin
curran until his death on Feb. 22, 1856. He *m.*
in St. Ann's Church, Dublin, on Oct. 31, 1833
Esther Katharyne, dau. of David Peter, Esq., whe
d. in 1863, and had issue—1. William Henry
Nassau (*bapt.* St. Ann's), M.B., T.C.D., *m.* Miss
Merelina F. Tindal, *o.s.p.*, Nov. 13, 1871 ; 2. Bedel
(*bapt.* T.C.), B.A., T.C.D., in H.O., *m.*, Sept. 29, 1868
Phoebe, dau. of Andrew Thompson, Esq., and has a
son, Bedell ; 3. Charles Edward Stuart, *m.* Fanny
(*d.* Nov. 4, 1883), dau. of William R. Box, Esq.
o.s.p., Dec. 7, 1887 ; 4. Adelaide Esther Katharyne
m. John H. Cooper, Esq., *d.* July 24, 1889, leaving
a son, Henry Austin Samuel; 5. Virginia Pauline
(*bapt.* T.C.), *m.* Samuel Cooper, Esq., who *d.* March
20, 1892.

CHAPTER VI.

RECTORS.

ANDREW NOBLE BREDIN, 1851-57,

eldest son of Major-General Andrew Bredin, R.A., was *b*. 1808. Having entered T.C.D., he graduated B.A., 1830, and M.A., 1832. He was Curate of St. Ann's, Dublin, and was one of the Stearne Catechists at St. Werburgh's. On Dec. 28, 1848, he was appointed to the Vicarage of Rincurran, Diocese of Cork, which he resigned Aug. 12, 1851, on being presented with the living of Taney, to which he had been collated on Aug. 1 in the same year. He held this parish until he was collated Prebendary of Dunlavin, on Dec. 23, 1857. He was installed on Jan. 9, and resigned in April following on being appointed Rector of Clonbullogue, Diocese of Kildare. He held this living until his death, which occurred a few months after, on July 18, 1858. He *m*., first, 1846, Miss Mary Wilhelmina Cooper, by whom he had issue—1. Arthur Francis Noble; 2. Margaret Florence Julia, *m*., first, 1879, Rev. Josiah Crampton, Rector of Killesher, son of Sir Philip Crampton, Bart., and secondly, Rev. Lewis Williams, Vicar of Llanwnda, North Wales; 3. Mary Henrietta, *d. unm.*, 1861; and secondly, Harriett, dau. of Capt. Peter Pemell, of Canterbury,

G

Kent, by whom he had issue—1. Andrew Nobl
William (*bapt.* T. C.), in H.O., B.A., Rector o
Sutton, Essex, *m.*, 1881, Pamela Adelaide Alice
dau. of Rev. Josiah Crampton (*vide ante*); 2. Har
riett Adelaide Pemell (*bapt.* T. C.), *d. unm.*, 1876
3. Ann Jane Pemell, *d. unm.*, 1873. (Hughes's *St
Werburgh's*, p. 92; Brady's *Records of Cork*, vol. i.
p. 239; vol. iii., p. 156; *Titles Book*; Cotton's *Fasti
&c.*, vol. v., p. 125.)

EDWARD BUSTEED MOERAN, 1857-67,

son of Edward Moeran, Esq., was *b.* at Cork, 1810
He was educated at Mr. Mulcahy's school, in Cork
under Mr. Farrell, and having entered T.C.D., Jul;
3, 1826, graduated B.A., 1831. He won Bisho]
Law's Mathematical Prize in 1832, and was i
Prizeman in the Fellowship Examination in 1838
He took out his M.A. degree in 1841, and his B.D
and D.D. degrees in 1853. He was ordained Deacoi
in St. Ann's Church, Dublin, on April 17, 1842
by the Bishop of Meath, and Priest in 1843 by th
Archbishop of Dublin. He was for a short tim
Curate of Bray, and was appointed Incumbent o
the Bethel (now Christ Church), Kingstown, ii
Feb., 1843. In 1852 he was elected Professor o
Moral Philosophy in T.C.D., and held the chair, a
well as his Chaplaincy, until 1857, when he wa
collated by the Archbishop of Dublin to the Rector;
of Taney. He resigned this parish in 1867, on bein;
appointed Rector of Killyleagh, Diocese of Down
to which he was presented by the Board of Trinit]

College. He was subsequently appointed Dean of
Down in 1876, and was one of the Bishop's ex-
amining chaplains. He *d.* on Oct. 13, 1887, and
was *bur.* at Killyleagh on Oct. 17. He *m.*, first,
Miss Christiana Mills, and had issue—1. Henry
Edward; 2. Marion De La Fea; and secondly, in
T. C., Feb. 7, 1865, Isabella, fourth dau. of John
Barton, Esq., of Stonehouse, Stillorgan Road, and
had issue—1. Francis Meredith (*bapt.* T. C.); 2.
Cecil Barton (*bapt.* T. C.); 3. Robert Warner; 4.
Archibald Edward; 5. Henry Hope; 6. Isabel Ethel
Jane; 7. Katherine Lillian.

Dr. Moeran was author of *Sermons on the Nature
of Faith; Examination of Colenso's Treatises on the
Pentateuch; and treatises on Mr. Baden Powell's
Study of the Evidences of Christianity; Mr. Jowett
on the Interpretation of Scripture; Romanism and
Ritualism,* &c., &c. He took a leading part in the
periodical entitled *The Catholic Layman,* for which
he wrote "The Dumb Village," and many other
papers.

WILLIAM ALFRED HAMILTON, 1867-—

fourth son of Henry Hamilton, Esq., J.P., formerly
of the 29th Regt. of Foot (who was third son of
the Right Rev. Hugh Hamilton, D.D., Lord Bishop
of Ossory, by his wife, Isabella, eldest dau. of Hans
Widman Wood, Esq.), by his wife Sarah, third dau.
of Rev. Michael Sandys, M.A.; was *b.* at Tullylish,
in the Co. Down. He was educated at Shrewsbury,
and having entered T.C.D., graduated B.A., 1846,

M.A., 1858, B.D. and D.D., 1877. He was ordained
Deacon, 1847, in Chester Cathedral by the Bishop
of Chester, and Priest on July 16, 1848, at Cambridge, by the Archbishop of Canterbury. He was
appointed Curate of St. Barnabas', Liverpool, by
the Rev. Thomas Nolan, and on Dec. 24, 1848,
Curate of Silso, Bedfordshire. In February, 1853,
he was presented by the Marquis of Drogheda to
the perpetual cure of Tullyallen, in the Diocese of
Armagh. In 1863 he was presented by the same
patron to Duleek, in the Diocese of Meath, but
never assumed the duties, as on Nov. 15 in that
year the same patron presented him to Monasterevan, in the Diocese of Kildare. He was Prebendary of Harristown, and a Rural Dean of Kildare
diocese. He was collated on Aug. 21, 1867, Rector
of Taney, on the presentation of the Archbishop of
Dublin. He was Canon of Christ Church Cathedral,
and Prebendary of St. Michan's, 1878-92, Rural
Dean of Taney, Chaplain to the Lord Lieutenant,
1869-92, and Chaplain to the Earl of Ennis-
killen. He m., Jan. 10, 1849, Henrietta Catherine,
third dau. of Henry St. George Cole, Esq., and
has issue—1. Henry Balfour, in H.O., M.A., T.C.D.,
Rector of West Leake, Nottingham, m., in T. C.,
Aug. 24, 1875, Hannah Sophia, dau. of John
Hubart Moore, Esq., and has issue—i. Alfred, ii.
John, iii. Augusta Cecilia ; 2. Alfred St. George ;
3. William Drummond, M.A., Oxon., m., in T. C.,
Aug. 5, 1891, Alice Josephine, third dau. of George
Kinahan, Esq., D.L., and has issue—i. George Alfred

Drummond; ii. Margaret Henrietta (*bapt.* T. C.);
4. Willoughby James, *m.*, in T. C., May 31, 1894,
Sophia Jane, third dau. of Charles Thompson,
Esq., J.P.; 5. Francis Cole Lowry (*bapt.* T. C.),
in H.O., B.A., Durham; 6. Blayney (*bapt.* T. C.); 7.
Gertrude May, *m.*, first, Sept. 1, 1875, Erskine
Wilmot Chetwoode, Esq., and had issue—i. Edward
Erskine, ii. Gertrude Florence Evelyn, iii. Rita
Kathleen, and secondly, in T. C., March 13, 1890,
Rev. Edward Mewburn Walker, Fellow of Queen's
College, Oxon., and has issue—i. John Drummond,
ii. Henrietta Frances; 8. Florence Eglantine; 9.
Catherine Henrietta, *m.*, in T. C., Oct. 25, 1886, her
cousin, Robert Pollock Hamilton, Esq., and has
issue (*bapt.* T. C.)—i. Charles Pollock, ii. Kathleen
Emma May, iii. Eva Maud.

At the close of 1885 a committee was formed for
the purpose of promoting the presentation of an
address and testimonial to the Rev. Canon Hamilton, in recognition of the high esteem in which he
was held by his parishioners. The movement was
most cordially received, and on March 31, 1886,
the Right Hon. John Thomas Ball,* on behalf of
the subscribers, presented the address and testimonial to Canon Hamilton. The address was
signed by ninety-one parishioners, and acknow-
ledged the earnestness and fidelity with which he
had discharged the duties of his office, the benefits
derived from his ministry and pastoral care, his

* Of Taney House, 1882-95, and, while Lord Chancellor of
Ireland, of Ardmore, Roebuck, 1876-80.

kindness and sympathy for those committed to his charge, and his exertions to promote the welfare of every class. ———

CURATES.

JOHN JOSEPH KNOX FLETCHER, 1852-55,
son of the Rev. John Fletcher, D.D., *b.* 1828, was educated at Dr. Graham's school, and having entered T.C.D. on Nov. 6, 1845, he took a scholarship in 1849, and graduated B.A., 1851, and M.A., 1864. He was ordained Deacon in 1852, and Priest at Cork, May 22, 1853. He was appointed Curate of Taney by Mr. Bredin in 1852, and discharged the duties from that time, although not licensed until Aug. 31, 1854. He resigned the Curacy of Taney in 1855 on being appointed Rector of Killiskey, Diocese of Kildare. He was subsequently Rector of Monasterevan, and Rural Dean, 1867-71, Prebendary of Harristown in the Cathedral of Kildare from 1867 until his death, Rector of Malahide, 1871-74, of Brockley, Somerset, 1874-86, Curate of Chelvey, Somerset, 1877-86, and Vicar of Whittlebury, with Silverstone, Diocese of Peterborough, from 1886 until his death. He *m.*, in T. C., June 14, 1855, Sidney, second dau. of Edward Colborn Mayne, Esq., formerly Capt. in the 95th Regt. of Foot, and had issue. (Crockford's *Clerical Directory*, 1891 ; Brady's *Records of Cork*, vol. iii., p. 185.)

CHARLES SEYMOUR LANGLEY, 1855-56,
son of Thomas E. Langley, Esq., by his wife

Fridzwide Seymour, was *b.* at Ballinasloe, April 3, 1830. He was educated at the school of the Rev. D. Flynn in Dublin, and entered T.C.D., July 1, 1848. He obtained a first honor in Classics, an honor in Ethics and Logics, a Divinity Premium, and a double Moderatorship in Classics and Logics. He graduated B.A., 1854, M.A., 1859, and took out his B.D. degree, 1864, and his D.D., 1868. He was ordained Deacon on July 16, 1854, at Gloucester, on letters dimissory from Limerick, and Priest on July 15, 1855, at St. Patrick's Cathedral, Dublin. He was appointed Curate of St. Michael's, Limerick, in 1854, and of Taney, by Mr. Bredin, in 1855. He resigned this curacy on being appointed in 1856 Rector of St. Mary's, Clonmel, where he remained until collated, Feb. 2, 1861, to the Rectory of Kilworth, Diocese of Cloyne. He was subsequently appointed a Canon of Cloyne Cathedral, and a Rural Dean. He *d.* April 9, 1885. He *m.* Maria, dau. of David Aston, Esq., M.D., of Dublin, and of his wife Maria Catharine, dau. of R. Watkins, Esq., of Prospect House, Roebuck, and had issue—1. Charles Seymour, L.C.S. Edin., *m.* Aug. 8, 1891, Katharine Phoebe, dau. of Capt. John Brasier Creagh, and has issue—Dorothy Kathleen Emily; 2. Mary Katharine (*bapt.* T. C.), *d.* Jan. 1, 1892; 3. Fridzwide Henrietta.

ROBERT WILLIAM WHELAN, 1857-58,

who was the second son of John Whelan, Esq., by his wife Abigail, dau. of Abraham Brownrigg,

Esq., was educated at Harcourt Street School under Mr. Lowton. He entered T.C.D., July 4, 1836, and graduated B.A., 1841, and M.A., 1850. He was ordained Deacon, 1851, and Priest, 1852, by the Archbishop of Dublin. He was Curate of St. Paul's, Dublin, for some years, and of Taney from 1857 to 1858. He was subsequently Curate of Derralossory and Laragh for one year, of Blessington from 1861 to 1862, of Hollywood from 1862 to 1863, and Incumbent of Malahide from 1863 to 1871. He was then appointed Rector of Maynooth, and held that living until 1889. He was Prebendary of Maynooth in St. Patrick's Cathedral from 1869 to 1889. He *m.* Eliza Frances, dau. of James Pratt, Esq., of Kinsale, Co. Cork, and had issue—1. Ernest Hamilton, in H.O., M.A., *m.* Miss Deborah Carnegie; 2. Richard Pratt (*bapt.* T. C.), *o.s.p.;* 3. William Brownrigg, B.A.; 4. James Pratt; 5. Percy Scott, in H.O., M.A., Warden of St. Columba's College; 6. Charles Pratt, *m.* Miss Annie Baldwin; 7. Fitzgerald; 8. Gertrude Sarah, *m.* Rev. E. S. Daunt; 9. Constance Isabella; 10. Kathleen Alice.

JOHN FAWCETT, 1858-61,

son of George Fawcett, Esq., was educated at Dr. Wall's school, and entered T.C.D., Jan. 11, 1853, as a Fellow Commoner. He graduated B.A., 1856, M.A., 1860. He was ordained Deacon by the Archbishop of Dublin, 1857, and Priest by the Bishop of Meath, 1858. He was appointed to the curacy of Monkstown in 1857, and of Taney, by Dr. Moeran, in 1858, which he resigned in 1861, on being appointed Perpetual Curate of Tullow (Carrickmines). He was subsequently Curate of Ballymoney (Connor), 1868, Curate of Ballymena, 1869, and afterwards went to England, where he was Chaplain of the Poplar and Stepney Sick Asylum, from 1874 to 1886, and Chaplain of the Stepney Union, from 1877 to 1886. He *m.*, 1851, Miss Dorothea Jane Maunsell Dunlevie, and had a dau., *bapt.* T. C., Isabella. (Crockford's *Clerical Directory*, 1886; Cox's *Clergy List*, 1867.)

JOHN HOBART SEYMOUR, 1862-65,

youngest son of Captain John Crossley Seymour, by his wife Frances Maria, dau. of Aaron Crossley Seymour, Esq., of Calcutta, was educated at Dr. Smith's school at Stillorgan, and having entered T.C.D., graduated B.A., 1853, and M.A., 1861. He was ordained Deacon, 1854, and Priest, 1855, by the Bishop of Down. He was Curate of Lisburn, 1854-56, and of Aghaderg, 1857, Incumbent of Glencraig, 1858-59, and Curate of Christ Church, Belfast, 1859-61. On Jan. 21, 1862, he was nominated Curate of Taney by Dr. Moeran, and licensed on the following day. He held the curacy until July, 1865, when he was nominated Curate of Trinity Church, Belfast. He was appointed Curate of Newcastle, Co. Down, in 1871, and was nominated Incumbent of that parish on Jan. 1, 1873. He was appointed Precentor of Dromore in June, 1894. He *m.*, first, May 16, 1856, Lily Anna Floyer, dau. of Alexander Jaffray Nicholson, Esq., M.D., of Dublin, who d. 1862, and has by her issue—1. John Nicholson, M.B. and B.CH., m., and has issue; 2. Clara; and secondly, June 4, 1867, Matilda, dau. of William Stevenson, Esq., of Belfast.

· ROBERT BAKER STONEY, 1866-68,

son of Robert J. Stoney, Esq., of Oakley Park, King's Co., by his wife Anne, dau. of J. Smith-wick, Esq., was educated at Parsonstown, Galway, and Dublin. He entered T.C.D., July 1, 1858, and graduated B.A., 1862, M.A., 1870, B.D., 1874, and D.D., 1891. He was ordained Deacon, 1863, and Priest, 1864, by the Bishop of Cork. He was Curate of Rahan, 1863-64, of St. Mary's, Shan-don, 1864-65, and was nominated to the curacy of Taney by Dr. Moeran in 1866, and licensed on April 18 in the same year. He resigned the curacy in 1868, and became Curate of Donnybrook. In 1872 he was appointed Incumbent of St. Matthew's, Irishtown. He was nominated Acting Chaplain to the Troops at the Pigeon House Fort in 1887, was appointed a Canon of Christ Church Cathedral in 1893, and the same year a Chaplain to the Lord Lieutenant in Ireland. He m. Kate Mabel, dau. of Richard Atkinson, Esq.,* of Gortmore, Dundrum, and has issue—1. Richard Atkinson, 2. Alice Mary.

Canon Stoney is the author of several papers and pamphlets, among others, of *An Easy Catechism for Members of the Church of Ireland*, which has been through numerous editions.

* See Tombstone IV., chapter iii.

EDWARD ARNOLD CARROLL, 1868-——,
son of William Carroll, Esq., of Eccles Street,
Dublin, was educated at Mr. Sargent's school, and
having entered T.C.D., graduated B.A., 1853, and
M.A., 1884. He was ordained Deacon, 1855, and
Priest, 1856, by the Archbishop of Dublin. He
was Curate of Holy Trinity Church, Rathmines,
from 1860 to July, 1864, and of Donadea, from
1865 to 1868. He was nominated Curate of Taney
by Dr. Hamilton in 1868, and licensed on April 1
of that year. He *m.*, April 27, 1859, Emily Elizabeth, eldest dau. of James Carmichael, Esq., Clerk
of the Crown for Tipperary, and has issue—1.
Arnold Edward; 2. Aylmer Singleton Arnold (*bapt.*
T. C.); 3. Edith Frances; 4. Elinor Emily Lindsay,
m., in T.C., April 6, 1892, Thomas Frederick Nesbitt
Irwin, Esq., and has issue (*bapt.* T. C.)—i. Frederick
Arnold, ii. Herbert Carmichael.

SECOND CURATES.

In addition to the curates already mentioned, a
second curate has been occasionally attached to the
parish. Amongst those who thus served under Dr.
Moeran was the Rev. James Walsh, D.D., Rector of
St. Stephen's, Dublin, and Canon of Christ Church
Cathedral. In recent years the following have
been appointed by Dr. Hamilton :—

- -JOHN EDWARD MURRAY, 1890-91,
son of the Rev. John Edward Murray, sometime
Rector of Edenderry, was *b.* in the King's Co., and

having entered T.C.D., graduated B.A., 1887. He
was ordained Deacon, 1888, and Priest, 1889, by
the Bishop of Down. He was Curate of St. Luke's,
Belfast, from 1888 to 1890, and was appointed
Curate of Taney in June, 1890. He resigned the
curacy in Dec., 1891, and has been since Curate of
St. Paul's, Leicester.

RALPH WALKER, 1892,

son of George Walker, Esq., was *b.* in the Co. Ros-
common, and was educated at Galway Grammar
School. He entered T.C.D., and graduated B.A.,
1889. He was ordained Deacon, 1890, by the
Bishop of Ossory, and Priest, 1894, by the Bishop
of London. He was Curate of Rathvilly from 1890
to 1891, and was appointed Curate of Taney, Jan.,
1892. He resigned in Nov., 1892, and was appointed Curate of St. Peter's, Paddington.

JAMES WILLIAM FFRANCK SHEPPARD, 1893---

son of Frank Sheppard, Esq., of St. Cronan's,
Roscrea, who was fifth son of Capt. James Shep-
pard, of Clifton, Roscrea, Co. Tipperary. He
entered T.C.D. in 1884, and having obtained a
Junior Moderatorship in Ethics and Logics, gradu-
ated B.A., 1889, and M.A., 1893. He was ordained
Deacon, 1891, and Priest, 1892, by the Bishop of
Killaloe. He was Curate of Tulla and of Lickmo-
lassy in 1891-92, and was appointed, Jan., 1893,
Curate of Taney.

CHAPTER VII.

CHRONOLOGICAL LIST FROM 1791.

1791. Sir Thomas Lighton, Bart., and John Giffard.

1792. Edward Mayne and Stephen Stock.

1793. Hon. William Tankerville Chamberlaine and Alexander Jaffray.

1794. James Potts and John La Touche Hume.

1795. } John Exshaw and Nathaniel Hone.
1796. }

1797. Valentine Dunn and Daniel Kinahan.

1798. } Richard Verschoyle and Henry Thompson.
1799. }

1800. Charles Haskins and Nathaniel Creed; June 3, William M'Kay, *vice* Nathaniel Creed, left the parish.

1801. Charles Haskins and Robert Norman.

1802. } Faithful William Fortescue and Robert
1803. } Norman.

1804. George Thompson and Robert Turbett.

1805. } Daniel Beere and John Townsend Sinnett.
1806. }

1807. } James Crofton and Walter Bourne.
1808. }

1809. } Peter Digges La Touche and William Ridge-
1810. } way.

1811.
1812. } William Ridgeway and Richard Verschoyle.
1818.

1814.   William Ridgeway and George Thompson.

1815.   William Ridgeway and Daniel Beere.

1816.
1817. } William Ridgeway and William Wood; Sept. 22, 1817, George Thompson, *vice* William Ridgeway, deceased.

1818.   George Thompson and Walter Bourne.

1819.
1820. } John White and Humphrey Minchin.

1821.   Barret Wadden and Robert Billing; Sept. 28, the resolution appointing Barret Wadden and Robert Billing rescinded, and John White and Humphrey Minchin reappointed.

1822.   Sir George Whiteford and James Crofton; Aug. 21, James La Farrelle, *vice* James Crofton, resigned.

1823.   John Maconchy and Henry Dawson.

1824.   Morris Hime and Daniel Kinahan.

1825.   Daniel M'Kay and Joseph M'Dermott.

1826.   Daniel M'Kay and William Augustus Minchin.

1827.   William M'Caskey and William Scott.

1828.   William Jervis Whitthorne, and Samuel Warren.

1829.   Arthur Burgh Crofton and John Goddard Richards.

1830.   John Blake and George Kinahan.

1831.   William M'Caskey and John Theophilus Boileau.

1832.   John Curry and Hutchins Williams.

1833. John Elliott Hyndman and James Turbett.

1834. Daniel Kinahan and Samuel Boxwell.

1835. Arthur Burgh Crofton and John West.

1836. John Blake and Daniel Kinahan.

1837. John West and William Walsh.

1838. John Blake and John Elliott Hyndman.

1839. William Walsh and Samuel Tipper.

1840. Daniel Kinahan and John West.

1841. Michael Charles Bernard and John Hill Lindé.

1842. William Lewis and John Blake.

1843. Robert Maunsell and John William Read.

1844. Henry Joseph Mason and John Lee Wharton.

1845. Manners M'Kay and Michael Charles Bernard.

1846. John La Touche White and Henry Lindsell Shade.

1847. John Lee Wharton and John Blake.

1848. Charles Pickering and Henry Thomas Price.

1849. Henry Birch and John Lee Wharton.

1850. William Stanley Purdon and Richard Thomas Bourne.

1851. James Lawrence Digges La Touche and Robert Ruskell.

1852. Robert Orme and George Daniell.

1853. John Thomas Lloyd and William Lewis.

1854. William Curtis and Henry Thompson.

1855. James Lawrence Digges La Touche and James Turbett.

1856. Edward Perceval Westby and Richard Downer Webb Bond.

1857. Alexander Dickson and John Porter.

1858. Charles Pickering and Henry Thomas Price.

1859. Edmund D'Olier and Edward Perceval Westby.

1860. Richard Manders and Edward Armstrong Vicars.

1861. Henry Birch and Edmund D'Olier.

1862. John Vincent and James Espinasse.

1863. John Maunsell and John Davis Garde.

1864. Edward Perceval Westby and Henry Roe.

1865. George Kinahan and Robert Turbett.

1866. Henry Birch and James Espinasse.

1867. Henry Roe and Martin Kirwan.

1868. Edward Perceval Westby and George Kinahan.

1869. John Reilly and Henry Birch.

1870. Edward Perceval Westby and Robert Ashworth Studdert.

1871. Robert Ashworth Studdert and William Andrew Hayes.

1872. William Andrew Hayes and John Reilly.

1873. John Reilly and Henry Birch.

1874. Edward Perceval Westby and Henry Birch.

1875. Edward Perceval Westby and William John Freke.

1876. William John Freke and John Walsh.

1877. Francis Rawdon Moira Crozier and Robert Henry Tilly.

1878. Robert Henry Tilly and Henry Darby Griffith.

1879. Henry Darby Griffith and Richard Henry Archibald M'Comas.

1880. Richard Henry Archibald M'Comas and Isaac William Usher.

1881.
1882. } Isaac William Usher and Isaac Ashe.

1883. Walter Reginald Crofton and Everard Hamilton.

1884.
1885. { Everard Hamilton and Thomas Manifold
1886. (Craig.
1887.

1888. Thomas Manifold Craig and Joseph St. Clair Mayne.

1889. Joseph St. Clair Mayne and Isaac Beckett.

1890. Isaac Beckett and Isaac William Usher.

1891. Isaac William Usher and Francis Elrington Ball.

1892. Francis Elrington Ball and John Gardiner Nutting.

1893. John Gardiner Nutting and Alexander Hamilton.

1894. } Alexander Hamilton and William Henry
1895. } Foster Verschoyle.

ALPHABETICAL LIST FROM 1791.

ASHE, ISAAC, 1881-82,

of the Central Asylum; M.D. & M.CHIR., T.C.D., F.K.Q.C.P.I.; eldest son of the Rev. Isaac Ashe, by his wife Jane, dau. of Robert Ellis, Esq.; *m.* Sarah, dau. of Henry Gore, Esq., and had issue—1. Isaac Leslie, Sch. & B.A., T.C.D.; 2. Arthur, Sch., T.C.D., *d.* July 4, 1892; 3. Robert William D'Estcourt;

H

4. Edward, *d.* Oct. 7, 1875; 5. Mary Kathleen Jane; 6. Sarah Ethel Barbara; 7. Lilian Evelyn. Dr. Ashe *d.* Nov. 19, 1891.

BALL, FRANCIS ELRINGTON, 1891-92,

of Taney House; J.P. Co. Dublin; second surviving son of the Right Hon. John Thomas Ball, and of his wife Catherine, dau. of the Rev. Charles Richard Elrington, D.D.

BECKETT, ISAAC, 1889-90,

of Altamont; J.P. Dublin; had issue, by his wife Georgina, 1. George Edmund, 2. Arthur, *bapt.* in T. C.

BEERE, DANIEL, 1805-6-15,

of Mount Anville; Secondary in Lord Treasurer's Remembrancer's Office, and Deputy Pursuivant of the Court of Exchequer; *m.*, 1791, Miss Butler, only dau. of Gerald Butler, Esq., of Ballyadams, Queen's Co., and had issue—1. George, Captain 1st West India Regt., *d.* at sea, leaving one son, Col. D. Beere; 2. Gerald, in H.O., *m.*, 1827, Mary, eldest dau. of General Armstrong, R.A., and had issue; 3. Edward, went to Australia, *m.*, and had issue; 4. Daniel, *m.*, and had issue; 5. Susan; 6. Charlotte, *m.*, in T. C., Oct. 3, 1820, William Maxwell Eason, Esq., and had a son, Henry Daniel, *bapt.* T. C.; 7. Anne; 8. Margaret; 9. Rosetta Adeline. Mr. Beere *d. circa* 1824.

BERNARD, MICHAEL CHARLES, 1841-45,

of Elm Lawn, Dundrum; B.A., 1832, M.B., 1835,
T.C.D., L.R.C.S.I.; third son of William Bernard,
Esq., of Clonmulah, Co. Carlow; *b.* May 20, 1810,
m., Feb. 23, 1841, Jane, youngest dau. of John
Leigh, Esq., of Broomhedge, Cheshire, and Bole
Street, Liverpool, and had issue (*bapt.* T. C.)—1.
Joshua Josiah, *d.* an infant, Feb. 9, 1843 (*bur.*
T. G.); 2. William Leigh; 3. Godfrey Mayne, *o.s.p.*,
April 16, 1870 (*bur.* T. G.); 4. Charles John;
5. Joseph St. Clair Smith; 6. Henry Hilton,
o.s.p., Dec. 11, 1887 (*bur.* T. G.); 7. Rachel
Isabel*; 8. Sarah Maria Elizabeth (now of Elm
Lawn); 9. Louisa Jane Victoria, *d. unm.*, Nov. 6,
1887 (*bur.* T. G.); 10. Eleanor Frances Henrietta;
11. Adeliza Susan Mary Wilhelmina, *d.* young,
May 13, 1864 (*bur.* T. G.); 12. Anna Travers
Crofton, *d.* young, March 14, 1876 (*bur.* T. G.).
Dr. Bernard *d.* April 24, 1881, and was *bur.* T. G.
(pp. 29, 64).

BILLING, ROBERT, 1821,

of Bird Avenue, Farranboley; Solicitor; son of
Thomas Billing, Esq.; *m.*, first, 1794, Elinor, dau.
of John Meyler, Esq., and had by her issue—1.
Theobald, *m.* Miss Ball; 2. William, *d.* young; 3.
Emily, *d.* young; 4. Eleanor; *m.*, secondly, 1805,
Martha, dau. of John Busby, Esq., and had by her
issue—1. Robert, *o.s.p.*; 2. Alfred (*bapt.* T.C.), *m.*
Miss Harriet Lewis; 3. Anna Lucinda, *m.*, in T. C.,

* See Mayne, Joseph St. Clair.

May 26, 1853, Daniel Maunsell, Esq. (see Maunsell,
Robert) ; 4. Eliza, *m.*, in T. C., Nov. 6, 1838, James
Stirling, Esq., afterwards of Ballawley Park, and
had issue—i. James Wilfred, Major R. Art., *m.*
Miss Hoste, dau. of Colonel Hoste; ii. Eliza Isabel,
m., in T. C., July 10, 1867, William Napier Magill,
Esq. ; iii. Matilda Lucy, *m.*, in T. C., Dec. 16, 1869,
Duncan Christopher Oliver Spiller, Esq. ; iv. Agnes
Jane, *m.*, in T. C., Sept. 2, 1874, Theophilus
Clements, Esq. ; v. Alice, *m.*, in T. C., Oct. 28,
1875, Henry Elsdale, Esq.; 5. Harriet. Mr. Billing
d. April 18, 1840.

BIRCH, HENRY, 1849-61-66-69-73-74,
of Drummartin Castle; Barrister-at-Law, *c.* 1830,
J.P. Co. Dublin; *m.* Miss Sayce.   He *d. s. p.* at
Monaincla, Roscrea, July 4, 1882, aged 76 years.

BLAKE, JOHN, 1830-36-38-42-47,
of Weston, Churchtown ; was the third son of
Isidore Blake, Esq., of Oldhead, Co. Mayo (see
Blake, of Towerhill, B.L.G., 1894); he *m.* Miss
Charlotte Blake, of Corbally, and had, amongst
other issue, Isidore John, Barrister-at-Law, who
had by his wife, Henrietta, issue, *bapt.* T. C.—i.
John Edward, ii. Isidore Anthony, iii. Richard
George, iv. Henry Eugene, v. Maria Wilhelmina,
vi. Charlotte Henrietta.

BOILEAU, JOHN THEOPHILUS, 1831,
of Drummartin ; he had issue by his wife, Elizabeth Dorothea, *bapt.* T. C.—1. Nassau Molesworth ;
2. Jasper Disbrisay ; 3. Samuel Brandram.

BOND, RICHARD DOWNER WEBB, 1856,
of Janeville, Roebuck; son of Andrew Bond, Esq.;
m., T. C., Aug. 9, 1855, Louisa Harriett, dau. of
James Pratt, Esq., of Farmhill, and had issue,
bapt. T. C.—1. Richard Pratt; 2. Charles John; 3.
William Henry. He *d.* at Bath, Nov. 21, 1864.

BOURNE, RICHARD THOMAS, 1850,
of Taney Hill; M.A., T.C.D., Barrister-at-Law, *c.*
1840; fifth son of Walter Bourne, Esq.; *m.*, in T. C.,
Feb. 24, 1846, Mary Sophia, dau. of John Hill
Lindé, Esq. (*q. v.*), and *o. s. p.*, Dec. 27, 1890.

BOURNE, WALTER, 1807-8-18,
of Taney Hill, and previously of Owenstown; Deputy
Clerk of the Crown of the North-East Circuit,
and Clerk of the Crown of the King's Bench;
b. 1766; *m.*, first, 1788, Elizabeth, dau. of Walter
Peter, Esq., by whom he had issue—Peter, *m.*
1820, Miss Ellen Gibbs (*d.* Sept. 18, 1882), and *d.*
Oct. 10, 1844, leaving issue; *m.* secondly, 1791,
Elinor, second dau. of Andrew Carmichael, Esq.,
by whom he had issue—1. Walter, Clerk of the
Crown for Co. Antrim, *m.*, in T.C., Aug. 6, 1821,
Louisa Arabella (*d.* Jan. 2, 1882), dau. of Humphrey
Minchin, Esq. (*q. v.*), and *d.* Nov. 19, 1881, having
had issue—i. Richard Carmichael, Surgeon 3rd
Dragoon Guards, *d.* April 15, 1871, ii. Humphrey
Minchin, Barrister-at-law (present owner of the
Bourne property at Dundrum), iii. Walter, M.D., *m.*
May 18, 1870, Geraldine Caroline, only dau. of Sir

John Judkin Fitzgerald, Bart., and has issue, iv. Andrew (*bapt.* T. C.), Solicitor, *m.* Miss Clarke, *o. s. p.*, Dec., 1893, v. William Henry, M.D., *o. s. p.*, June 22, 1856, vi. John (*bapt.* T. C.), vii. Charles Henry, viii. Eleanor (*bapt.* T. C.), *m.*, 1849, Anthony Beaufort Brabazon, Esq., M.D., and has issue, ix. Frances, x. Louisa, xi. Julia Adelaide (*bapt.* T. C.); 2. Thomas Daniel, Clerk of the Crown for Co. Monaghan, *o. s. p.*, Jan. 31, 1877; 3. William, in H.O., Rector of Rathcormack, *m.*, 1833, Elizabeth, eldest dau. of Charles Frizell, Esq., M.D., of Castle Kevin, Co. Wicklow, and *o. s. p.*, April 5, 1851; 4. Andrew, *m.* Miss Charlotte Bolton, *o. s. p.*, March 6, 1886; 5. Richard Thomas (*q. v.*); 6. Jane, *m.*, 1812, Richard Carmichael, Esq., M.D., and *d.* Nov. 21, 1864; 7. Ellen, *d. unm.*, July 16, 1876; 8. Marianne, *d. unm.*, April 20, 1878; 9. Eliza, *m.* 1828, Thomas Belton, Esq., and *d.* Jan. 18, 1880; 10. Frances Margaret, *m.*, in T.C., July 5, 1827, Bridges John Hooke, Esq., of the 34th Regt. of Infantry, and has issue, including Bridges Carmichael (*bapt.* T. C.); 11. Anna, *m.*, 1826, Rev. Lyndon Henry Bolton, and *d.* May 14, 1886, leaving issue; 12. Emily, *m.*, in T. C., Aug. 23, 1831, Keith Claringbould Hamilton Hallowes, Esq., and has issue. Mr. Bourne *d.* Nov. 18, 1848.

BOXWELL, SAMUEL, 1834,

of Campfield House; *m.*, 1802, Miss Jane Tinckler, and *o. s. p.*, 1852.

CHAMBERLAINE, HON. WM. TANKERVILLE, 1793, of Churchtown, and of Stephen's Green, Dublin, was the eldest son of Michael Tankerville Chamberlaine, Esq. He graduated B.A., T.C.D., 1774, and was called to the Irish Bar in 1779. He was returned in 1792 to the Irish Parliament as member for the Borough of Clonmines (Co. Wexford). He was appointed a Justice of the Common Pleas, Dec. 6, 1793, and a Justice of the King's Bench, June 20, 1794. He *d.* at his residence in Churchtown on May 12, 1802, and was *bur.* in St. Ann's Church, Dublin. He *m.*, 1780, Lucy, eldest dau. of Higatt Boyd, Esq., of Roslare, Co. Wexford, and had issue four sons and six daughters. (See pedigree of Chamberlaine family, *Irish Builder*, vol. xxix. (1887), p. 265.)

The following obituary notice of him appears in the *Gentleman's Magazine*, vol. lxxii., pt. i., p. 585 :—

"To the most profound legal knowledge he joined an inflexible integrity and firmness of mind, which were so eminently displayed in the late unfortunate rebellion, that he will live for ever in the hearts of a grateful nation. He possessed brilliant talents with an infinity of wit; but such was the benevolence of his disposition, that in his most cheerful hours he was never heard to utter an expression that could cause a pang in the heart of anyone; and though suffering excruciating pain from the gout, he always preserved his usual equanimity of temper. His manners were gentle and conciliating. He discharged the duties of every station with exemplary fidelity ; and universally respected, he died universally regretted."

The *Dublin Evening Post*, May 15, 1802, says he was "a good man, an able lawyer, and an honest judge."

In an inscription on a monument erected in St.
Ann's Church, Dublin, to him and to his friend
Lord Downes (who desired that he should be
buried with him), he is stated to have excelled in
promptness and penetrating force of intellect. See
Blacker's *Sketches of Booterstown*, p. 322.

CRAIG, THOMAS MANIFOLD, 1884 TO 1888,
of Rockmount; son of Richard Craig, Esq., *m.*
Annie, dau. of Thomas Gorton, Esq., of Burton-
on-Trent, Staffordshire, and had issue—1. Arthur
Richard Thomas, *d.* Feb. 28, 1890 (*bur.* T. G.);
2. Ernest Manifold; 3. Myra Eleanor; 4. Nora
Mary, *m.*, in T. C., June 3, 1891, Thomas Du Bedat
Whaite, Esq., A.M.D. Mr. Craig *d.* Dec. 2, 1890,
and was *bur.* in T. G.

CREED, NATHANIEL, 1800,
of Owenstown, and of Great Ship Street, Dublin;
Livery Lace Manufacturer; was *b.* 1750, *m.*, in
St. Mary's Church, Dublin, Sept. 30, 1790, Miss
Rebecca Donolan, and had issue—1. William
Nathaniel, *d.* June 13, 1815; 2. James Joseph, *d.*
April 18, 1825; 3. Nathaniel, *d.* Jan. 17, 1805; 4.
Maria, *m.*, T. C., Dec. 23, 1819, James Allen Hey-
land, Esq. (*d.* Dec. 11, 1837), and *d.* Dec. 8, 1830.
Mr. Creed *d.* April 17, 1805, and was *bur.* in T. G.,
with the above members of his family (p. 32).

CROFTON, ARTHUR BURGH, 1829-35,
of Roebuck Castle;* J.P. and High Sheriff, 1842, of

* See under John, Baron Trimleston, chapter viii.

Co. Dublin; eldest son of James Crofton, Esq.
(*q.v.*); *m.*, in T. C., Oct. 7, 1828, Catherine (*d.* April 14,
1882), dau. of Willcocks Huband, Esq., by his wife
Frances, eldest daughter of Arthur Chichester
Macartney, Esq., by his wife Anna, dau. of Samuel
Lindesay, Esq., and had issue (*bapt.* T. C.)—1.
George James, *d.* ; 2. Frances, *d.* ; 3. Louisa, *d.* ; 4.
Matilda, *d.*; 5. Letitia Augusta Laughton, *m.* David
Boyle Hope, Esq., Sheriff of Roxburghshire, Ber-
wickshire, and Selkirk, and has issue—i. James,
ii. Kathleen, iii. Hilda. Mr. Crofton *d.* Dec. 29,
1850.

CROFTON, JAMES, 1807-8-22,

of Roebuck Castle,* and of the Irish Treasury;
m., 1797, Frances (*d.* Jan. 8, 1811, *bur.* T. G.), dau.
of Arthur Stanley, Esq., and had issue—1. Arthur
Burgh (*q.v.*) ; 2. George, Lieut., 17th Lancers, *d.*
in India; 3. Louisa, *bur.* T. G., June 25, 1822;
4. Anne, *bur.* T. G., April 29, 1817; 5. Frances,
d.; 6. Eliza, *d.* an infant, *bur.* T. G. Mr. Crofton
was *bur.* T. G., June 5, 1828† (p. 31).

CROFTON, WALTER REGINALD, 1883,

of Roebuck Lodge; *c.* to the English Bar, Inspector

* See under John, Baron Trimleston, chapter viii.

† Mr. Crofton and his son, Mr. Arthur Burgh Crofton,
were Commissioners for the construction of the Royal Harbour of George IV. at Kingstown, then called Dunleary, and
their names appear on the monument erected in 1823 to
commemorate the laying of the first stone by the Lord Lieutenant (Earl Whitworth), on May 31, 1817.

of Irish Prisons, J.P. Co. Dublin; eldest son of the
Right Hon. Sir Frederic Crofton, C.B., by his wife
Anna Maria, only dau. of the Rev. Charles Shipley;
m., 1880, Georgina Louisa, dau. of Rev. John
Harrison, late Vicar of Bishopstone, Sussex.

CROZIER, FRANCIS RAWDON MOIRA, 1877,

of Roebuck Hall; M.A., T.C.D., Solicitor; son of
Thomas Crozier, Esq., of Seafield, Stillorgan Road;
m. Catherine Sophia (*d.* Feb. 16, 1887), dau. of Rev.
William Magee, Rector of Dunganstown, and has
issue—1. Thomas Francis, 2. William Magee (*bapt.*
T. C.), 3. George Francis, 4. Francis Rawdon Moira
(*bapt.* T. C.), 5. Louis Herbert (*bapt.* T. C.), 6. Kathleen Amelia.

CURRY, JOHN, 1832,

of Drummartin House and of Sir John Rogerson's
Quay; Timber Merchant; *m.*, Kilgobbin Church,
Oct. 6, 1824, Eliza, fourth dau. of Alexander
Brenan, Esq., Six Clerk in Chancery, of Kingston
Lodge, and had a son, Benjamin Shafton, and a
dau., Anne Elizabeth, *bapt.* in T. C. Mr. Curry *d.*
circa 1837.

CURTIS, WILLIAM, 1854,

of Churchtown.

DANIELL, GEORGE, 1852,

of Mount Dillon; Captain, R.N.; third son of Henry
Daniell, Esq., and Isabella, dau. of Robert Tighe,
Esq., of South Hill (see Daniell, of New Forest;

B.L.G., 1894); *b.* Aug. 31, 1797, *m.*, June 23, 1842, Alicia Catherine (*d.* March 3, 1885), eldest surviving dau. of the Right Hon. Francis Blackburne,* and had issue, a son, Francis Henry Blackburne (*bapt.* T. C.), Fellow of Trinity College, Cambridge, *c.* to the English Bar, who *m.*, Aug. 16, 1877, Caroline Sophia, eldest dau. of William Bence Jones, Esq., of Lisselan, Co. Cork, and has issue —i. George Francis Blackburne, ii. William Arthur Blackburne, iii. Francis Reginald Blackburne, iv. Henry Edmund Blackburne, v. Alice Caroline Blackburne. Captain Daniell *d.* Nov. 2, 1856.

Captain Daniell had a distinguished naval career; he joined as First-class Volunteer in the *Africaine*, June 24, 1810, and served in the action between her and the French frigates, *Astrée* and *Iphigenie*, on Sept. 13, 1810, when she was captured. He was prisoner in the Mauritius until Dec. 6, 1810, when the island was taken by the British. He afterwards served in the Mediterranean, and in 1813-14 took part in cutting out attacks at Languillia and Alassio, on the coast of Genoa, in the capture of Leghorn, in the attacks on forts at Spezzia, and in other operations preceding the surrender of Genoa. He was at Plymouth in 1815, when the *Bellerophon* was there with Napoleon, and, in a letter in the possession of his son, mentions that Napoleon was very observant of everything on board the English ships, and particularly of the exercises of the sailors. He took

---

* See Right Hon. Francis Blackburne, chapter viii.

part in the expedition of the *Leven* and *Barracouta*,
which were sent to explore the African coast, and
which made the first survey of Delagoa Bay and of
the coast up to Madagascar. At the Battle of Navarino he commanded the cutter of the *Mosquito* in an
attack on fireships, when two of the boat's crew
were killed and three wounded, and was promoted
to the rank of Commander for his conduct on that
occasion, besides receiving the Navarino medal.
He commanded the *Despatch* in the West Indies
from June 7, 1832, to Oct. 6, 1835, and received
the thanks of the British Consul and merchants at
Para, in Brazil, for the protection to life and property afforded during a revolution there. The
Portuguese Government also conveyed their thanks
through their Ambassador in London to Lord
Palmerston, and the Lords of the Admiralty expressed approval of his conduct in a despatch to
the Commander-in-Chief on the West Indian and
North American station. He was promoted to the
rank of captain on June 28, 1838, being amongst
those who received commissions at the coronation
of our present Sovereign.

DAWSON, HENRY, 1823,

of Drummartin Castle, and of Hume Street, Dublin; *b.* 1782; Barrister-at-Law, *c.* 1806; *m.*, first,
1807, Miss Letitia Stapleton (*d.* Aug., 1808), and
had issue, William, *d.* Jan., 1818; *m.*, secondly,
1811, Miss Emily Dunne, and had issue—1.
Thomas; 2. Henry, *d.* Oct., 1868; 8. Richard;

4. William Augustus (*bapt.* T. C.), in H.O., *d.* July, 1857 ; 5. Elinor, *m.*, T. C., Feb. 28, 1835, William Jacob, Esq. ; 6. Louisa (*bapt.* T. C.) ; 7. Catherine (*bapt.* T. C.) ; 8. Emily Vesey (*bapt.* T. C.). Mr. Dawson *d.* Jan., 1833, and is *bur.* in Stillorgan Churchyard.

DICKSON, ALEXANDER, 1857,

of Moreen; Barrister-at-Law, *c.* 1841 ; *m.*, but *o. s. p.*

D'OLIER, EDMUND, 1859-61,

of Roebuck Cottage ; B.A., T.C.D. ; had issue by his wife, Maria Louisa, *bapt.* T. C.—1. Edmund ; 2. Isaac Bertram ; 3. Cathcart Rutherford ; 4. Emily Elizabeth Violet ; 5. Margaret Ethel ; 6. Theodora Alice ; 7. Rosanna Beatrice.

DUNN, VALENTINE, 1797,

of Dundrum, and of Castle Street, Dublin ; Ironmonger ; *m.*, 1791, Miss Barbara Sinnett, and *d. circa* 1822.

ESPINASSE, JAMES, 1862-66,

of Rockmount Cottage ; Captain 1st Royal Regt., son of William Espinasse, Esq., by his wife Susan Mangin ; *m.* Julia (*d.* June 19, 1877, *bur.* T. G.), dau. of William Stephens, Esq., of St. Kitts, West Indies, and had issue—1. William, *m.* Margaret, dau. of Robert Bailie, Esq., and has issue—i. Robert, ii. James, iii. Mary, iv. Dora ; 2. Reuben, *m.* Miss Madeline Gilmor, and *d.* at Melbourne, June 27, 1893, leaving one son, Bernard ; 3 Mary, *d.*, Dec. 29, 1879 (*bur.* T. G.). Capt. Espinasse *d.* March 1, 1874, and was *bur.* in T. G. (p. 34).

EXSHAW, JOHN, 1795-96,

of Roebuck and Grafton Street, Dublin ; bookseller and publisher. He was Sheriff of Dublin in 1779-80, and Lord Mayor in 1780-90, and for part of 1799-1800. He *d.* Jan. 6, 1827.

His death is thus recorded in the *Gentleman's Magazine*, vol. xcvii., pt. i., p. 94 :—

"At his seat at Roebuck, John Exshaw, Esq., senior Alderman and the oldest magistrate in the County of Dublin. Alderman Exshaw was elected to the aldermanic gown in the year 1782. In 1790 he contested the election for the City of Dublin in the Irish Parliament, but did not succeed. During the disturbances in 1797-98, he commanded the Stephen's Green Yeomanry,* which formed a fine and well-disciplined battalion, upwards of 1,000 strong : he was likewise Adjutant-General to the entire yeomanry forces in the Dublin district, and was considered an excellent officer, reversing the adage, *cedunt arma togæ*. On one occasion, during these disturbances, the command of the Dublin Garrison devolved upon

---

* On St. Patrick's Day, 1797, " the first regiment of Royal Dublin Volunteers, commanded by Captain Alderman Exshaw, received two very elegant stands of new colours from the hands of Miss Exshaw (daughter of the captain commandant) at her father's house in Grafton Street, very richly embroidered with great taste by this young lady, which she presented with a most becoming modesty, accompanied with a short but handsome speech."—*Hibernian Magazine*, 1797, pt. i., p. 217.

him for a short time in consequence of the absence of the troops of the line. Alderman Exshaw was one of the police magistrates of the 2nd Division; this office, in consequence of the late arrangements, dies with him. He was likewise the publisher of the *Hue and Cry*, the emoluments of which are stated to be about £1,000 a year."

FORTESCUE, FAITHFUL WILLIAM, 1802-3,

of Ballaly, and Milltown Grange, Co. Louth; Barrister-at-Law, *c.* 1796; Member for the Borough of Monaghan in the Irish Parliament, 1797-1800; only son of William Fortescue, Esq. (see *History of the Family of Fortescue*, by Lord Clermont, 1880, p. 212), *m.*, Nov., 1796, June, second dau. of John Adair, Esq. (see Adair of Bellegrove, B. L. G., 1846), and *o. s. p.*, 1824.

FREKE, WILLIAM JOHN, 1875-76,

of Bellemont; B.A., T.C.D.; son of James Freke, Esq., by his wife Anne, dau. of the Rev. Michael Sandys; *m.*, 1843, Frances Mary (*d.* June 3, 1880, *bur.* T. G.), dau. of Thomas Johnson, Esq., and had issue—1. Percy Evans, *m.*, in T. C., July 15, 1885, Kathleen Maria, dau. of William Richard Hamilton, Esq., M.D., and has issue (*bapt.* T. C.), Raymond Forbes; 2. Katherine Mary. Mr. Freke *d.* Nov. 17, 1879, and was *bur.* in T. G. (pp. 34, 37).

GARDE, JOHN DAVIS, 1863,

of Mount Dillon; Crown Solicitor, Cos. Longford and Cavan; *m.* Catherine McVeagh, dau of Henry Lumsden, Esq., D.L., of Auchindoir, Aberdeenshire,

and had issue—1. Richard Davis, *m.* Ida Mary,
dau. of Colonel Paton, D.L., of Granholm, Aberdeenshire ; 2. Susan Elizabeth, *m.* Edward Perceval
Westby, Esq., D.L. (*q. v.*) ; 3. Katherine Georgina,
m. John Smyly, Esq., M.A. ; 4. Henrietta Lumsden ;
5. Mary Olivia. Mr. Garde *d.* in 1889.

GIFFARD, JOHN, 1791,

of Woodbine Hill, Dundrum ;* Accountant-General
of His Majesty's Customs in Dublin ; High Sheriff
of Dublin,† 1793-94 ; a Captain in the Dublin
Militia. He *m.*, June, 1769, Sarah, dau. of William
Morton, Esq., and had issue—1. Ambrose Hardinge,‡ LL.D., T.C.D., Chief Justice of Ceylon,
and a Knight ; *m.*, 1808, Harriet, dau. of Lovell
Pennell, Esq., *d.* April, 1827, leaving issue ; 2.
John, *d.* young ; 3. William,§ Lieut. 82nd Regt.,
murdered by the rebels in May, 1798 ; 4. Stanley
Lees,‖ M.A., LL.D., Barrister-at-Law of the Middle
Temple, for twenty-five years editor of the *Standard*,
d. Nov. 6, 1858, having *m.*, first, 1814, Susannah
Meares, dau. of Francis Moran, Esq., of Down-
hill, Co. Mayo, by whom he had issue—i. John

* Woodbine Hill is mentioned in the *Post-Chaise Companion*, 1803, p. 3, as being on the main road opposite Dundrum Castle.

† " His chariot was pearl blue ; the carriage and wheels
dark brown, picked in with orange, blue, and white."—*Anthologia Hibernica*, vol. ii., p. 315.

‡ See *Dictionary of National Biography*, vol. xxi., p. 290.

§ See *Gentleman's Magazine*, vol. lxviii, pt. i., p. 535.

‖ See *Dictionary of National Biography*, vol. xxi., p. 296.

Walter de Longueville (*bapt.* T. C.), M.A., Oxon., a Judge of the County Courts in England, *m.* Emilie, dau. of D. B. Scott, Esq., and *d.* Oct. 23, 1888, leaving issue, ii. Francis Osborne (*bapt.* T. C.), B.A., Oxon., in H.O., *m.* Anna, dau. of Rev. Richard Ryan (*vide post*), and *d.* Dec., 1894, leaving issue, iii. Hardinge Stanley, Baron Halsbury, sometime Lord High Chancellor of England, *m.*, first, Caroline, dau. of W. C. Humphreys, Esq., and, secondly, Wilhelmina, dau. of Henry Woodfall, Esq., and has issue, iv. Sara Lees, *m.* J. Houston Browne, Esq., v. Susanna, *m.* T. Aldwell, Esq., and having *m.* secondly, 1830, Mary Anne, dau. of Henry Giffard, Esq., R.N., by whom he had two sons and two daus.; 5. Harriet, *m.*, first, Major George King, and secondly, Rev. James Phelan, *d.* Dec. 24, 1858; 6. Mary Lees, *m.* Rev. Richard Ryan (see p. 71), who had, in addition to the children there mentioned, Anna Maria (*vide ante*), *bapt.* in Rathconnell Church. Mr. Giffard *d.* May 5, 1819.

John Giffard, of Drummartin, or Woodbine Hill, was *b.* in 1745, and was the only son of John Giffard and Dorcas O'Morchoe (anglicised "Murphy"), of Oulartleigh, a family of great antiquity in the county of Wexford. Mr. Giffard's father, John Giffard, was the head and representative of the Giffards of Halsbury and Brightleigh, one of the oldest families in the West of England, full and detailed particulars of which are to be found in the County Histories of Devon, Heralds Visitations, and many other works, such as the *Worthies of*

Devon, by the learned Dr. Prince. The last
Giffard of Halsbury was Roger Giffard, Esq., who
sold that property, and died in 1763. This Roger
Giffard was the uncle (his father's younger brother)
of Mr. John Giffard, the subject of this sketch.
The other great family property, Brightleigh, with
its vast possessions, was diverted from the regular
channel of succession by the act of John Giffard,
Esq., of that place, who in 1712 illegally disin-
herited his little grandson, John Giffard, the father
of John Giffard, of Drummartin. Retaining only
a portion of his patrimonial estates, this Mr. John
Giffard was bred to the law, and died at the com-
paratively early age of 47, while engaged in attempt-
ing the recovery of his family estates, leaving one
son (as before mentioned), John Giffard, a baby in
arms.

This orphan child, deprived thus early of his
father, and of his mother six years later, was
adopted by Counsellor Ambrose Hardinge, a friend
of his father, who brought him up as his adopted
son, until he too could help him no longer, by reason
of liabilities incurred through an act of charity to a
near connection. Thus deprived of all help from
his friends and relations, and ousted from his lawful
possessions in England, Mr. John Giffard went
forth to seek his own fortune, which, though at first
hard and necessitous, he encountered with a forti-
tude worthy of the race from which he sprung.
Steadily he set himself to overcome the many diffi-
culties which faced him, until at length he obtained

a lucrative appointment in the Customs, and was subsequently made Accountant-General of the Customs in Dublin. He became a leading member of the Dublin Corporation, and took an active and prominent part in all local affairs. When the Volunteer movement was started in 1778, he was one of the earliest to join, and the first company of Dublin Volunteers was formed at his house. In 1793 he entered the City of Dublin Militia on its enrolment, and continued a Captain until 1802. On the occasion of Emmet's rebellion in 1803, he applied for permission to raise a corps of Yeomanry in the neighbourhood of Dundrum, and in ten days had enlisted 150 Volunteers, and was able to march them fully armed and respectably disciplined to a review in the Phœnix Park. While High Sheriff he detected the Back Lane Parliament, and, at risk of his life, entered and dispersed the meeting. A strong Protestant and supporter of the English Government, he had good reason for being decided in his views, as he had seen his son murdered by the rebels in Kildare, and also as his wife's nephew, Captain Ryan, had been killed in assisting to arrest Lord Edward Fitzgerald. As the owner of a paper called the *Dublin Journal*, he materially assisted the Government, and was one of the most resolute advocates for the Union with England.

With such opinions, it is needless to say, he has been the subject of much misrepresentation from political opponents, and Gilbert in his *History of Dublin*, vol. ii., p. 53, gives an account of his career,

extracted from Sir Jonah Barrington's *Personal
Sketches*, which in many respects is ungenerous and
unjust. He says, however, in the conclusion that,
notwithstanding Giffard's strong political and religious prejudices, he never allowed the acerbities
of party feeling to impede the dictates of benevolence ; and in private life he was always found to
be a steadfast and generous friend.*

See obituary notice in *Gentleman's Magazine*,
vol. lxxxix., pt. i., p. 481, and under Halsbury in
B. P., 1895.

GRIFFITH, HENRY DARBY, 1878-79,

of Margaretta, Roebuck; General, C.B., Colonel
5th Lancers, Equerry to the Queen, commanded
the Scots Greys all through the Crimea, and was
wounded at Balaclava. He was son of General
Matthew Chitty Darby Griffith (see Griffith of Pad-
worth, B. L. G., 1894), and *m.* Miss Bainbridge
(*d.* May, 1893). He *d. s. p.*, Nov. 17, 1887.

* His son, Dr. Stanley Lees Giffard, in a letter written in
1837 (*Dublin University Magazine*, vol. x., p. 622) to vindi-
cate his father's memory from an attack made on him in
connection with his command of a detachment of the Dublin
Militia at the "Battle of the Diamond," in the Co. Armagh,
in Sept., 1795, says that, though the part which his father
acted in Irish politics was not very obscure, he was never
accused of a single act of persecution, and that he frequently
expressed his thankfulness that he had passed through the
whole of the civil war from 1795 to 1799, generally holding
an independent military command, without being under the
necessity of inflicting severity in a single instance.

HAMILTON, ALEXANDER, 1893-94-95,

of Bellemont; Barrister-at-Law, J.P. Co. Dublin; son of Gustavus Hamilton, Esq., *m.*, T. C., Aug. 14, 1883, Anita Ellen Mary, dau. of William Richard Hamilton, Esq., M.D. (p. 37), and has issue—1. Muriel Maud; 2. Mildred Anita; 3. Anita, *d.* an infant, *bur.* T. G.

HAMILTON, EVERARD, 1883 TO 1887,

of Sydenham Terrace, now of Ballinteer Lodge; B.A., T.C.D., Solicitor; son of John Hamilton, Esq. (who was son of Gustavus Hamilton, Esq., above mentioned), by his wife, Adelaide Margaret, dau. of William Maffett, Esq., *m.*, T. C., April 21, 1881, Elinor Anna, dau. of Andrew Nolan, Esq., M.D., and has issue, *bapt.* T. C.—1. Gustavus Everard; 2. Helen Mary Adelaide; 3. Sylvia Grace Victoria.

HASKINS, CHARLES, 1800-1,

of Roebuck, and of Summer Street, Dublin; a clothier; *m.*, 1788, Miss Mary Kelly.

HAYES, WILLIAM ANDREW, 1871-72,

of Summerville; B.A., T.C.D.; *m.*, first, 1851, Miss Elizabeth Carolin; secondly, Miss Mary Eleanor Pratt, and had issue, *bapt.* T. C.—1. Thomas William Patrick; 2. Madaline Eleanor Rebecca; 3. Eva Sarah. His dau. Grace *m.*, T. C., Sept. 7, 1882, Brandram Henry Sydenham Boileau, Esq. Mr. Hayes *d.* May 12, 1889, and is *bur.* T. G. (p. 86).

HIME, MORRIS, 1824,

of Roebuck ; had issue by his wife, Sophia (who *d.*
Nov. 20, 1841)—1. Maurice Caldwell, in H.O., *m.*
Harriot, dau. of the Rev. Bartholomew Lloyd, D.D.,
Provost of T.C.D., and had issue—i. Bartholomew
Clifford, Sch., B.A. & Mod., T.C.D., *d.;* ii. John Rhames,
B.A. & Mod., T.C.D., C.E., *d.* ; iii. Humphrey, Estate
Agent in Toronto ; iv. Maurice William, B.A. and
Vice-Chancellor's Prizeman, T.C.D., in H.O., Army
Chaplain, *d.* in India ; v. Frederick, General, R.E. ;
vi. Robert Douglas, B.A., T.C.D., Indian Civil Ser-
vice, *d.;* vii. Albert, Hon. Colonel, R.E. ; viii.
Sophia, *m.* John H. Chapman, Esq., F.R.C.P.I. ;
2. John Rhames, *m.* Miss Susan Black, and *d.* Oct.
11, 1843, leaving issue—i. Henry William Lovett,
Col. R.A. ; ii. Maurice Charles, LL.D., Barrister-at-law,
Head Master of Foyle College, *m.*, first, Mary Stuart,
dau. of the Rev. George Robinson, Rector of Tar-
taraghan, Co. Armagh ; secondly, Rebecca, dau. of
Professor James Apjohn, M.D., and has issue—John
Godfrey Whiteside, Charles Richardson, Mary
Henrietta, Frances Charlotte ; iii. Thomas Whiteside, *m.* Miss Annie Tate ; iv. Frances Harriot, *m.*
Rev. F. S. Aldhouse, M.A., Head Master of Drogheda
Grammar School ; 3. Eliza, *m.* Edward Smith, Esq.;
4. Clarissa, *m.*, in T.C., May 31, 1817, George Gilling-
ton, Esq. ; 5. Sophia, *m.* Surgeon Henry Haffield ;
6. Sarah, *m.* Rev. Edward Hearn, Rector of Hurst
Green, Lancashire ; 7. Harriot, *m.* Rev. John
Whiteside, brother of Lord Chief Justice Whiteside. Mr. Hime *d. circa* Jan., 1828.

HONE, NATHANIEL, 1795-96,

of Hannahville, Dundrum; an Alderman of Dublin, High Sheriff, 1798-99, and Lord Mayor, 1810-11 ; J.P. Co. of Dublin, and sometime Governor of the Bank of Ireland. He *m.*, 1784, Miss Hannah Dickinson, and had issue—1. Henry; 2. Addison ; 3. Nathaniel ; 4. Hannah (*bapt.* T. C.), *m.* Frederick Moore, Esq. ; 5. Sarah (*bapt.* T. C.). He *d.* April 8, 1819.

"A gentleman very much lamented, and who possessed many amiable qualities."—*Saunders' News-Letter*, April 9, 1819.

HUME, JOHN LA TOUCHE, 1794,

of Roebuck; was third son of George Hume, Esq., of Humewood, by Anne, dau. of Thomas Butler, Esq. (See Hume, of Co. Wicklow, B.L.G., 1894.) He *d.* Jan., 1827. He was *m.*, and left issue—1. John Samuel, *d.* Sept. 1, 1854 ; 2. Louisa; 3. Elizabeth; 4. Anna Maria, *m.* Robert Mayston, Esq.

HYNDMAN, JOHN ELLIOTT, 1833-38,

of Roebuck Lodge,* and of Bachelor's Walk, Dublin; Merchant ; Coroner of Dublin; High Sheriff, 1834-35 ; *m.*, 1820, Miss Mary Hutchinson, and had issue—1. George Hutchinson (*bapt.* T. C.) ; 2. Elliott, *m.* Miss Elizabeth Curtis LaNauze, *o. s. p.;* 3. Thomas Warwick (*bapt.* T. C.), in Australia ;

---

* Lewis, in his *Topographical Dictionary of Ireland*, vol. ii., p. 518, says that this was formerly the manor house, and about fifty years before that date (1837) the only house in the neighbourhood, with the exception of the Castle.

4. John; 5. Mary (*bapt.* T. C.), *d. unm.*; 6. Everina;
7. Elizabeth, *m.* Rev. —— Stephens; 8. Matilda.
Mr. Hyndman *d.* April 21, 1859.

JAFFRAY, ALEXANDER, 1793,

of Roebuck; he *d.* at Cheltenham, on March 20,
1818, in the 84th year of his age.

"He was formerly an eminent merchant in the City of
Dublin, and the first elected Governor of the Bank of Ireland. He was descended from an ancient and respectable
family in the Co. of Aberdeen, and was one of the surviving
great-grandsons of Robert Barclay, of Urie, in Scotland,
author of the learned *Apology for the People called Quakers*,
in the principles of which sect he was educated. When he
arrived at an age to form his own decisions, he became a
member of the Established Church; but through life he
retained that simplicity and integrity of mind and conduct
for which they have been justly celebrated. To these were
added, a cultivated understanding, a generous and affectionate
heart."—*Annual Register*, vol. lx., p. 199; also see *Gentleman's Magazine*, vol. lxxxviii., pt. i., p. 473.

KIRWAN, MARTIN, 1867,
of Orchardton.

KINAHAN, DANIEL, 1797-1824,

of Roebuck Park, previously of Churchtown, and of
Merrion Square, Dublin; *b.*, 1756, *m.*, first, 1791,
Martha (*d.* 1800), dau. of George Paine, Esq., and
had issue—1. George (*q.v.*); 2. John, in H.O., M.A.,
T.C.D., Rector of Knockbreda, Co. Down, *b.* 1792,
m., Stillorgan Church, Sept. 25, 1823, Emily, dau.
of John George, Esq., and sister of the Right Hon.
Mr. Justice George, and *d.* Aug., 1866, leaving

issue; 3. Daniel (*q. v.*); 4. Robert Henry, M.A., T.C.D., J.P., High Sheriff, 1851, and Lord Mayor of Dublin, 1853, *b.* 1799, *m.*, Dec. 22, 1822, Charlotte, dau. of Edward Hudson, Esq., M.D., of Fields of Odin, Rathfarnham, and *d.* April 29, 1861, leaving issue;* 5. Prudentia, *m.*, T. C., June 10, 1814, Rev. Charles Henry Minchin (see Minchin, Humphrey), and *d.* 1868 ; 6. Martha, *d.* 1798. Mr. Kinahan *m.*, secondly, 1805, Miss Julia Carr, and *d.* July, 1827. He was *bur.* in St. Mary's Churchyard, Dublin.

KINAHAN, DANIEL, 1834-36-40,

of Belfield, Roebuck ; Classical Gold Medallist, T.C.D., M.A., Barrister-at-Law ; third son of Daniel Kinahan, Esq. (*q. v.*), *b.* 1797, *m.*, 1825, Louisa Anne Stuart (*d.* Jan. 6, 1887), dau. of John Miller, Esq., by whom he had issue—1. Daniel Miller, *d.* 1848 ; 2. John Robert, M.D., T.C.D., *d.* 1863 ; 3. George Henry, *m.*, 1855, Henrietta Anne (*d.* 1889), dau. of Samuel Gerrard, Esq.; 4. James Bond, *d.* 1857; 5. Charles Alfred (*d.* 1892), *m.*, 1864, Louisa, dau. of Rev. Charles Minchin ; 6. Thomas William (*bapt.* T. C.), M.A., T.C.D., J.P., *m.*, 1864, Florence Sarah (*d.* July 11, 1881), dau. of Justin Macarthy, Esq. ; 7. Willoughby (*bapt.* T. C.), *d.* 1845 ; 8. Wensley (*bapt.* T. C.), *d.* 1845 ; 9. Louisa Stuart ; 10. Julia Miller, *d.* 1886; 11. Henrietta Martha (*bapt.* T. C.), *d.* 1865 ; 12. Anna, *m.*, 1865, John Kinahan, Esq., M.D. ; 13. Maria Charlotte, *d.* 1890 ;

* See Sir Edward Hudson-Kinahan, Bart., chapter viii.

14. Katherine Stuart (*bapt.* T. C.), *m.*, 1876, H. Leonard, Esq.; 15. Lucy Wensley.   Mr. Kinahan *d.* June 9, 1859.

KINAHAN, GEORGE, 1830,

of Roebuck Park; M.A., T.C.D., J.P.; eldest son of Daniel Kinahan, Esq. (*q. v.*), *b.* 1791, *m.*, 1815, Maria Jane (*d.* 1850), dau. of Alderman Cash, and had issue—1. Daniel, M.A., T.C.D., J.P., *m.*, 1851, Harriett, dau. of J. Hone, Esq., and *d.* 1860, leaving issue (*bapt.* T. C.)—i. George Percy Daniel, *m.* Amalinda Rosa, dau. of Major John Atkinson, 89th Regiment; ii. Annie Julia, *m.*, July 23, 1873, Charles Bent Ball, Esq., M.D.; iii. Maria Jane ; iv. Harriett Lucy Nanette, *m.*, May 17, 1894, James Caverhill, Esq.; 2. George (*q. v.*); 3. John Cash (*bapt.* T. C.) *d.;* 4. Robert William (*bapt.* T. C.), *d.* in Canada ; 5. Charles Henry, Major 63rd Regt., *d.* April 13, 1878; 6. Isabella; 7. Julia ; 8. Maria, *m.*, T. C., Feb. 2, 1843, Joseph Hone, Esq., of Ashton Park, Monkstown; 9. Emily; 10. Henrietta Eleanor, *m.*, T. C., May 14, 1845, Rev. George Bennett; 11. Matilda Louisa (*bapt.* T. C.); 12. Charlotte Mary (*bapt.* T. C.); 13. Adelaide, *m.*, T. C., Oct. 9, 1860, Herbert William Clifford, Esq., M.D. Mr. Kinahan *d.* in 1853.

KINAHAN, GEORGE, 1865-68,

of Roebuck Park; J.P., D.L., and High Sheriff, 1873, of the City of Dublin, J.P., and High Sheriff, 1879-80, of the Co. of Dublin ; second son of George Kinahan, Esq. (*q. v.*), *m.*, 1863, Margaret, dau. of

Rev. Daniel Dickinson, M.A., Rector of Seapatrick, Co. Down, and has had issue (*bapt.* T. C.)—1. George Daniel, *d.* an infant; 2. George Dickinson, *d.* March 13, 1878; 3. Arthur Edward, B.A., Cantab.; 4. Margaret Charlotte Emily, *m.*, T. C., May 24, 1892, Ivon Henry Price, Esq., LL.D., T.C.D., District Inspector, R.I.C.; 5. Maria Georgina; 6. Alice Josephine, *m.*, T. C., August 5, 1891, William Drummond Hamilton, Esq., M.A., Oxon.; 7. Emily Elizabeth; 8. Isabella Frances; 9. Violet Georgina; 10. Lilian Grace; 11. Olive Rosa.

LA FARELLE, JAMES, 1822,

of Friarsland and of the Stamp Office, Dublin; *m.*, Dec., 1817, Eliza, dau. of John Greene, Esq., of Leeson Street, and Greenfield, Co. Kildare, and had issue, *bapt.* T. C.—1. Thomas; 2. Mary Anne.

LA TOUCHE, JAMES LAWRENCE DIGGES, 1851-55,

of Mountainview, Churchtown; Barrister-at-Law, J.P. Co. Dublin; son of James Digges La Touche, Esq. (eldest son of William La Touche, Esq., D.L., and Grace, dau. of John Puget, Esq.), and Isabella, dau. of Sir James Lawrence Cotter, Bart., *m.* Miss Elizabeth Pye, and *o. s. p.*

LA TOUCHE, PETER DIGGES, 1809-10,

of Belfield, Stillorgan Road, fifth son of James Digges La Touche, Esq., M.P., by his second wife, Martha, dau. of William Thwaites, Esq., *m.*, 1789, Charlotte, dau. of George Thwaites, Esq., and had issue—1. Peter Digges, *m.* Mary Anne Moore, dau. of Dodwell

Browne, Esq., of Rahins, Co. Mayo, and had issue :
i. Peter Dodwell Digges, in H. O., *m.* Miss Elizabeth
Digges La Touche, ii. David Henry Digges, *o. s. p.*,
iii. William Nassau Digges, iv. John James Digges,
LL.D., Deputy Keeper of the Public Records of
Ireland, *m.* Miss Anne Pringle, v. Everard Neal
(Major), *m.* Miss Clementine Eagar, vi. Mary
Elizabeth, *d. unm.*, vii. Charlotte Sophia, viii. Louisa,
d. unm., ix. Janet, *d. unm.*, x. Margaret Adelaide,
d. unm., xi. Isabella Florence, *m.* Rev. Theodore
James Cooper, xii. Marianne, *d.*, *m.* Madison Wall
Fisher, Esq., xiii. Octavia, *d. unm.;* 2. John James
Digges, in H. O., *o. s. p.*, July 13, 1835; 3. George
Digges, Barrister-at-Law, *m.*, first, Miss Emily
Grueber, and had issue two children ; secondly,
Feb. 18, 1841, Frances, dau. of Rev. Cæsar Otway,
and had issue two children ; 4. Theophilus Digges,
o. s. p., June 24, 1858; 5. William Digges, M.D., *o. s. p.*,
Oct. 7, 1834 ; 6. Elizabeth, *d. unm.*, Dec. 11, 1872;
7. Emily, *m.* John Brenan, Esq. (*d.* Aug. 2, 1865),
d. Dec. 3, 1841; 8. Frances, *d. unm.*, Nov., 1826 ;
9. Charlotte, *d.* young ; 10. Henrietta, *d. unm.*,
Dec. 8, 1859 ; 11. Grace, *d. unm.*, March 4, 1834 ;
12. Gertrude, *d. unm.*, March 21, 1880 ; 13. Martha,
d. young ; 14. Sophia, *d. unm.*, March 4, 1840.   Mr.
La Touche *d.* Feb. 2, 1820.

LEWIS, WILLIAM, 1842,
of Harlech, Roebuck ; Solicitor ; *d. circa* 1850.

LEWIS, WILLIAM, 1853,
of Harlech, Roebuck ; Solicitor ; had a son by his
wife Jane, Harvey, *bapt.* in T. C.

LIGHTON, SIR THOMAS, BART., 1791,
of Merville and of Stephen's Green, Dublin. A
banker of the firm of Lighton, Needham, and Shaw,
of Foster Place. He represented the Borough of
Tuam in the Irish Parliament from 1790 to 1797,
and the Borough of Carlingford from 1798 to 1800.
He was created a Baronet on March 1, 1791, and
took the title of Sir Thomas Lighton, of Merville,
Dublin. He was High Sheriff of the Co. Dublin,
1790. He was son of John Lighton, Esq., of
Raspberry Hill, Co. Tyrone, by Elizabeth, his wife,
dau. of John Walker, Esq., of Tisdern, Co. Tyrone.
He *m.*, Dec. 11, 1777, Anna (*d.* June, 1804), dau. of
William Pollock, Esq., of Strabane, by whom he
had issue—1. Thomas, who succeeded to the
Baronetcy on the death of his father, and *m.*, Dec.
14, 1811, Miss Sylvia Brandon (*d.* May 24, 1817);
he *d.* May 11, 1816 (*bur.* T. G.), and left an infant
son, Thomas, *b.* Nov. 1813, who succeeded to the
Baronetcy on the death of his father, and *d.* April
20, 1817 ; 2. James, *d.* April, 1806 (*bur.* T. G.) ; 3.
John, in H.O., Rector of Donaghmore, Co. Donegal,
succeeded to the Baronetcy on the death of his
infant nephew, *m.*, Jan. 23, 1817, Mary Hamilton
(*d.* June 28, 1826), second dau. of Christopher
Pemberton, Esq., M.D., and *d.* April 5, 1828, leaving
issue—i. John Hamilton, *b.* May, 26, 1818, succeeded to the Baronetcy on the death of his father,
and *o. s. p.*, April 29, 1844 : ii. Christopher Robert,
M.A., in H.O., Vicar of Ellastone, succeeded to the
Baronetcy on the death of his brother, *b.* May 28,

1819, *m.*, June 2, 1843, Mary Anne Elizabeth, only dau. of Rev. Digby Joseph Stopford Ram, and *d.* April 12, 1875, leaving Christopher, the present Baronet, and other issue; iii. Thomas, *b.* Sept. 26, 1820, *o. s. p.*, May 3, 1852; iv. Andrew, M.A., *b.* Dec. 26, 1822, *m.*, May 25, 1860, Eliza Amelia, youngest dau. of Henry Sumner Joyce, Esq.; v. Mary, *d.* young; 4. Henry Chester; 5. Elizabeth (*d.* Jan. 18, 1848), *m.*, Aug., 1803, Sir Samuel Hayes, Bart.; 6. Anne, *m.* Charles Rea, Esq., of Fort Royal, Co. Donegal; 7. Charlotte, *m.* Rev. John Sweeny; 8. Mary, *d.* Nov., 1794, *bur.* T. G. Sir Thomas *d.* April 27, 1805, and was *bur.* in T. G. on April 29.

The following interesting account of his life appears in the obituary notices in the *Annual Register*, vol. xlviii., p. 496 :—

"At Dublin, Sir Thomas Lighton, Bart. and Banker, who was one of the many instances that 'honesty is the best policy.' He was very early in his life an humble trader, in the town of Strabane, in the North of Ireland, and proving unsuccessful, he went in search of better fortune to the East Indies, as a soldier in the company's service. He was a man of talent, and of a strong mind, and rendered himself extremely useful by having, in a very short time, acquired a knowledge of the Oriental languages. It was his good fortune to be confined in the same prison with the late General Matthews, who, previous to his unfortunate catastrophe, entrusted to the care of Mr. Lighton jewels and property to an immense amount, to be delivered to his family if he should effect his escape; and to ensure his zeal and punctuality, he presented him with a considerable sum. Being some time afterwards employed as an interpreter, he took advantage of the first opportunity that offered to escape. After assuming various disguises, and encountering many perilous adventures, he arrived in London, and, waiting on Mrs. Matthews, delivered to her the last letter of her husband, together with the treasure. By her his fidelity is said to have been rewarded with £20,000. He immediately wrote to Ireland, to inquire for a beloved wife and child, whom he had left behind him, and sent a sum of money to discharge his debts. He found that his wife, whom he had left young, handsome, and unprotected, had, by honest industry, supported herself and her daughter, then ten years of age, and given her an education superior to her humble means. He now took a handsome house in Stephen's Green, Dublin; the seat belonging to the late Lord Chief Baron Foster, father of the Irish Chancellor of the Exchequer, near Dublin, was purchased, and new carriages were built for him. But an inactive life had no charms for him, and he embarked the greatest part of his fortune in a banking house, which has been very successful. Lady Lighton, whose amiable manners endeared her to all ranks, died some time since, and left a numerous family."

LINDE, JOHN HILL, 1841,

of Drummartin House; *m.*, 1823, Charlotte Maria, dau. of Sir Henry Jebb, and had issue—1. William Edward (*bapt.* T. C.); 2. Mary Sophia, *m.*, T. C., Feb. 26,1846, Richard Thomas Bourne, Esq. (*q. v.*); 3. Florence Reeves (*bapt.* T. C.); 4. Adelaide Louisa Jebb, *m.*, July 9, 1857, Herbert Panmure Ribton, Esq. (who was murdered at Alexandria, June 11, 1882), and had issue, Ada.

LLOYD, JOHN THOMAS, 1853,

of Farmley (now Lynwood); Barrister-at-Law; eldest son of Rev. Edward Lloyd, of Castle Lloyd,

by his wife, Dania Connor, *m.*, Sept. 17, 1832,
Elizabeth Grace (*d.* 1874), second dau. of Rev. E.
Thomas, Rector of Ballinacourty, and had issue—
1. Edward, *m.* Miss Dora Harvey, and *o. s. p.*, May,
1850 ; 2. Richard, *m.* Miss Dorothea Harvey ; 3.
William, *d.* 1876; 4. Francis; 5. Jane Georgina, *m.*,
1855, James Howlin, Esq., J.P., of Ballycronigan,
Co. Wexford (Howlin, of Ballycronigan, B.L.G.,
1894), and has issue—i. James, ii. Jane Georgina,
iii. Nina ; 6. Dania ; 7. Edwina; 8. Eliza Alice
(*bapt.* T. C.).   Mr. Lloyd *d.* 1853.

MANDERS, RICHARD, 1860,

of Rockmount, and subsequently of Brackenstown,
Swords ; *m.* Caroline, sister of Henry Roe, Esq.,
D.L. (*q. v.*), and had issue—1. Richard, *m.* Alice
Dorothea, dau. of Henry Smith Wright, Esq., M.P. ;
2. Henry Robert (*bapt.* T. C.), in H.O., Vicar of
Horbury Junction, Wakefield; 3. George Edward
Roe (*bapt.* T. C.) ; 4. John Frederick ; 5. Caroline,
m. C. P. Laudon, Esq., Indian Telegraphic Service;
6. Kate Charlotte.   Mr. Manders *d.* 1884.

MASON, HENRY JOSEPH, 1844,

of Summerville, Dundrum.

MACONCHY, JOHN, 1823,

of Roebuck ; eldest son of John Maconchy, Esq., of
Co. Derry (see Maconchy of Rathmore, B.L.G.,
1894), *b.* May 30, 1793, *m.*, March 4, 1816, Deborah,
dau. of Stewart King, Esq., and had issue—1.
George, afterwards of Rathmore, *m.* Louisa Eliza-

beth, dau. of John Goddard Richards, Esq. (*q. v.*) ;
2. John Stewart, *m.* Henrietta Frances, dau. of Rev.
Charles William Doyne; 3. Elizabeth, *m.* Rev.
Frederick FitzJohn Trench; 4. Helen (*bapt.* T. C.),
m. James Chaigneau Colvill, Esq. ; 5. Barbara, *m.*
Lt.-Col. Thomas Harper Colvill. Mr. Maconchy
d. Dec. 10, 1843.

MAUNSELL, JOHN, 1863,

of Rockmount, Dundrum, now of Edenmore,
Raheny; Solicitor, J.P. Co. Limerick; son of Robert
Maunsell, Esq. (*q. v.*), *m.*, first, 1851, Catherine
Lucinda (*d.* Feb. 3, 1862, *bur.* T. G.), dau. of Thomas
Lloyd, Esq., D.L., and had issue—1. Edmund
Robert Lloyd, M.A. and LL.B., T.C.D., Barrister-at-
Law, *b.* Oct. 18, 1852, *m.*, 1879, Annie Rachel,
dau. of Joseph Emerson Dowson, Esq., and *d.* Nov.
2, 1886 (*bur.* T. G.), leaving issue; 2. John Drought,
late Capt. Durham Light Infantry, now Army Pay
Department, *m.* Miss Euphemia Bushe; 3. Frederick
William, *m.* Eleanor, dau. of P. O'Brien, Esq., C.E.,
and *d.* May 10, 1894 ; 4. Eyre Lloyd, *d.* Nov. 19,
1894; 5. Annie Mary. Mr. Maunsell *m.*, secondly,
Emily Roche, only child of Archibald John
Stephens, Esq., Q.C., LL.D., Recorder of Winchester,
and by her had issue—Archibald John Stephens
(*bapt.* T. C.), Capt., Royal Warwickshire Regt. ;
and thirdly, Annie, dau. of Rev. George Peacocke.

MAUNSELL, ROBERT, 1843,

of Ballawley Park, and of Merrion Square, Dublin ;
Solicitor ; ninth son of Daniel Maunsell, Esq. (see

K

Maunsell of Ballywilliam, B.L.G., 1894), *b.* Aug.
9, 1795, *m.*, first, Anne, eldest dau. of the Rev.
John Lloyd, and by her had issue—1. Daniel, *m.*,
T. C., May 26, 1853, Anne Lucinda, dau. of Robert
Billing, Esq. (*q. v.*); 2. John (*q. v.*); 3. Elizabeth,
m., T. C., June 10, 1851, Robert Mayne, 37th Regt.
M. N. I., son of John Mayne, Esq., and grandson
of Judge Mayne (*q. v.*); 4. Isabella, *m.* William
Boyne Butt, Esq., M.D.   Mr. Maunsell *m.*, secondly,
Frances (*d.* July, 1844, *bur.* T. G.), eldest dau. of
Francis Dwyer, Esq., and by her had issue (*bapt.*
T. C.)—1. Francis Richard; 2. Albert Edward;
3. Fanny Barbara Maria; and thirdly, Louisa, dau.
of James Douglas, Esq., and had issue—George
Meares, Captain.   Mr. Maunsell *d.* 1876.

MAYNE, EDWARD, 1792,

of Churchtown and of Stephen's Green, North,
Dublin, was the eldest son of Charles Mayne, Esq.,
of Freame Mount, Co. Monaghan, by his wife
Dorothea, dau. of Edward Mayne, Esq., of Mount
Ledboro, Co. Fermanagh (see B. L. G., 1868, p.
998).   He entered T.C.D., and having won a
Scholarship in 1775, graduated B.A. in 1777.   He
was called to the Bar in 1781.   He was appointed
a Justice of the Common Pleas, Feb. 21, 1805, and
was transferred to the King's Bench, Oct. 24, 1816.
He resigned on Dec. 1, 1818, and *d.* in 1829.   He
m., 1780, Sarah (*d.* 1853), dau. of John Fiddes, Esq.,
and had issue—1. Charles, in H. O., M.A., T.C.D.,
Rector of Kilmastulla, *m.* Susan (*d.* 1865), dau. of

William Henn, Esq., and *d.* 1873, having had issue—i. William, *m.* Emily, dau. of Thomas Murray, Esq., *d.* 1876, ii. Charles, iii. Edward John, iv. Susan, *d. unm.*, June 6, 1894, v. Eliza, *m.* John Going, Esq., of Cragg, Co. Tipperary; 2. Edward, *m.* Eliza, dau. of William Henn, Esq., and *d.* 1878, having had issue—i. Edward, *m.* first, Miss Janette Woodall; secondly, Miss Georgie Taylor (*d.* 1881), and *d.* 1888, ii. Susan, *d. unm.*, 1864; 3. John, *m.* Anna, dau. of the Very Rev. Dean Graves, and *d.* 1829, having had issue—i. Edward Graves, *o. s. p.*, ii. John Dawson, iii. Elizabeth, *m.* Henry Colles, Esq.,* iv. Sarah, *m.* her cousin Dawson Mayne, Esq. (p. 132); 4. Richard (*bapt.* T. C.), K.C.B., Chief Commissioner London Metropolitan Police, 1829-68, *m.* at Danbury, Aug. 31, 1831, Georgina (*d.* April 12, 1872), dau. of Thomas Carvick, Esq., of Riffham Lodge, Essex, and *d.* Dec. 26, 1868, having had issue—i. Carvick Cox, *d.* Sept., 1851, ii. Richard Charles, Rear-Admiral, R.N., C.B., M.P. for Pembroke Boroughs 1886-92, *m.*, 1870, Sabine, eldest dau. of Thomas Dent, Esq., and *d.* May 29, 1892, iii. Edward William, *d.* Aug., 1844, iv. Robert Dawson, *m.* Emma Elizabeth, dau. of Professor Malden, *d.* June, 1887, v. Charles Edward, *d.* Nov., 1873, vi. Georgina Marianne, *m.*, 1870, Horace Brooke, Esq., vii. Sarah Fanny, *m.*, 1877, Charles E. Malden, Esq., viii. Katherine Emily, *d.* 1868; 5. William, *o. s. p.*, 1867; 6. Dawson, *m.* Miss Mary Hewitt, *o. s. p.*,

* See Abraham Colles, M.D., chapter viii.

1872 ; 7. Robert, *o.s.p.*, 1843 ; 8. Dorothea, *m.* John Mayne, Capt. 9th Dragoons, and had issue— i. Dawson, *m.* his cousin Sarah, dau. of John Mayne, Esq. (p. 131), ii. Robert, *m.*, T. C., June 10, 1851, Elizabeth, dau. of Robert Maunsell, Esq. (*q. v.*), iii. John Colburn, Madras Light Infantry, *o. s. p.*, in India, iv. Helen, v. Dora, *m.*, 1862, Colonel Gustavus Charles Walsh, 14th Bengal Native Infantry, son of John Walsh, Esq., of Dundrum Castle, and had issue, John Russell, *m.* Miss Norcott, third dau. of Arthur Norcott, Esq., of Park, Doneraile, Co. Cork, and Dorothea Helen ; 9. Sarah, *m.*, 1830, Rev. R. French Lawrence, *d.* 1832 ; 10. Kate, *m.* Major Basil Heron, R.A., *d.* 1869 ; 11. Margaret, *m.* at Berne, Oct. 29, 1823, Thomas E. Beatty, Esq., M.D. ; 12. Fanny, *d. unm.*, 1872.

MAYNE, JOSEPH ST. CLAIR, 1888-89,

of Sunnybank ; Barrister-at-Law ; son of James Arthur Mayne, Esq., Solicitor, *m.*, in T. C., Aug. 4, 1869, Rachel Isabel, eldest dau. of Michael Charles Bernard, Esq., M.D. (*q. v.*).

McCASKEY, WILLIAM, 1827-31,

of Hermitage, Roebuck, and of Church Street, Dublin ; Iron Manufacturer ; *d.* June 9, 1834 (p. 39).

M'COMAS, RICHARD HENRY ARCHIBALD, 1879-80,

of Homestead, Ballawley ; Junior Moderator and M.A., T.C.D., Barrister-at-Law, *c.* 1875 ; third son of

Archibald M'Comas, Esq., M.A., of Cliff Castle,
Dalkey, and Elgin Road, Dublin, by his wife Jane,
dau. of W. Jones, Esq.; *m.*, Jan. 28, 1875, at St.
Mary's, Donnybrook, Susannah Alice, dau. of C.
Goodman, Esq., of Lapsdowne Road, and had issue
(*bapt.* T. C., excepting Mabel)—1. Edwin Archibald;
2. Harold; 3. Cyril Henry; 4. Gerald; 5. Reginald; 6. Rupert; 7. Mabel Christine Jane; 8.
Sybil Frances; 9. Olive.

M'Dermott, Joseph, 1825,

of Castleview, Roebuck; Solicitor; *m.*, 1811, Miss
Mary Stone, and *d.* 1837, leaving issue—1. John
(*bapt.* T. C.); 2. Joseph (*bapt.* T. C.) ; 3. Fanny;
4. Anne Joanna (*bapt.* T. C.).

M'Kay, Daniel, 1825-26,

of Moreen and Stephen's Green ; Solicitor ; eldest
son of William M'Kay, Esq. (*q. v.*), *m.*, April 16,
1811, at Rhuabon Church, North Wales, Eliza,
dau. of Edward Rowland, Esq., of Gurthen, in the
Co. of Denbigh, and had issue—1. William ; 2.
Manners (*q. v.*) ; 3. Rowland ; 4. Louisa Jane ; 5.
Eliza Maria. He *d.* Dec. 5, 1840, and was *bur.* in
St. Ann's Church, Dublin.

M'Kay, Manners, 1845,

of Moreen ; Capt. Dublin Militia, formerly of 3rd
Dragoon Guards, J.P. Co. Dublin ; second son of
Daniel M'Kay, Esq. (*q. v.*), *m.* Alice Georgina (*d.*
Nov. 22, 1853), dau. of Thomas Bunbury, Esq., of

Lisbryon, Co. Tipperary, and *d.* June 12, 1854, leaving issue (*bapt.* T. C.)—1. Mary Eliza, *m.* Major James Lenox MacFarlane, J.P.; 2. Alice Georgina; 3. Sarah Jane, *m.* George Selby, Esq.

M'KAY, WILLIAM, 1800, of Moreen,* and of Merrion Square; Solicitor, Pursuivant to the Court of Chancery, Deputy Clerk of the Faculties, and Clerk of the Recognizances in Chancery; *m.*, 1794, Miss Mary Bartley, and had issue—1. Daniel (*q. v.*); 2. John; 3. Anne. He *d.* Oct., 1812. He held the position of Assistant Clerk of the Council, and was amongst the officers of the Irish Houses of Parliament to whom annuities were granted at the Union.—Gilbert's *History of Dublin,* vol. iii., p. 371.

MINCHIN, HUMPHREY, 1819-20-21, of Roebuck Lodge;† J.P. Co. Dublin, High Sheriff

* "Near the four-mile-stone is Moreen, a most pleasing situation. It is within three miles of the sea, of which it has a grand view, also of the city and adjoining county for many miles. This place is remarkable for having a desperate battle fought in it some centuries ago by two of the neighbouring families, who, on their revenge being satiated, mutually agreed to erect a church in the valley where the engagement was had, and from thence called the Cross Church of Moreen; on the rocky ground adjoining, with great industry and expense, is erected a neat, compact house, with gardens, lawns, plantations, and suitable offices, belonging to William M'Kay, Esq."—*Post-Chaise Companion,* 1803, p. 391.

† In 1798, at the time of the rebellion, Mr. Humphrey Minchin was residing at the Grange, Rathfarnham. A party of the rebels entered his house, headed by his gardener and

of Dublin, 1795-96; *b.* Nov., 1750, *m.*, first, Frances
Catherine, dau. of Major Sirr, and had issue—1.
Charles Henry, in H. O., *m.*, T. C., June 18, 1814,
Prudentia, dau. of Daniel Kinahan, Esq. (*q. v.*),
and had issue; 2. Joseph, *m.* May 22, 1804, Miss
Louisa Hall, and had issue; 3. Frances, *m.* Major
Kingsmill Pennefather; 4. Elizabeth, *m.*, 1797,
Captain Townsend Monckton Hall, of the 28th
Regt. of Foot; 5. Emma, *m.* James Walcot Fitz-
gerald, Esq. ; 6. Louisa Arabella, *m.*, T. C., Aug. 6,
1821, Walter Bourne, Esq., jun. (*q.v.*). Mr. Minchin
m., secondly, 1812, Miss Arabella Ashworth. He
d. in 1830, and was *bur.* in St. Werburgh's. (See
Hughes's *St. Werburgh's*, pp. 42, 140.)

MINCHIN, WILLIAM AUGUSTUS, 1826,

of Ballinteer; *b.* 1768, *m.*, first, 1796, Mary, dau. of
John Ferrar, Esq., of Limerick, and had issue—1.
Augustus, in H. O., Rector of Buncrana, Co. Done-
gal, *m.* Miss Anne Tittle (who *m.*, secondly, in T. C.,
Feb. 6, 1879, James Arthur Mayne, Esq.), and *d.*

gate-keeper, about seven o'clock in the evening, when he
and his family were in Dublin. They carried off various
articles of furniture in two of his carts, and his gardener
declared that all Ireland had risen that night, and that he
would return in a day or two, and take possession of the
house and demesne for his own. Mrs. Minchin's aged
father and a female servant were the only Protestants in the
house, and the gate-keeper's wife threatened to cut their
throats ; but some other women who assisted her in plunder-
ing the house, dissuaded her from it. Assassins were posted
on the avenue to shoot Mr. Minchin ; but fortunately he did
not return from Dublin that evening.—Musgrave's *Memoirs of
the Rebellion* (Dub., 1801), p. 224.

1873 ; 2. John, *o. s. p.*, Oct. 14, 1850 ; 3. William,
o. s. p., April, 1825, *bur.* T. G. ; 4. Anne, *d.* Sept.,
1819, *bur.* T. G. ; 5. Rosetta, *d.* 1849, *bur.* Newtown-
breda ; 6. Mary, *m.*, T. C., Sept. 19, 1834, her cousin,
Michael Ferrar, Esq. (*d.* Feb., 1884), and *d.* Dec.
3, 1858, leaving issue—i. William Hugh, F.T.C.D.,
m. Miss Banks, and *d.* May, 1871, leaving issue—
Benjamin, M.D., Mary Howard, *m.* —— Binns,
Esq., Annie, *m.* Rev. J. Paterson Smyth, and Elsie,
ii. Augustus Minchin, *m.* Miss Hughes, and has
issue, iii. Michael Lloyd, *m.* Miss O'Donnell, and
has issue—Michael Lloyd, Beatrice Minchin, *m.*
Wolseley Haig, Esq., B.C.S., Gwendolyn Howard
Minchin, *m.* J. M. Holms, Esq., B.C.S., iv. Howard
Minchin, *o. s. p.*, 1872, v. Henry Stafford, in
America, *m.*, and has issue, vi. John in Natal, *m.*,
and has issue, vii. Mary Minchin, *m.* Dr. Hardy,
and has issue, viii. Rosetta Minchin. Mr. Minchin
m., secondly, 1810, Miss Charlotte Burrowes, who
d. March, 1853 (*bur.* T. G.), and had by her issue—
1. Robert, *o. s. p.*, Jan. 2, 1878 (*bur.* T. G.) ;
2. George Howard, *m.* Miss Matilda Beck (*d.* Aug.,
1859, *bur.* T. G.), and *d.* Dec. 30, 1877, *bur.* T. G.,
leaving issue—i. William Augustus, ii. Charlotte
Matilda, *m.* —— Hunter, Esq., and has issue. Mr.
Minchin *d.* Jan. 3, 1841, and was *bur.* T. G.

NORMAN, ROBERT, 1801-2-3,

of Dundrum ; *m.*, 1782, Miss Anne Jennings, and
had issue—1. Anne, *m.*, T. C., April 3, 1802, George
Hughes, Esq. ; 2. Charlotte, *m.*, T. C., March 12,
1810, George Corbett, Esq.

NUTTING, JOHN GARDINER, 1892-93,

of Gortmore; D.L. Dublin, J.P., and High Sheriff, 1895, Co. Dublin; son of John Nutting, Esq., *m.* Mary Stansmore, dau. of Restel R. Bevis, Esq., of Manor Hill, Birkenhead, and has issue—1. Harold Stansmore; 2. John Godfrey Stansmore; 3. Arthur Ronald Stansmore; 4. Dorothy Stansmore; 5. Mary Stansmore (*bapt.* T. C.).

ORME, ROBERT, 1852,

of Mount Anville, and of Owenmore, Co. Mayo, and Enniscrone, Co. Sligo; J.P. and D.L. Co. Sligo; second son of William Orme, Esq., Belleville, Co. Mayo, *m.,* Feb. 16, 1843, Sydney Frances, dau. of Major Christopher Carleton L'Estrange, of Market Hill, and had issue—1. Robert William (*bapt.* T. C.), now of Owenmore; 2. Christopher Guy; 3. Albert; 4. Janet Georgina (*bapt.* T. C.), *m.* Claude Brownlow, Esq. Mr. Orme *d.* 1877. (See Orme of Owenmore, B.L.G., 1894.)

PICKERING, CHARLES, 1848-58,

of Roebuck Grove; Solicitor; his dau. Sarah *m.,* T. C., Sept. 13, 1853, John M'Donald Royse, Esq., and his dau. Jane Adelaide *m.,* T. C., Feb. 19, 1856, Charles Furlong Harding, Esq.

PORTER, JOHN, 1857,

of Weston House, Churchtown; *m.,* 1850, Miss Lydia Georgina Duff.

Potts, James, 1794,

of Richview, Roebuck, was the proprietor of *Saunders'*
News-Letter. He *m.*, 1761, Miss Elizabeth Irwin,
and *d.* May, 1796. His death is thus recorded in
Walker's *Hibernian Magazine* for that year (p.
384):—

"Most sincerely and justly lamented, James Potts, Esq.,
an eminent printer and bookseller ; his conduct and character as a man of business have been for many years under
the observation of his fellow-citizens, who have long known
him an upright, inoffensive, unassuming, and courteous
trader."

In Gilbert's *History of Dublin* (vol. i., p. 276),
some information will be found about Potts's connection with *Saunders' News-Letter.* He carried on
a violent newspaper warfare with Mr. John Giffard
(*q. v.*), and a paragraph reflecting on "the dog in
office"—as Giffard was called—having appeared
in *Saunders'*, Giffard and his son Hardinge horse-
whipped Potts outside Taney Church, on Sunday,
October 19, 1794. Criminal proceedings were taken
by Potts, and the case was tried in the following
July. A full report appears in the *Hibernian
Magazine* for that year (p. 144). Mrs. Campbell,
wife of the Rev. Matthew Campbell, was one of
the principal witnesses. Hardinge Giffard was acquitted, but Mr. John Giffard had to pay £20 to the
poor of Taney, £20 to the poor of Stillorgan, and
£10 to the Dublin Marshalsea.

Price, Henry Thomas, 1848-58,

of Drummartin Lodge; *m.*, 1838, Miss Emma Hall,

PURDON, WILLIAM STANLEY, 1850,
of Arbour House, Windy Arbour; *m.*, 1838, Miss
Sarah Porter, *o. s. p.*

READ, JOHN WILLIAM, 1843,
of Lyndhurst, Churchtown.

REILLY, JOHN, 1869-72-73,
of St. Bridgid's, Roebuck; Barrister-at-Law, *c.*1842,
Clerk of Records and Writs in Chancery; eldest
son of James Miles Reilly, Esq. (see Reilly of
Scarvagh, B.L.G., 1894), *b.* 16 Nov., 1817, *m.*, 14
Aug., 1845, the Hon. Augusta Sugden, youngest
dau. of Edward, first Lord St. Leonard's, and had
issue—1. Emily; 2. Kathleen Matilda, *m.*, T. C.,
July 7, 1870, Capt. Matthew John Bell; 3. Wini-
fred, *m.*, first, Hon. John Montague Stopford;
secondly, Arthur, fifth Earl of Arran. Mr. Reilly
d. July 1, 1875.

RICHARDS, JOHN GODDARD, 1829,
of Roebuck, and of Ardamine, Co. Wexford; Barrister-at-Law, J.P., D.L., Co. Wexford, High Sheriff,
1824; eldest son of Solomon Richards, Esq., the
celebrated Dublin surgeon (who purchased the Roebuck estate, still held by the Richards family, from
Lord Trimleston), by his wife, Elizabeth, dau. of
Rev. Edward Groome. He *m.*, first, July 16, 1821,
Anne Catherine (*d.* May 10, 1835), dau. of Hon.
Robert Ward, by whom he had issue—1. Solomon
Augustus (*bapt.* T. C.), *m.*, June 10, 1856, Sophia

Mordaunt, dau. of Rev. Bernard John Ward, and *d.*
Jan. 13, 1874, leaving issue; 2. Robert Edward (*bapt.*
T. C.), in H.O., M.A., Principal of the Gloucester,
Bristol, and Oxford Training College; 3. William
Hamilton (*bapt.* T. C.), Col., late 55th Regt. of
Foot, *m.*, Aug., 1858, Margaret Isabella, dau. of
Major Samuel Hill Lawrence, and has issue; 4.
Louisa Elizabeth, *m.*, 1843, Geo. Maconchy, Esq.,
of Rathmore, and *d.* 1864, leaving issue (p. 128);
5. Mary Anne (*bapt.* T. C.), *m.*, Nov. 5, 1850, Samuel
Johnson, Esq., J.P., of Janeville, Co. Wexford, and
had issue; 6. Emily Sophia (*bapt.* T. C.), *m.*, April,
1849, Rev. Philip Walter Doyne, and had issue.
Mr. Richards *m.*, secondly, May 5, 1840, Mary,
dau. of Sir William Rawson, by whom he had no
issue, and *d.* April 13, 1846.

RIDGEWAY, WILLIAM, 1809 TO 1817,

of Runnymede, Balally. He graduated T.C.D., B.A.
in 1787, LL.B., 1790, and LL.D. in 1795. He was *c.*
to the Bar in 1790, and was some time Seneschal of
the Liberties of St. Patrick's. He *m.*, 1797, Miss
Catherine Ledwich. In Walker's *Hibernian Magazine* for 1807, p. 445, it is mentioned that—

" He was complimented with his freedom of the Corporation at large, partly by claim as being son-in-law to the
celebrated Irish historian, the Rev. Dr. Ledwich, and that it
was unanimously carried with some compliments on Mr.
Ridgeway's professional and private worth and abilities."

He *d.* Aug. 27, 1817. His death is thus announced

in the *Gentleman's Magazine*, vol. lxxxvii., pt. ii., p. 572:—

"Of a fever, while attending his professional duty on circuit at Trim, Mr. William Ridgeway, an eminent Irish lawyer, and a most worthy man."

ROE, HENRY, 1864-67, of Mount Anville; D.L. Dublin; son of Henry Roe, Esq., *m.*, 1857, Miss Charlotte Theodosia Jane D'Olier, and had issue—1. Richard, *o.s.p.;* 2. George Henry; 3. Charlotte D'Olier, *m.*, Sept. 4, 1878, Lord Granville Armyn Gordon; 4. Elizabeth, *m.*, T. C., Feb. 20, 1882, George Augustus Hotham Howard, Esq.; 5. Maude Mary; 6. Florence Madeline. He *d.* Nov. 21, 1894.

"Many of the citizens of Dublin will learn with feelings of deep regret of the death of Mr. Henry Roe, which occurred recently in London. He was the representative of a family whose name was long identified with the business life of Dublin, and whose numerous gifts to charitable objects were always cheerfully given, and given, too, with no niggard hand. He spent himself nearly £200,000 in restoring the fabric of Christ Church Cathedral, which is an enduring testimony of his public spirit and his attachment to the Church."—*Daily Express*, Nov. 26, 1894.

In the *Daily Express* of Nov. 28th, a letter appeared from Dr. Hamilton, which told of Mr. Roe's gifts to Taney Church :—

"The restoration of Christ Church Cathedral, magnificent in its design, and perfect in its completion, was not the only work of the kind which Mr. Roe carried out. His gifts to Christ Church, Taney, his parish church, were no less

generous in their character, and I and my congregation
must ever retain his name in grateful recollection. Soon
after I became Rector of the parish, I brought under his
notice the desirability of improving the musical portion of
the service, and he, in reply, offered to present the church
with an organ, which he did at considerable cost. There,
however, his gifts did not end. Entirely without solicitation,
he undertook to build a chancel, which was much required.
It is needless to mention that he had the work done in the
best manner, regardless of expense, not alone building the
chancel, but furnishing it with five stained-glass windows of
beautiful design; and by this addition he converted our
church into the handsome edifice it now is."

Ruskell, Robert, 1851,

of Ballinteer House; his dau. Jemima *m.*, T. C.,
Nov. 23, 1856, Godfrey Parr, Esq.; he *d. circa*
1855.

Scott, William, 1827,

of Drummartin and of Stafford Street, Dublin;
High Sheriff of Dublin, 1829-30. He had a son by
his wife Sarah Jane, *bapt.*, T. C., William Frederick
Augustus. Mr. Scott *d. circa* 1853.

Shade, Henry Lindsell, 1846,

of Larchfield, Churchtown, and Parliament Street,
Dublin; *m.*, 1828, Miss Rachel Jane Powell, and
had a son, *bapt.* T. C., Charles Francis.

Sinnett, John Townsend, 1805-6,

of Churchtown and of Merchant's Quay, Dublin;
Wholesale Silk Merchant, *m.*, 1791, Miss Emelia
Dunn, and *d. circa* 1836.

Stock, Stephen, 1792,

of Churchtown. He *d.* Dec., 1800, but was not then residing in the parish. His death is thus recorded in Walker's *Hibernian Magazine* :—

" Most sincerely and deservedly lamented, at his house near Dublin, Stephen Stock, Esq., late of Dame Street, an eminent woollen draper, and only brother to the Lord Bishop of Killala ; his study was ever to ameliorate the condition of the poor by a distribution of the essential comforts of life, which renders his death a public loss, while they afford a bright example to the affluent."

Studdert, Robert Ashworth, 1870-71,

of Clonlea, Ballinteer, now of Kilkishen House, Co. Clare ; J.P., D.L., and High Sheriff in 1848 of that county, Barrister-at-law, *c.* 1841, late Major, Clare Militia; son of Thomas Studdert, of Kilkishen House (see Studdert of Bunratty, B.L.G., 1894), *b.* Dec. 31, 1817, *m.*, Jan. 18, 1849, Maria, eldest dau. of Rev. William Waller, and had a son Thomas, *b.* 1850, *d.* 1869.

Tilly, Robert Henry, 1877-78,

of Clonlea, Ballinteer, and of Shanahoe, Mount-rath; son of Robert Tilly, Esq., of Chantilly, Loughlinstown, *m.*, May 7, 1844, Mary Anne, eldest dau. of James William Cusack, M.D. (see Cusack of Gerardstown, B.L.G., 1894), and had issue—1. Hubert ; 2. Florence ; 3. Beatrice. He *d.* Dec. 13, 1890, at Shanahoe.

TIPPER, SAMUEL, 1839,

of Roebuck and of Ormond Quay, Dublin ; Paper Manufacturer ; had issue by his wife, Elizabeth, *bapt.* T. C.—1. William Gore ; 2. Samuel ; 3. Lucy Ellen.

THOMPSON, GEORGE, 1804-14-17-18,

of Clonskeagh Castle,* and of the Treasury, Dublin Castle, was the second son of David Thompson, Esq., of Oatlands, Co. Meath, by his wife, Anne, fourth dau. of George Higginbotham, Esq., of Larghy, Co. Derry, by his wife Anne, dau of Robert Acheson, Esq. He was *b.* Aug. 16, 1769, and *m.*, first, Eleanor, dau. of John Wade, Esq., of The Lodge, Co. Meath, and had issue—1. David, J.P., Co. Dublin, *o. s. p.*, 1875 ; 2. Thomas Higginbotham, J.P. Cos. Galway and Dublin, *m.*, in T. C., Feb. 6, 1836, Martha, only dau. of Thomas Wallace, Esq., K.C., M.P.,† and *d.*, May 27, 1886, having had issue—i.

* Clonskeagh Castle was built by Mr. Henry Jackson, who also erected the adjoining iron works at an expense, D'Alton, in his *History of the County Dublin* (p. 808), says, of £20,000. Jackson took a prominent part in the rebellion, and was an active member of the Executive Committee of the United Irishmen. He was never brought to trial, but underwent a prolonged term of imprisonment. His daughter married Oliver Bond, who was convicted of high treason, July, 1798. (Fitzpatrick's *Secret Service under Pitt*, pp. 7, 127, 187.) In Whittock's *Guide to Dublin*, Lon., 1846, p. 139, it is stated that Jackson was obliged to emigrate to America, and that from him General Jackson, President of the United States, was descended.

† See Thomas Wallace, K.C., chapter viii.

George, *bapt.* T. C., *d.* 1865 ; ii. Thomas Wallace, *d.* 1864 ; iii. Robert Wade Thompson, B.A., T.C.D., Barrister-at-Law, called 1873, J.P. Co. Dublin, late Capt. Dublin Artillery Militia, *m.*, T. C., March 10, 1876, Edith Isabella, dau. of Rev. William Jameson, by his wife Eliza, dau. of Arthur Guinness, Esq., of Beaumont, Co. Dublin, and has issue—Thomas William, Hamlet George, William Jameson, Edith, Freida Catherine, Madeline Geraldine, Alice Isabella ; iv. Hamlet Wade, 25th K.O.B. Regt., *d.* 1866; v. Arthur William, Major Dublin Artillery Militia ; vi. Katherine, *m.* Colonel Rowan, J.P., of Belmont, Tralee, and *d.* 1876 ; vii. Ellen, *m.* Rev. W. T. Turpin, M.A. ; viii. Anne, *m.* Major de Wet ; ix. Louisa, *m.* Capt. O'Sullivan de Tedeck, of the Chateau de Tedeck, Belgium ; 3. George William ; 4. Margaret Hannah (*bapt.* T. C.), *d. unm.;* 5. Anne Mary, *m.*, T. C., Dec. 2, 1828, David Peter Thompson, Esq., of the King's Co., J.P., who had, among other issue, Ellen, *m.*, T. C., Jan. 17, 1866, Major-General Henry Alexander Little, C.B. ; 6. Louisa Elizabeth (*d.* 1841), *m.*, T.C., May 25, 1832, Edmund ffloyd Cuppage, Esq., of Claregrove, Co. Dublin, and had issue—i. Alexander (*bapt.* T. C.) ; ii. George William (*bapt.* T. C.), of Riverston, Co. Meath, *m.* Louisa, dau. of Edward Vernon, Esq., D.L., of Clontarf Castle ; iii. Hamlet Wade, Capt. 43rd Light Infantry, *m.* Hannah Gerrard, dau. of David Peter Thompson, Esq.; iv. Ellen, *d. unm.* Mr. Thompson *m.*, secondly, Catherine, dau. of General Robert Alexander, of Derry, and, thirdly, Jeanett, fourth dau.

of William Butler, Esq., of Drame, Co. Kilkenny,
by Hon. Caroline Massy, sixth dau. of Hugh, 1st
Lord Massy, and by her had a son, Massy Wade
(*bapt.* T. C.), *o. s. p.* Mr. Thompson *d.* May, 1860.

Mr. George Thompson's father was the fifth son
of William Thompson, Esq., of Clonfin, Co. Longford, who *m.* Miss Metge, of Athlumney Castle, Co.
Meath, and was grandson of Capt. William Thompson, of Yorkshire, one of three brothers who accompanied King William III. to this country in 1688.
The King gave Capt. Thompson certain confiscated
lands, and he settled and married in Co. Longford.
(See Thompson of Clonfin, B. L. G., 1894.)

THOMPSON, HENRY, 1798-99,

of Roebuck, and of Ormond Quay, Dublin. He *d.*
Nov., 1800. The following obituary notice appears
in Walker's *Hibernian Magazine* of that date :—

" Suddenly in his carriage, on the road to Bath, Henry
Thompson, Esq., of the city of Dublin, an eminent merchant ; he was strict in the discharge of every duty as a
husband, parent, friend, and Christian, and his death, like
his life, was serene and calm ; his temper was mild and
gentle, and his disposition uncommonly affectionate and uncommonly generous ; to his friends he is an irreparable loss,
and to the poor he never can be replaced. He lived beloved
and died lamented by all who had the pleasure of his acquaintance."

THOMPSON, HENRY, 1854,

of Greenmount, Ballaly.

TURBETT, JAMES EXHAM PUREFOY, 1833.

of Owenstown; only son of Robert Turbett, Esq.
(*q. v.*), *b.* 1790, *m.*, Dec. 12, 1823, Sophia (*d.* Dec.
13, 1882, *bur.* T. G.), dau. of the Hon. and Very
Rev. George Gore, Dean of Killala, third son of
the second Earl of Arran, and of his wife, Anne,
dau. of Robert Burrowes, Esq., of Stradone, and
had issue (*bapt.* T. C., excepting Mary)—1. Robert
Exham (*q. v.*); 2. James (*q. v.*); 3. George William,
of Roebuck Hill, and subsequently of Owenstown,
m. Ellen, dau. of the Rev. John Morton, and
d. Feb., 1894, *bur.* T. G., having had issue (*bapt.*
T. C.)—i. James Gore, ii. Richard George, iii.
Charles Morton, iv. John Routledge, v. Eyre
Anthony Weldon, vi. Royston Cecil Gladwyn,
vii. Ethel Clementina Burrowes, *d.* April, 1889,
bur. T. G., viii. Eleanor Sophia Georgett; 4.
Thomas, of Scribblestown House, *m.* Florence,
dau. of Jolliffe Tufnell, Esq., F.R.C.S.I.; 5. John
Gore, *o. s. p.*, April, 1850, *bur.* T. G.; 6. Mary
Anne, *m.*, T. C., Nov. 6, 1844, John Pollock Ferrier,
Esq.; 7. Sophia Frances, *m.*, T. C., June 6, 1849,
Robert Manders, Esq., of Landscape, and had
issue—i. Frances Sophia, *m.*, T. C., Oct. 13, 1887,
George Medlicott Vereker, Esq., ii. Gertrude Caroline
(*bapt.* T. C.), *m.* General J. Davis, C.B., iii. Cecilia
Maude (*bapt.* T. C.), *m.*, T. C., Jan. 4, 1888, Capt.
Edward Hamilton Gordon, of the 2nd Gordon
Highlanders; 8. Jane, *m.*, T. C., July 19, 1853,
Richard Manders, Esq., and had issue—i. Arthur,
ii. Reginald, iii. Helena Frances, *m.*, T. C., Nov. 23,

1876, Henry Lumsden Forbes, Esq., of Invery, Guild-
ford, iv. Augusta Margaret Elizabeth, *m.* F. Coryton,
Esq., of Liss House, Hants, v. Harriett Jane, *m.*,
T. C., July 25, 1882, Spencer C. Blackett, Esq., late
21st Hussars; 9. Louisa, *m.*, T. C., Aug. 12, 1858,
Gordon James Douglas, Esq.; 10. Emily, *m.*, T. C.,
Aug. 25, 1859, John Graburn, Esq.; 11. Cecilia;
12. Eleanor, *m.*, T. C., July 30, 1872, Major Warren
Richard Colvin Wynne, R.E., and *d.* Dec. 14, 1873,
bur. T. G.; 13. Ada, *m.*, T. C., April 19, 1872,
Henry Hazell Unett, Esq., of Huntingdon Hall,
Yorks. He *d.* Oct. 27, 1868, and was *bur.* in T. G.

TURBETT, JAMES, 1855,

of Oaklawn, Roebuck; son of James Exham Turbett, Esq. (*q. v.*) ; *m.* Harriet, dau. of John Powys,
Esq., of West Wood Manor, Staffordshire.

TURBETT, ROBERT, 1804,

of Greenmount; *b.* 1760, *m.* Miss Marianne Purefoy,
(who *m.*, secondly, T. C., Aug. 31, 1831, William
Noble, Esq., of Arnageel, Co. Louth, and *d.* July,
1834, *bur.* T. G.), and *d.* Jan. 21, 1831, *bur.* T. G.
(p. 44), leaving issue one son, James Exham Purefoy (*q. v.*).

TURBETT, ROBERT EXHAM, 1865,

of Belfield, Roebuck; M.A.; son of James Exham
Turbett, Esq. (*q. v.*) ; *m.* Lucy, dau. of Benjamin
Lefroy, Esq., of Cardenton House, Athy, and *d.*
March, 1889, *bur.* T. G., having had issue (*bapt.* T. C.,
excepting Kathleen)—i. Robert James, ii. Langlois
Benjamin, iii. George Frederic Gore, iv. Kathleen.

USHER, ISAAC WILLIAM, 1880-81-82-90-91,

of Tudor House; L.R.C.P., Edin., 1863; L.R.C.S.I., 1862; eldest son of Isaac Usher, Esq., by his wife, Frances, dau. of John Parker, Esq. (See Ball Wright's *Memoirs of the Ussher Families*, Dub., 1889, p. 19.)

VERSCHOYLE, RICHARD, 1798-99, 1811-12-13,

of Mount Merrion; J.P. and High Sheriff in 1819 of the Co. Dublin. He was a Commissioner for the construction of Kingstown Harbour, and his name appears on the monument near the pier (see p. 105). He was the second son of Joseph Verschoyle of Donare (see Verschoyle of Kilberry, B.L.G., 1894), and *m*. Miss Barbara Fagan. He *d. s. p.* at Brighton on Aug. 27, 1827, and was *bur.* there. In an inscription on a tablet erected to his memory in Booterstown Church, he is described as a man of strong religious character, with a mind richly stored with intellectual knowledge. (See Blacker's *Sketches of Booterstown*, p. 30.)

VERSCHOYLE, WILLIAM HENRY FOSTER, 1894-95,

of Woodley; J.P. Co. Dublin; second son of John James Verschoyle, Esq., of Tassaggart, Co. Dublin, by his wife, Catherine Helen, dau. of the Rev. William Foster (see Verschoyle of Castleshanaghan, B.L.G., 1894); *m.*, June 16, 1888, Frances Harriett Hamilton, youngest dau. of Edward James Jackson, Esq., of Upwell, Co. Norfolk, and of the

Priory, St. Andrew's, N.B., and widow of Captain
W. Unett, 21st Hussars, and has issue—1. George
John Foster (*bapt.* Stillorgan Church); 2. William
Arthur; 3. Kathleen Laura (*bapt.* T. C.).

VICARS, EDWARD ARMSTRONG, 1860,

of Trimleston Lodge; Government Inspector of
Military Schools in Ireland; eldest son of Richard
Vicars, Esq., and brother of Captain Hedley Vicars
(97th Regt.), and Clara, Lady Rayleigh; *m.* Julia
Frances, dau. of George Eckersall, Esq., of St.
Catherine's, near Bath, and had issue—1. Hedley
(*bapt.* T. C.), in H. O., Rector of Huntingdon; 2.
George Rayleigh (*bapt.* T. C.), in H. O., Curate of
Whitley Bridge, Yorkshire; 3. Edward, in Foreign
Office; 4. May Catherine (*bapt.* T. C.), *d.* 1892; 5.
Isabel Mary (*bapt.* T. C.); 6. Evelyn Clara (*bapt.*
T. C.); 7. Lilian Frances; 8. Margaret Annie; 9.
Marion Julia.   Mr. Vicars *d.* June 9, 1870.

VINCENT, JOHN, 1862,

of Charlton, Roebuck.

WADDEN, BARRET, 1821,

of Roebuck, and of Palace Street, Dublin; Silk
Manufacturer; *m.*, 1809, Miss Elizabeth M'Connell,
and *d. circa* 1823.

WALSH, JOHN, 1876,

of Dundrum Castle; son of John Walsh, Esq., and
brother of the Hon. Frederick William Walsh, who
was called to the Bar 1836, made a Q.C. 1855,

and Bencher of the King's Inns 1871, appointed Judge of the Court of Bankruptcy, 1875, and *d.* 1886, and of Colonel Gustavus Charles Walsh (see under Mayne, Edward, p. 132).

WALSH, WILLIAM, 1837-39,

of Drummartin; *m.*, 1809, Miss Anne Shannon.

WARREN, SAMUEL, 1828,

of Churchtown; *m.*, 1825, Miss Catherine Watson, and *d. circa* 1850.

WEST, JOHN, 1835-37-40,

of Cedar Mount, Mount Anville; *m.*, 1803, Caroline, dau. of John Busby, Esq., and had issue—1. John, in H. O., M.A., D.D., T.C.D., ordained Deacon at Glasnevin, Aug. 24, 1829, by the Bishop of Kildare, Priest at Ferns, March 7, 1830, Curate of Monkstown, and of St. Ann's, Dublin, Vicar of St. Ann's, Domestic Chaplain to Archbishop Whately, Archdeacon of Dublin, Dean of St. Patrick's, *m.* Elizabeth Margaret, eldest dau. of the Most Rev. Charles Dickinson, D.D., Bishop of Meath, and *d.* July 5, 1890, leaving issue; 2. Samuel, *d.* young; 3. Eliza, *m.* Rev. Elias Thackeray Stevenson, *d.;* 4. Lucy, *d. unm.* 1892. Mr. West *d. circa* 1850.

WESTBY, EDWARD PERCEVAL, 1856-59-64-68-70-74-75,

of Roebuck Castle,* and of Kilballyowen and Roscoe, Co. Clare; D.L., and J.P., Co. Clare; J.P.

* See under John, Baron Trimleston, chapter viii.

Co. Dublin ; High Sheriff, Co. Clare, 1854 ; eldest
son of Nicholas Westby, Esq., and of his wife, the
Hon. Emily Susan, eldest dau. of William, Lord
Radstock, *m.*, first, Elizabeth Mary, dau. of the
Right Hon. Francis Blackburne,* who *d.* 1863,
and had issue—1. William Francis Perceval, *o. s. p.*,
1870 ; 2. Francis Vandeleur (*bapt.* T. C.), High
Sheriff of Co. Clare, 1895, *m.*, 1888, Janet Louisa,
second dau. of George Orme, Esq., of Castle
Lacken, and has issue ; 3. Emily Jane Laura
(*bapt.* T. C.). Mr. Westby *m.*, secondly, T. C.,
June 16, 1864, Susan Elizabeth, dau of John
Davis Garde, Esq. (*q. v.*), and *d.* April 23, 1893.

Wharton, John Lee, 1844-47-49,

of Sweetmount ; Solicitor ; *m.*, 1843, Miss Eliza
Wilme, and had issue, *bapt.* T. C.—1. George
Henry ; 2. Esther Jane ; 3. Elizabeth Georgiana ;
4. Jane Julia Anna Wilme. He *d.* June 17, 1866.

White, John, 1819-20-21,

of Ballaly.

White, John La Touche, 1846,

of Readsvale, Dundrum ; l.r.c.s., Edin., l.a., Dub. ;
m., T. C., Nov. 2, 1844, Frances Dorothea (*d.* July
8, 1874), youngest dau. of Sir Henry Jebb, and had
issue, *bapt.* T. C.—1. Henry Francis La Touche ;
2. Mary Jane Ribton Jebb. He *d.* June 25, 1870,
and was *bur.* T. G. (p. 45).

* See Right Hon. Francis Blackburne, chapter viii.

WHITEFORD, SIR GEORGE, 1822,

of Annaville, Churchtown, and Mount Salem, Mountrath; Silk and Poplin Manufacturer. He was an Alderman of Dublin, and was High Sheriff in 1821, when George IV. visited Ireland. He then received the honour of Knighthood. He was Lord Mayor in 1833-34. He *m.* 1811, Miss Anne Bergin, who *d.* Dec., 16, 1847. He went subsequently to reside in the Queen's Co., and *d.* Jan. 14, 1865.

WHITTHORNE, WILLIAM JERVIS, 1828,

of Churchtown; Solicitor.

WILLIAMS, HUTCHINS, 1832,

of Bloom Villa, Farranboley, and of Merrion Square, Dublin.

WOOD, WILLIAM, 1816-17,

of Churchtown and of Bishop Street, Dublin; a Merchant. High Sheriff of Dublin, 1818-19. He *m.*, 1803, Miss Mary Williams, and *d. circa* 1836.

NOTE.—The information in these notes has been obtained mainly from private sources and from the Parochial Registers, but in some cases from wills and grants in the Public Record Office, from B. P. and B. L. G., and from Dublin Directories and Newspapers.

CHAPTER VIII.

THE following biographical and genealogical notes on some of the more remarkable persons who have resided in the parish, and who are not included amongst the Churchwardens, are necessarily brief, in order to come within the limits of this History; and it is therefore possible only to give a mere outline of the lives of the distinguished men who are mentioned. It is hoped, however, that these notes may serve to prevent their connection with the parish being forgotten. The dates after the names give with such accuracy as is possible the period of residence.

THE FAMILIES OF FITZWILLIAM AND HERBERT, circa 1442-1895.

The members of these noble families, who have resided in Mount Merrion,* deserve prior and prin-

---

* Amongst the temporary residents at Mount Merrion have been Archbishop King and the Right Hon. John Fitz-Gibbon, afterwards and better known as Lord Clare. In Mant's *History of the Church of Ireland*, vol. ii., p. 272, *et seq.*, there are letters from Archbishop King written in August and September, 1714, which are dated from Mount Merrion. "His temporary country residence, near Dublin," says Bishop Mant, " by the kindness of Lord Fitzwilliam." He mentions in one of them that he went to see his neighbour, Lord Kildare, at Stillorgan. Lord Clare occupied Mount Merrion *circa* 1787-9. (See Blacker's *Sketches of Booterstown*, pp. 182, 426.)

cipal mention as the chief parishioners of Taney, and as lords of the soil of a great portion of the parish. It is, however, thought unnecessary to insert their pedigrees, which will be found, of the Fitzwilliam family in B. E. P., 1866, p. 214, and of the Herbert* family under Pembroke in B. P., 1895, p. 1119. Blacker's *Sketches of Booterstown* is also replete with information on the subject, and at p. 108 he gives a pedigree of the Fitzwilliam family.

RIGHT HON. FRANCIS BLACKBURNE, 1827-51.

This great lawyer resided for many years at Roebuck Hall.† He was the only surviving son of Richard Blackburne, Esq., of Footstown, in the Co. Meath, by his wife Elizabeth, dau. of Francis Hopkins, Esq., of Darvistown, in the same county. He was *b.* Nov. 11, 1782, and having entered T.C.D., took a Scholarship in 1801; he won the gold medal for the most distinguished collegiate career, and graduated B.A. in 1803. He subsequently in 1852 took out his LL.D. degree. He

---

* On the death of Richard, seventh Viscount Fitzwilliam, without issue in 1816, the principal part of the Fitzwilliam estates passed to George Augustus, eleventh Earl of Pembroke, whose grandfather Henry, ninth Earl of Pembroke, *m.* Mary, eldest dau. of Richard, fifth Viscount Fitzwilliam. The Fitzwilliam title devolved upon John, eighth Viscount, who *o. s. p.*, 1833, when the title became extinct.

† Mentioned by D'Alton as the only place in the neighbourhood which did not present a "sombre, unsocial appearance." (*History of the Co. Dublin*, p. 809.)

was *c.* to the Bar in 1805, and was made a King's
Counsel in 1822. He was appointed a Sergeant in
1826, and was Attorney-General from 1830 to 1835,
and from 1841 to 1842, when he was raised to the
Bench. He was Master of the Rolls from 1842 to
1846, Lord Chief Justice from 1846 to 1852, and
Lord Chancellor in 1852. He was appointed the
first Lord Justice of Appeal in 1856, and held that
office until again appointed Lord Chancellor in
1866. He resigned the Chancellorship in 1867.
He was Vice-Chancellor of the University of Dublin from 1852. He *m.*, 1809, Jane (*d.* 1872),
dau. of William Martley, Esq., M.D., and had issue
—1. William Martley, *m.* Mary, dau. of the Rev.
William Thorpe, D.D., *d.* May 8, 1868, leaving
issue; 2. Francis, *o. s. p.*, 1863; 3. Edward, of Rathfarnham Castle, Q.C., J.P. Co. Dublin, *m.*, 1857,
Georgiana, dau. of Robert Graves, Esq., of Merrion
Square, and has issue ; 4. Frederick John, of Renny
House, Co. Cork, *m.*, 1856, Annette, dau. of Eardley
Hall, Esq., of Wilmington, Essex, *d.* Oct., 1863,
and had issue ; 5. John Henry, *m.*, 1857, Elizabeth,
dau. of Anthony Crofton, Esq. ; 6. Arthur, *o. s. p.* ;
7. Alicia Catherine, *m.* Captain George Daniell, R.N.
(p. 106); 8. Jane Isabella, *m.*, T. C., Oct. 25, 1845,
Thomas Rice Henn, Esq., Q.C., Recorder of Galway,
of Paradise Hill, Co. Clare ; 9. Elizabeth Mary
(*bapt.* T. C.), *m.* Edward Perceval Westby, Esq., D.L.
(p. 151) ; 10. Adelaide Frances (*bapt.* T. C.), *d. unm.*
Mr. Blackburne *d.* Sept. 17, 1867, and was *bur.* at
Mount Jerome.

In the *Imperial Dictionary of Universal Biography* (vol. i., p. 600) Dr. John Francis Waller thus wrote of Mr. Blackburne :—

" His statements were masterpieces of forensic eloquence, singularly lucid, simple, and brief ; he placed every fact before the Court in the clearest light, and drew his conclusions with a force that was irresistible ; while the power of his calm, self-possessed, and solemn eloquence was deeply impressive. But in his judicial position all these faculties attained their perfection. His calmness rose to imperturbable deliberation, his self-possession to dignity, and the quiet, melodious tones of his voice gave force to the dispassionate and impartial judgments which he delivered."

It is impossible, however, within the scope of this History to give any extract which would do justice to Mr. Blackburne's attainments, and to the consummate ability and dignity with which he filled all the highest judicial offices. To form a true estimate of his character and of his services to his country, the reader must consult larger works, and is referred to the *Life of Francis Blackburne*, by his son (Lon., 1874), and to biographical notes in the *Dictionary of National Biography* (vol. v., p. 122), and in Burke's *Lord Chancellors of Ireland*.

RIGHT HON. ABRAHAM BREWSTER, 1855-74.

This distinguished leader of the Irish Bar, who became Lord Chancellor of Ireland, resided at Roebuck. Grove,* from the year 1855 until his

* Previously called Roebuck House. Mr. Brewster purchased the place from the representatives of Sir John Power (*q. v.*).

death. He was son of William Bagenal Brewster, Esq., by his wife Mary, dau. of Thomas Bates, Esq., and was *b.* in April, 1796. He entered T.C.D., and graduated B.A., 1817, and M.A., 1847. He was *c.* to the Bar in 1819, and was made a K.C. in 1835. He was appointed Law Adviser in 1841, Solicitor-General in 1846, and was Attorney-General from Jan., 1853 to 1855. In July, 1866, he was appointed Lord Justice of Appeal, and in March in the following year Lord Chancellor, which office he continued to hold until the resignation of the Government in Dec., 1868. He *d.* July 26, 1874, and was *bur.* at Tullow, Co. Carlow. He *m.* Mary Anne (*d.* Nov. 24, 1862), dau. of Robert Gray, Esq., by whom he had issue—1. William Bagenal, Colonel; 2. Elizabeth Mary, *m.* Henry French, Esq., and had issue one son, Robert Abraham, who has assumed the name of Brewster. —See *Dictionary of National Biography*, vol. vi., p. 299, and Burke's *Lord Chancellors of Ireland*.

"One of the ablest advocates which the Irish Bar has produced during the present century. . . . His management of the public business was always honest, firm, and unswerving, and no imputation of favouritism was ever made against him."—*The Times*, July 28, 1874.

"It is of course impossible to learn from a report the effect or force of a legal argument; but those who have been the contemporaries of Mr. Brewster can speak of the strength and power of his handling of cases on either side of the Hall of the Four Courts, the incisive force of his points, the weight of his argumentation, and his readiness for every emergency. Whether it was a new trial motion, a bill of exception, or a dry legal argument, he was ever ready, ever fortified; and when he gave up Common Law business, and confined himself to Chancery instead, he assumed and took the lead of that Court, which he maintained until the repose of the Bench gratefully rewarded him."—*Dublin University Magazine*, 1874 (p. 652).

RIGHT HON. WILLIAM BROOKE, 1852-81.

This eminent lawyer, churchman, and philanthropist resided at Taney Hill House for nearly thirty years. He was the eldest son of William Brooke, Esq., M.D., by his wife Angel, dau. of Captain Edward Perry, and was b. in 1796. He was educated at the Rev. John Fea's School, and having entered T.C.D., he won a Scholarship in 1812, and graduated B.A. in 1814, taking the Gold Medal awarded for a distinguished collegiate career. In 1871 the degree of LL.D. *honoris causâ* was conferred on him by the University. He was c. to the Bar in 1817, made a King's Counsel in 1835, and a Bencher of the King's Inns in 1846. In the same year he was appointed a Master of Chancery. In 1874, when the Great Seal of Ireland was in Commission, he acted as one of the Commissioners, and was then created a Privy Councillor. After the passing of the Irish Church Act he took a prominent and active part in the formation of a Constitution for the Irish Church, and in the debates of the Synod on the Revision of the Prayer Book. He was elected one of the Diocesan Nominators of the Diocese of Dublin. He *m.*, first, 1819, Emily Margaret, only dau. of Robert Rogers Wilmot, Esq., by his wife Eliza (who *d.* 1850), dau. of

the Rev. John Chetwode, of Glanmire, Co. Cork,
and had issue—1. Robert Wilmot, Lt.-Colonel,
60th Rifles, *m.*, first, Elizabeth, only daughter of
Sir Duncan Macgregor, к.с.в., and had issue—
Graham Wilmot, Eardley Wilmot, Lieut. 60th
Rifles; and secondly, Bertha, dau. of Sir Crawford
Caffin, к.с.в., and has issue—Robert Wilmot, Craw-
ford Wilmot; 2. Henry Edward, in H.O., *m.* Maria,
dau. of Rev. John A. Jetter, Vicar of Trowbridge,
Salop, and has issue—William Montagu, Henry
Sinclair, in H.O., Margaret Graham; 3. Charles
Francis, Lieut. 40th Regt., fell in the New Zealand
War, 1860; 4. Caroline Hamilton, *m.* Bartholomew
Clifford Lloyd, Esq., q.c., and has issue—Clifford,
William Chetwode, Lt.-Col., Humphrey Wilmot,
Alfred Robert, Major, Arthur Brooke, Frederick
Charles, Captain, Emily, *m.* Major Wynne, Con-
stance, Florence, Caroline, *m.* Captain Anson
Schomberg, R.N. He *m.*, secondly, in 1853, Cathe-
rine Anne Daschkaw (*d.* Oct. 25, 1882), dau. of
Rev. William Bradford, by his wife Matilda, dau.
of Edward Wilmot, Esq. He *d.* Aug. 19, 1881,
and was *bur.* at Mount Jerome.

" One of the best friends of the Church of Ireland, a distinguished member of the Bar, and a kindly, upright Irish
gentleman. . . . His death will be received with a
general feeling of regret by all who knew his sterling worth,
kindly qualities, and charitable disposition."—*Dublin Evening Mail, Aug.* 22, 1881.

A very handsome monument to Master Brooke's
memory was erected in 1882 in St. Patrick's

Cathedral by a number of his friends. The idea of the design is borrowed from a Venetian window. In the centre on a white marble tablet is the following inscription :—

" In loving memory of the Right Honble. William Brooke, LL.D., for many years a Master of the High Court of Chancery, and subsequently a Commissioner of the Great Seal of Ireland. Born July 22, 1796, died Aug. 19, 1881.

" Throughout a long and useful life he ' adorned the doctrine of God our Saviour in all things,' and having to its close rejoiced in the faithfulness of Him whose word was his constant support, he died in perfect peace. ' Casting all your care upon Him ; for He careth for you.'—1 Peter v. 7."

MR. JUSTICE BURTON, 1825-47.

The Hon. Charles Burton was for many years a parishioner, and lived at Mount Anville.* This distinguished judge was an Englishman by birth, descended from the ancient family of Burton of Leicestershire (see B.L.G., 1846), and was *b.* Oct. 16, 1760. He was *c.* to the Irish Bar in 1792, and was made a King's Counsel in 1806. He was appointed successively 3rd Sergeant on Oct. 30, 1817, 1st Sergeant on Dec. 1, 1818, and a Justice of the King's Bench on Dec. 2, 1820. He *m.*, 1787, Miss Anna Andrews, who *d.* March 10, 1822, and had an only daughter, Eliza Felicia, who *m.* at

* It is now the Sacred Heart Convent. Judge Burton purchased the place from the representatives of Mr. Daniel Beere (p. 98), and after the Judge's death his representatives sold it to Mr. Dargan (*q. v.*), who sold it to the trustees of the convent.

M

St. Peter's Church, Dublin, Nov. 8, 1819, John Beatty West, Esq., Q.C., M.P. for the City of Dublin (*d.* 1842), and who had a son, Charles Burton, and several daughters. Judge Burton *d.* on Dec. 10, 1847, and was *bur.* in St. Peter's.

"He filled the very highest place as a lawyer. . . . As a judge he fully sustained the high character he acquired at the bar. Calm, dignified, and impartial, he turned neither to the right nor left in dealing out rigid justice."—*Annual Register*, lxxxix., p. 272; also see *Gentleman's Magazine*, vol. xxix. (N. S.), p. 198.

ABRAHAM COLLES, M.D., 1816-42.

Mr. Colles, one of the most eminent of the great surgeons of Dublin, resided at Donnybrook Cottage,* which is in the townland of Roebuck, for many years. He was the second son of William Colles, Esq., was *b.* in Kilkenny on July 23, 1773, and was educated at the Endowed School in that town. He came to Dublin, and took out the Diploma of the College of Surgeons in 1795; he then proceeded to Scotland, and took out the degree of M.D. in the University of Edinburgh, and subsequently studied in London. On his return to Dublin, he was appointed Resident Surgeon to Steevens' Hospital, of which institution he was afterwards the Visiting Surgeon. In 1804 he was appointed Lecturer on Anatomy and Surgery in the Royal College of Surgeons, and in 1826 became Professor of Surgery.

* Now called St. Margaret's. Mr. Colles sold the house to Judge Plunket (*q. v.*).

He was twice President of the College. In 1835 he resigned his professorship on account of ill-health, and the College presented him with a superb piece of plate, and placed his portrait in their board-room, and his bust in their museum. He was offered a baronetcy in 1839, but declined the honour. He *d.* on Dec. 1, 1843, and was *bur.* at Mount Jerome. He *m.*, 1807, Sophia, dau. of the Rev. Jonathan Cope, Rector of Aghascragh, Co. Galway, and had issue—1. William, M.D., M.CH., *honoris causâ*, Regius Professor of Surgery, T.C.D., *m.*, 1859, Penelope, dau. of Cadwallader Waddy, Esq., M.P., and *d.* 1892, leaving issue—i. Abraham Richard; ii. Margaret, *m.*, 1891, Rev. William Beaufoy Stillman; iii. Sophia Cope, *m.*, 1890, Rev. Herbert Kennedy; 2. Henry Jonathan Cope, Barrister-at-Law, *m.*, 1845, Elizabeth, dau. of John Mayne, Esq. (p. 131), and *d.* Dec. 25, 1877, leaving issue—i. Abraham, M.D., *m.*, 1875, Emily, dau. of Major Alexander Dallas, and granddau. of Rev. Alexander R. C. Dallas, M.D., F.R.C.S.I.; ii. John Mayne, LL.D., *m.*, 1885, Bessie, dau. of Rev. Charles Dickinson, and granddau. of the Most Rev. Charles Dickinson, D.D., Bishop of Meath; iii. Henry J. Cope; iv. Anne Sophia, *m.*, 1866, Hon. Mr. Justice Bewley; v. Frances, *m.*, 1868, the Right Hon. Edward Gibson, Baron Ashbourne; vi. Minnie, *m.*, 1888, W. S. Burnside, Esq., F.T.C.D., and *d.* 1890; vii. Henrietta Elizabeth, *m.*, 1874, Henry Falconer Grant, Esq.; viii. Ethel, *m.*, 1888, Joseph H. Moore, Esq.; 3. Abraham, B.A., *m.* Anna, dau. of Francis

Hopkins, Esq., of Mitchelstown, J.P., *d.* 1879 ; 4.
Thomas, *d.* March 30, 1829 ; 5. Richard, B.A., Barrister-at-Law, of Melbourne, *m.*, 1841, Frances, dau.
of John Wilmett, Esq., of Bordeaux, Advocate, *d.*
1883 ; 6. Graves Chamney, M.A., Solicitor, *m.*, first,
Mary Anne, dau. of Robert Harrison, Esq., M.D. ;
secondly, Saremna, dau. of Rev. John Blower, *d.*
1893 ; 7. Mary Anne, *m.*, in T. C., Aug. 21, 1832,
Lt.-Col. James Harrison, Madras Artillery, *d.* 1850 ;
8. Sophia ; 9. Frances Jane, *m.* James Wall, Esq.,
of Knockrigg, County Court Judge, Co. Tipperary,
d. 1888 ; 10. Maria Jane Cope, *d.* 1887.

" The leading features of Mr. Colles's character were solid
judgment, manly directness, perfect probity, the soundest of
understandings, and the kindest of hearts. In every relation
of life he was amiable and upright, nor were his talents more
remarkable than his gentleness and modesty."—*Dublin
University Magazine*, vol. xxiii., p. 688.

Also see biographical notices in Webb's *Compendium of
Irish Biography*, p. 86 ; *Dictionary of National Biography*,
vol. xi., p. 333 ; and *Imperial Dictionary of Universal Biography*, vol. i., p. 1090.

WILLIAM DARGAN, 1851-65.

A History of the parish would be incomplete
without some mention of this well-known and remarkable man, who resided at Mount Anville for
a considerable time. He was a native of the Co.
Carlow, and was *b.* in 1799. He was placed in a
surveyor's office, and soon acquired a knowledge of
his profession. Having been employed under Tel-
ford in the construction of the Holyhead Road, he

returned to Ireland, and commenced business on his own account. He was the original promoter of the Dublin and Kingstown Railway—the first line made in Ireland—and became the contractor for its construction. He was subsequently the contractor for the Ulster Canal, the Dublin and Drogheda, Great Southern and Western, and Midland Great Western Railways. The Dublin Exhibition of 1853 owed its existence to his generosity; he advanced enormous sums for its promotion, and lost by it £20,000. At the opening of the Exhibition he was publicly complimented by the Queen,* and was afterwards offered a baronetcy, which he declined. He was a J.P. and D.L. of Dublin. He *d*. Feb. 7, 1867, and was *bur*. at Glasnevin. He left a widow, who *d*. June, 1894, but had no children.

" To follow the career of Mr. Dargan would be to comment on almost every great undertaking in the land. We believe the estimate is not overstated which attributes to him the

* The *Dublin Evening Mail*, Aug. 31, 1853, thus describes the Queen's reception of Mr. Dargan :—''Her Majesty received Mr. Dargan with manifest delight. She advanced rapidly to the edge of the platform, warmly congratulated him on the success of his splendid undertaking, and expressed her great pleasure on seeing him on that occasion. The Queen stretched forth her hand as if for the purpose of shaking hands with Mr. Dargan ; but that gentleman's modesty not permitting him to respond to a distinction as great as it was unexpected, he hesitated for an instant, when Her Majesty kindly laid her hand upon his arm, and shook it warmly. The immense assemblage burst out into a unanimous and enthusiastic cheer, which was repeated again and again."

construction of over one thousand miles of railway, and one
hundred miles of canals, embankments, and tunnels. He
is one of the most remarkable instances on record—not in-
frequent as such instances are in modern times—of men who
are the architects of their own fortunes, and the promoters,
at the same time, of the progress and prosperity of the
country to which they belong. He possesses, in truth, in a
singular degree, the qualities which can alone place a man
in the van of civilization and industrial progress. Prompt,
sagacious, clear-sighted, and far-seeing, he estimates character by instinct, and is thus seldom mistaken in those whom
he selects to carry out his object."—*Imperial Dictionary of
Universal Biography*, vol. ii., p. 26.

Le Fanu, in his *Seventy Years of Irish Life*, in
speaking of Mr. Dargan (p. 208), says :—

"I have never met a man more quick in intelligence, more
clear-sighted, and more thoroughly honourable."

Also see *Dictionary of National Biography*, vol.
xiv., p. 54; *Gentleman's Magazine*, vol. ccxxii.,
p. 388.

The Queen, when in Ireland for the opening of
the Great Exhibition, visited Mr. Dargan at Mount
Anville. This event, memorable as the only occasion on which the parish has been honoured by a
visit from Her Majesty, is thought worthy of record,
and an account, somewhat abridged, taken from the
Dublin Evening Mail of Aug. 31, 1853, is here
inserted :—

"Her Majesty proceeded at a quarter to five o'clock to
visit Wm. Dargan, Esq., at his residence Mount Anville. At
half-past four o'clock, the two chariots, each drawn by four
splendid bays, driven by postilions wearing the Royal livery
and attended by five outriders, drove round to the principal

entrance of the Viceregal Lodge. Her Majesty, Prince Albert, the Prince of Wales, Prince Alfred, and the Countess of St. German's entered the first carriage. His Excellency the Lord Lieutenant, the Hon. Miss Bulteel, and the Earl of Granville occupied the second carriage. In a barouche were the officers of the staff in attendance on Her Majesty. The route taken was along the quays, Dame Street, Grafton Street, Nassau Street, Stephen's Green, North and East, Leeson Street, Donnybrook Road by Clonskeagh, and on by Roebuck to Mount Anville, the residence of Mr. Dargan, where Her Majesty and party arrived at half-past five. The *cortége* proceeded up the splendid avenue of the princely residence at a slow pace. The carriages having been drawn up in front of the principal entrance, the Royal party alighted, and Her Majesty, Prince Albert, the Prince of Wales, and Prince Alfred were received by Mr. and Mrs. Dargan. The manner of Her Majesty was exceedingly gracious and courteous, and that of Prince Albert most polite and cordial. Mrs. Dargan having been presented to Her Majesty and Prince Albert, by whom she was most warmly and graciously received, the Royal party were after a time conducted through the splendid mansion to the lofty tower adjoining, from which they obtained a view, not to be surpassed for grandeur, beauty, and variety in the United Kingdom. Her Majesty and His Royal Highness expressed their warmest admiration of the scenery. After paying a visit of more than half-an-hour's duration, the Royal party prepared to return, and the Queen and Prince Albert took leave most graciously of Mr. and Mrs. Dargan. In returning the party proceeded at a rapid pace by the route leading through Kilmainham to the Park, and arrived at the Lodge shortly after seven o'clock."

RIGHT HON. WILLIAM, BARON DOWNES, 1811-26.

The parish has never had a more distinguished resident than Lord Downes, who lived at Merville for some years ; and, as has been mentioned in an earlier part of this History, he took an active interest in its affairs, and was instrumental in procuring the means of building the present church. His life has been fully recorded in other works, and it is only necessary to state here that he was called to the Bar in 1776, was M.P. for the Borough of Donegal, was appointed a Justice of the King's Bench, 1792, Lord Chief Justice, 1803, and Vice-Chancellor of the University of Dublin, 1806. He resigned the office of Chief Justice in 1822, and was created an Irish Peer in the same year. He *d.* March 3, 1826, and was *bur.* in St. Ann's Church, Dublin, in the same tomb with his friend Judge Chamberlaine (p. 103). (See Blacker's *Sketches of Booterstown*, pp. 122-4, 319-23 ; also biographical notice by Blacker in the *Dictionary of National Biography*, vol. xv., p. 395.)

Right Hon. Anthony Foster, *circa* 1770.

Chief Baron Foster resided at, and there is reason to believe was the builder of, Merville,* and from him the adjoining road is called Foster Avenue. He was the son of John Foster, Esq., of Dunleer, Co. Louth, by his wife Elizabeth, youngest dau. of William Fortescue, Esq., of Newrath, Co. Louth, and was *b.* in 1705. He entered T.C.D., and

---

* His town residence was " Kerry House," Molesworth Street, in which he was succeeded by his distinguished son, the last Speaker of the Irish House of Commons.—Gilbert's *History of Dublin*, vol. iii., p. 260.

graduated B.A. in 1726. He was called to the Bar in 1732, and made a King's Counsel in 1760. He represented the Borough of Dunleer in Parliament for over twenty years, until returned for the Co. Louth in 1762. He continued to sit for that county until 1765, when he was appointed Chief Baron of the Exchequer. He was created a Privy Councillor. In 1776 he resigned the office of Chief Baron, and *d.* on April 3, 1778. He *m.*, first, Feb. 25, 1736, Elizabeth (*d.* July 30, 1744), younger dau. of William Burgh, Esq., of Dublin, and had issue—1. John,* last Speaker of the Irish House of Commons, created Baron Oriel in 1821, *m.*, 1764, Margaret Amelia, dau. of Thomas Burgh, Esq., M.P., of Bert, Co. Kildare, and *d.* Aug. 23, 1828; 2. William,† D.D., Bishop of Cork, and subsequently of Kilmore and of Clogher, Chaplain to the Irish House of Commons, *m.* Catherine Letitia (*d.* 1814), dau. of Rev. Henry Leslie, and *d.* 1797 ; 3. Margaret, *m.* Right‡ Rev. and Hon. Henry Maxwell,§ Bishop of Meath, and *d.* 1792. He *m.*, secondly, July 29, 1749, Dorothea, dau. of Thomas Burgh, Esq., of Oldtown, M.P., Naas, and by her had no issue. (See Foster's *Peerage*, 1881, under Massereene; and Foster, Rev. Sir Cavendish, Bart. ; and in B. P., 1830, under Ferrard, Viscount.)

---

* See *Dictionary of National Biography*, vol. xx., p. 56.

† See Cotton's *Fasti*, &c., vol. i., p. 234 ; vol. iii., pp. 83, 170, and Brady's *Records of Cork*, vol. iii., p. 81.

‡ Thus styled in the Meath Register.

§ See Cotton's *Fasti*, &c., vol. iii., pp. 123, 174, 284.

Chief Baron Foster did not confine his attention to his profession ; he took a practical interest in agriculture, and was remarkable in the age in which he lived for advanced views on the management of property. Arthur Young calls him a "prince of improvers," and gives a long account of a visit which he paid in July, 1776, to the Chief Baron on his estate at Collon in the Co. Louth. He says that twenty years previously it was a waste sheep-walk, covered with heath, and inhabited by people as miserable as can be conceived, and describes this barren wilderness, at the time of his visit, as a sheet of corn, a country smiling with cultivation, and planted with a happy and industrious tenantry. The operations in reclaiming the estate were of a magnitude such as Young had never heard of before ; enormous quantities of lime had been laid on the land, miles of fences and roads had been constructed, many acres of plantations had been made under the direction of the Chief Baron's son, and " a new race of tenantry had been nursed up." The Chief Baron gave Young " a variety of information uncommonly valuable ;" he told him that he had found raising rents quickened the industry of the tenantry, set them searching for manures, and made them better farmers, and was of opinion—an opinion which would not find much acceptance in the present day—that it was one of the greatest causes of the improvement of Ireland.—Arthur Young's *Tour in Ireland*, ed. by A. W. Hutton, Lon., 1892, vol. i., pp. 110 *et seq*.

Mr. Justice Fox, 1812-19.

The Hon. Luke Fox, one of the Justices of the Common Pleas, resided at Trimleston for several years. He was the son of Michael Fox, Esq., and was *b.* in Leitrim in 1757. He entered T.C.D. on July 8, 1773, and having won a Scholarship in 1777, graduated B.A. in 1779. He was *c.* to the Bar in 1784, and appointed a King's Counsel in 1795. He sat in the Irish Parliament as member for the Borough of Fethard, in the Co. Wexford, from 1795 to 1797, for the Borough of Clonmines, in the same county, from 1797 to 1799, and for the Manor of Mullingar from 1799 to 1800. He was appointed a Justice of the Common Pleas, March, 1801, and continued to occupy that position until he resigned in 1816. He *d.* suddenly at Harrogate, where he had gone for the benefit of his health, on Aug. 26, 1819. He *m.* in 1791, at Rathfarnham Castle, Miss Annesley, niece to the Right Hon. Lord Viscount Loftus.

Sir John Franks, 1836-51.

Sir John Franks, of St. Brigid's,* was the second son of Thomas Franks, Esq., of Ballymagooly, by

---

* St. Brigid's was occupied by Sir John's elder brother, Matthew Franks, Esq., who purchased it in 1806, before it became his residence. It has since remained in the possession of the Franks family, and is now the residence of his grand-nephew, Thomas Cuthbert Franks, Esq., Solicitor, ex-President of the Incorporated Law Society, and J.P. Co. Dublin. (See Franks of Carrig, B.L.G., 1894.)

Catherine, dau. of Rev. John Day, and sister of the
Hon. Mr. Justice Day. He was *b.* in 1770, and
having entered T.C.D., he graduated B.A., 1788, and
LL.B., 1791. He was *c.* to the Bar in 1792, and
went the Munster Circuit. In 1822 he was made
a King's Counsel, and in 1825 he was appointed
Judge of the Supreme Court of Calcutta. He was
presented to the King on his appointment, and
received the honour of Knighthood. He returned
from India in 1835. He *m.*, first, Catherine, dau.
of Thomas Franks, Esq., of Carrig, Co. Cork, and
had issue—1. John, D.L., *m.* Eleanora, dau. of
William Whitmore, Esq., and *d.* 1881, leaving
issue ; 2. Matthew, 11th Dragoons, *m.* Louisa, dau.
of Captain Roche, and *d.*, leaving issue; 3. Margaret,
m. Ven. John Hawtayne, Archdeacon of Bombay ;
4. Catherine, *m.* Thomas Montgomery, Esq. ; 5.
Lucy, *m.* Henry Holroyd, Esq. He *m.*, secondly,
Jane, dau. of John Marshall, Esq. ; and thirdly,
Sarah Wollaston (*d.* Feb. 22, 1874, *bur.* T. G.),
dau. and co-heir of William O'Regan, Esq. Sir
John *d.* Jan. 10, 1852, and is *bur.* in T. G. (p. 34).

" Upon his appointment to the Indian Bench in 1825, he
was presented with an address from all his brethren of the
Munster Bar, breathing the most cordial sentiments of affection and respect ; and before his final departure from the
East, he was presented with similar testimonies to his
ability and worth. . . . As a companion his conversa-
tion was always attractive. In addition to his stores of
general knowledge, derived from books and from the experience of a long life, he brought a quality of his own which
individualized his thoughts and diction—a peculiar aboriginal

wit, quiet, keen, and natural to the occasion, and, best of all, never malignant."—*Gentleman's Magazine*, vol. xxxvii. (N. S.), p. 408; also see *Dictionary of National Biography*, vol. xx., p. 198.

Sir Edward Grogan, Bart., 1875-91.

Sir Edward Grogan resided at Ballintyre for nearly twenty years. He was the eldest son of John Grogan, Esq., by his wife Sarah, dau. of Charles Dowling Medlicott, Esq. (B.P., 1895, p. 641.) Having entered T.C.D., he graduated b.a., 1828, m.a., 1833. He was c. to the Bar in 1840. In 1841 he was elected m.p. for Dublin, and represented the City for nearly a quarter of a century until 1865. He was created a Baronet, April 23, 1859, and was a d.l. of Dublin. He *d.* Jan. 26, 1891, and was *bur.* at Mount Jerome. He *m.*, July 27, 1867, Catherine Charlotte, eldest dau. of Sir Beresford Burston MacMahon, Bart., and had issue—1. Edward Ion Charles, the present Baronet ; 2. Maria Katharine Nina ; 3. Sarah Madeleine ; 4. Aileen Edward Sybil Teresa.

" His keen and close attention to business, and his uncompromising adherence to the party to which he had attached himself by conviction, commanded the respect of friends and opponents alike."—*Daily Express*, Jan. 27, 1891.

Lieut.-General Henry Hall, c.b., 1839-75.

General Hall, who resided at Merville from 1839 until his death, was the fourth son of the Venerable Francis Hall, Archdeacon of Kilmacduagh, by

Christiana Traill, niece of the Right Rev. Dr.
Traill, Bishop of Down. (See Hall of Mairwara,
B.L.G., 1863.) He was *b.* Sept. 11, 1789, entered
the Army in 1804, and went to India in the following year. He was successively lieutenant, captain,
major, and colonel in the Bengal Army. He saw
much active service, and displayed great bravery in
several expeditions against the native chiefs. In
1822 he was appointed Governor of Mairwara, and
in the subjugation and civilization of that province
exhibited remarkable administrative ability. He
continued to hold that position until 1835, when he
returned from India. He was made a c.b. in 1838,
and became a Major-General, and subsequently, in
1858, a Lieutenant-General. He was j.p. for the
Cos. of Dublin and Galway. He *d.* Aug., 1875.
He *m.*, 1827, Sarah (*d.* 1847), eldest dau. of
General Fagan, Adjutant-General of the Bengal
Army, and had issue—1. Henry Edward, Captain
13th Light Infantry, served in the Crimean War
and Indian Mutiny, *m.*, Nov. 23, 1858, Annie, only
child of Col. T. Moore, Bengal Army, and *d.* Feb.,
1869, having had issue—i. Henry Thomas, Captain
18th Hussars, *m.* Lizzie Annie, eldest dau. of Major
John Joseph Lopdell, of Raheen Park, Galway; ii.
Charles Henry Edward; iii. Arthur Francis; iv.
Clara Annie Isabella; 2. Christopher James Traill,
o. s. p., 1854; 3. Eliza Margaret (*d.* July 14, 1885),
m., T. C., Jan. 30, 1855, the Rev. Macnevin Brad-
shaw, m.a., sometime Rector of Clontarf; 4. Annie,
d. unm.

A full account of General Hall's career as a
soldier and as an administrator will be found in the
Story of Mairwara (Lon., 1868). The author, in
speaking of his character, says (p. 127) :—

"In advanced years he retains and exhibits the energy,
the assiduity, the benevolence, the active beneficence, and
the unfailing judgment, which in other days achieved for
him such great results in India."

Sir Robert Harty, Bart., 1826-32.

Sir Robert Harty was only for a short time a
parishioner, owing to his premature death; but the
residence of his family, since his decease, at Prospect Hall has identified the name of Harty with
Dundrum.   Sir Robert was a well-known citizen
of Dublin.   He was an Alderman; High Sheriff
in 1811, and Lord Mayor in 1830.   He was
elected M.P. for the City in 1831, and on Sept. 30
of that year was created a baronet.   He *m.*, March
21, 1807, Elizabeth (*d.* June 9, 1875), eldest dau.
of John Davis, Esq., of Eden Park, and had issue
—1. Robert, the present baronet, *m.*, Jan. 6, 1857,
Sophy, dau. of Rev. Samuel G. Fairtlough, Rector
of Ahinagh, Co. Cork, and had issue—i. Robert
Way, *o. s. p.*, July 22, 1879; ii. Caroline Elizabeth
Josephine; iii. Isabella Henrietta; 2. Marcus, C.E.,
o. s. p., Dec., 1879 ; 3. Charles Allsop, *o. s. p.*, July
20, 1840 ; 4. Henry Lockington, J.P. Co. Dublin, of
Casino,* *m.*, 1854, Anna (*d.* March 11, 1880), dau.

* Casino was the country residence of Dr. Robert Emmet,
the father of Thomas Addis and Robert Emmet, and his
name appears in the applotments for the Church cess, under

of Henry Davis, Esq., and has issue—i. Allsop
Frederick; ii. Lionel Lockington; iii. Paulina
Rhoda; iv. Elizabeth Kathleen; 5. Louisa Matilda,
m., Aug. 11, 1846, George Haigh, Esq. (*d.* 1883),
of Bemerside, Yorkshire; 6. Elizabeth Henrietta;
7. Adelaide Emma Jane, *m.*, T. C., Dec. 13, 1859,
George Henry Haigh, Esq. (*d.* 1887), Grainsby
Hall, Lincoln. Sir Robert *d.* Oct. 10, 1832.

SIR ROBERT KANE, 1856-73.

Sir Robert Kane resided at Wyckham for a num-
ber of years. He was *b.* in 1810, and having
entered T.C.D., graduated B.A., 1835, and LL.D.,
1868. He was a Fellow of the King and Queen's
College of Physicians, a Fellow of the Royal
Society, and a Member of the Royal Irish Academy.
He was appointed President of the Queen's College,
Cork, in 1845, and Director of the Museum of Irish
Industry in the same year. In 1846 he received
the honour of Knighthood. He *d.* in Dublin on
Feb. 16, 1890. He *m.*, 1838, Katharine (*d.* 1886),
dau. of Henry Baily, Esq.

SIR EDWARD HUDSON HUDSON-KINAHAN, BART., 1873-92.

This well-known citizen of Dublin, who was for
many years one of her most prominent public men,

the townland of "Farmbolie," from 1794 until his death,
which occurred in Oct., 1802. His son Robert returned to
Ireland about that time from the Continent, where he had
gone after the rising of 1798, and remained at Casino in
seclusion for some months. It is said he formed hiding-
places between the floors of the rooms.—Webb's *Compendium of Irish Biography*, p. 169.

purchased Wyckham in 1873, and resided there until his death. He took an active part in every movement for the advancement of the material prosperity of his city and country, and was a munificent supporter of all charitable institutions. In his political opinions he was a Conservative, and, as a much esteemed member of his party, his counsel and assistance were sought and greatly valued in all times of emergency. He was the second son of Robert Henry Kinahan, Esq., Lord Mayor of Dublin, 1853, by his wife, Charlotte, dau. of Edward Hudson. Esq., M.D. (p. 121), and was b. Nov. 27, 1828. He was a J.P. for the City and Co. of Dublin, and for the Co. of Cork. He was High Sheriff of Dublin, 1868, of the Co. Dublin, 1875, and of the Queen's Co., 1892. He was created a baronet, Sept. 26, 1887, and assumed, by royal license, Oct., 1887, the prefix of Hudson. He d. at Maryborough, where he was attending the Assizes as High Sheriff of the Queen's Co., on March 8, 1892, and was bur. at Mount Jerome. He m., May 12, 1863, Emily Isabella, dau. of the Rev. Daniel Dickinson, M.A., Rector of Seapatrick, Co. Down, and had issue— 1. Edward Hudson, the present baronet; 2. Robert Henry ; 3. Daniel Dickinson ; 4. George Frederick (bapt. T. C.); 5. Cecil Barton (bapt. T. C.); 6. Margaretta Emily, d. June 12, 1873 ; 7. Charlotte Hudson, m., T. C., Jan. 22, 1895, Cornelius Richard O'Callaghan, Esq.; 8. Grace Elizabeth ; 9. Emily Margaretta ; 10. Gertrude Isabella Margaret; 11. Ellen Louisa Maria ; 12. Eileen Julia.

N

In speaking of Sir Edward, the *Daily Express*, March 9, 1892, said :—

" Few men who have taken so prominent a part in public life during times of great political excitement have won and retained to so large an extent the respect and honour of their fellow-citizens of all creeds and classes. Although a very firm, courageous, and consistent upholder of Conservative principles, he was never obtrusive in his political attitude, and the bitterest and most sensitive opponent could not find the slightest occasion for offence in his expression of his opinions."

Hon. Patrick Plunket, 1842-59.

The Hon. Patrick Plunket, Judge of the Court of Bankruptcy, resided at Donnybrook Cottage,* from 1842 until his death. He was the fifth son of William Conyngham, first Baron Plunket, some-time Lord Chancellor of Ireland, by his wife, Catherine, only dau. of John M'Causland, Esq., M.P. (B. P., 1895). He was *b*. in 1799, and having entered T.C.D., graduated B.A., 1821, and M.A., 1832. He was called to the bar in 1824. He was appointed a Commissioner of Bankrupts in 1837, and, under legislation in 1858, became a Judge of the Court of Bankruptcy. He *d*. July 31, 1859. He *m*., May 24, 1838, Maria, dau. of John Atkinson, Esq. (p. 28), and had issue—1. William Conyngham, Lieut. 22nd Regt. ; 2. Charles John Cedric, *m*., Aug. 4, 1881, Alice, third dau. of Francis P. Cupiss, Esq., F.R.C.S. ; 3. Constance Gertrude Maria, *m*., Feb. 9, 1866, Richard Mayne Tabuteau, Esq.

* Now called St. Margaret's (see p. 162).

Sir John Power, 1814-55.

Sir John Power, who was one of O'Connell's most influential supporters, resided at Roebuck House* for over forty years. He was a D.L. and J.P. of Dublin, and was created a Baronet, Oct. 18, 1841. He d. June 26, 1855. He m., Sept. 26, 1799, Mary (d. 1834), eldest dau. of Thomas Brenan, Esq., and had issue—1. James, the second Baronet, D.L. and J.P., M.P. for Co. Wexford, m. Jane Anna Eliza, dau. of John Hyacinth Talbot, Esq., D.L. and M.P., and d. Sept. 30, 1877, leaving issue (see B.P., 1895); 2. Mary, d. unm.; 3. Catherine, m. Sir Nicholas FitzSimon, M.P.; 4. Margaret, m. Francis Augustus Codd, Esq.; 5. Annetta, m. Thomas S. Coppinger, Esq.; 6. Eliza, m. John Hyacinth Talbot, Esq.; 7. Emily; 8. Ellen, m. Joseph Barry, Esq.

"Simple-hearted and sincere in his manner, upright and liberal in every transaction of life, unbounded and discriminating in his charities, his memory will be long cherished by his family and friends."—*Dublin Evening Post*, June 28, 1855.

"Sagacious, active, and energetic, he dispensed with wise munificence an ample fortune. . . . . He respected conscientious difference of sentiment, and lived on terms the most friendly with those of opposite views."—*Freeman's Journal*, June 27, 1855.

Whitley Stokes, M.D., 1806-31.

Dr. Whitley Stokes resided in Dundrum for many years, and is buried in Taney Graveyard,

* Now called Roebuck Grove (see p. 157).

with several members of his family. His distinction as a collegian was not less than the eminence he enjoyed as a physician; and he is one of the few instances in which a Fellow of T.C.D. filled the chair of Regius Professor of Physic. He was *b.* in 1763, and was educated at the Endowed School, Waterford. He entered T.C.D., and having won a Scholarship, graduated B.A., 1783, M.A., 1789, and M.D., 1793. He became a Fellow in 1788, and was appointed King's Professor of Practice of Medicine in 1793. In 1816, on becoming a Nonconformist, he resigned his Fellowship, and was appointed Lecturer in Natural History. In 1830 he was appointed Regius Professor of Physic. He was instrumental in founding the College Botanical Gardens, and also took a leading part in establishing the Zoological Gardens. As a physician he had a large practice, and much distinguished himself by his treatment of fever during severe epidemics in 1817 and 1827. He *d.* at his house in Harcourt Street on April 13, 1845. He *m.* Mary Anne (*d.* July 13, 1844, *bur.* T. G.), only dau. of William Picknoll, Esq., and had issue—1. Whitley; 2. William, Honorary M.D., Dub.; D.C.L., Oxon.; LL.D., Cantab.; LL.D., Edin.; three times President of the College of Physicians of Ireland, Regius Professor of Physic, T.C.D., *d.* Jan. 7, 1878; 3. Gabriel; 4. Henry; 5. John; 6. Harriet, *d.* June 10, 1825, *bur.* T. G.; 7. Mary Anne, *d.* Oct. 14, 1838, *bur.* T. G.; 8. Eliza; 9. Sarah; 10. Ellen Honoria, *d.* Aug. 6, 1880, *bur.* T. G. (see p. 43).

Dr. Stokes was a son of the Rev. Gabriel Stokes, D.D., Chancellor of Waterford Cathedral, and Rector of Ardtrea, in the Diocese of Armagh (Cotton's *Fasti*, vol. i., pp. 148, 191, vol. iv., p. 146), who *m.* Miss Sarah Boxwell, and had issue—1. Whitley; 2. William, M.D., formerly of Killeshandra, who was *bur.* T. G., Oct. 20, 1806; 3. Gabriel, *m.* Miss Merrit, and was *bur.* T. G., April 18, 1848, leaving issue Gabriel, *bur.* T. G., June 13, 1853; 4. Harriet; 5. Eliza, *bur.* T. G., March 25, 1846.

"A man who conferred many and great benefits on society in Ireland, and whose body, soul, and spirit were for years devoted to the pursuit of means to promote the moral interests and develop the physical resources of his country, and who was so far in advance of the times in which he lived, that it is now only we can appreciate what he strove for during a long life; and we are now reaping the benefits of that for which he endured years of toil, obloquy, and even persecution to accomplish. . . . Doctor Stokes was through a long life a strenuous advocate of the liberties, not only of his country, but of mankind. He was the uncompromising enemy of tyranny, whether despotic or democratic. He was the first successful teacher of medicine in Ireland, as well as the founder of clinical medical instruction."—*Dublin University Magazine*, vol. xxvi., p. 202.

The above extract is taken from a most interesting memoir in the *University Magazine;* also see a biographical notice in Webb's *Compendium of Irish Biography*, p. 502, and Stubbs's *History of the University of Dublin*, pp. 294, *et seq.*

JOHN EDWARD VERNON, 1854-87.

Mr. Vernon, as agent to the Pembroke Estates, resided for many years at Mount Merrion. He was

the eldest son of the Rev. John Fane Vernon, by
his wife Frances, dau. of the Right Rev. John
Kearney, D.D., Bishop of Ossory. (See Vernon of
Clontarf, B.L.G., 1895.) He was *b.* in 1816, and
having entered T.C.D., graduated B.A., 1838, and
M.A., 1865. He was J.P., D.L., and High Sheriff,
1864, of Cavan, and J.P. for the Cos. Dublin,
Wicklow, and Monaghan. He was some time a
Director and Governor of the Bank of Ireland. In
1881 he was appointed one of the Land Commis-
sioners. He *d.* March 7, 1887. He *m.*, first, July
2, 1846, Harriet, youngest dau. of the Right Rev.
John Leslie, D.D., Bishop of Kilmore, by his wife
Isabella, dau. of the Hon. and Right Rev. Thomas
St. Lawrence, Bishop of Cork, and had issue—1.
John Fane, M.A., Barrister-at-Law, J.P., and High
Sheriff, 1890, Co. Cavan, and J.P., Co. Dublin, *m.*,
May 11, 1882, Thomasina Georgina, dau. of Rev.
Canon Henry Joy Tombe, D.D. ; 2. Edward Saunder-
son, *m.*, 1882, Miss Georgina Rich ; 3. Isabella
Frances, *m.*, T. C., June 24, 1875, Henry Chichester
Tisdall, Esq. ; 4. Charlotte Diana, *d.* Dec. 19, 1867.
He *m.* secondly, T. C., Nov. 17, 1857, Maria Esther,
eldest dau. of the Hon. George F. Pomeroy-Colley,
and had issue (*bapt.* T. C.)—1. George Arthur
Pomeroy, LL.D. ; 2. Walter Pomeroy, *d.* Oct. 10,
1890 ; 3. Anna Lilian ; 4. Helen Rose ; 5. Blanche.

" A public man of high talents and character. . . His
appointment as a Land Commissioner was one for which his
natural talents, experience, independence, and strict probity
fitted him. As agent of the Pembroke Estates, he had long
been noted for his practical recognition of the duties as well

as the rights of property, and no Irish estate was better administered. . . . His death brings to a close a most useful life, and cannot but be regarded as a distinct loss to his country."—*Dublin Evening Mail*, March 8, 1887.

JOHN, BARON TRIMLESTON, *circa* 1534.

D'Alton states that John, the 3rd Baron of Trimleston, resided in the Castle of Roebuck.* He was the grandson of Robert, 1st Baron of Trimleston, who *m.* Elizabeth, dau. and heiress of Christopher le Brune, of " Rabo " or Roebuck, and, there is no doubt, was the owner of the estate which remained in the possession of the Trimleston family until the beginning of the present century. In 1509 he was appointed second Justice of the King's Bench in Ireland, in 1522 Vice-Treasurer of Ireland, in 1524 High Treasurer of Ireland, and in 1534 Lord Chancellor of Ireland. He *m.* four times, his first wife being Jane, dau. of John Bellew, Esq., of

* Brewer, in his *Beauties of Ireland*, p. 213, says the building was nearly destroyed in the wars of 1641, whilst the property of Matthew Barnewall, Lord Trimleston, but has been since restored. Lewis, in his *Topographical Dictionary of Ireland*, ed. 1837, vol. i., p. 518, says it was occupied by James II. and the Duke of Berwick when they encamped in the neighbourhood. He mentions that it was repaired about 1790 by the then Lord Trimleston, who fitted up one of the apartments, a noble room, 50 feet in length, as a theatre, and that it was purchased about ten years afterwards by Mr. James Crofton (p. 105), who pulled down a portion of the buildings; and modernised the remainder, of which the room mentioned, then used as a drawing-room, was the only remaining part of the old castle.

Bellewstown, and *d.* in 1538.   (D'Alton's *History of the County Dublin*, p. 809 ; B.P., 1895 ; Burke's *Lord Chancellors of Ireland*, p. 38.)

THOMAS WALLACE, K.C., 1820-47.

Mr. Wallace, who purchased Belfield, Stillorgan Road, which is still in the possession of his son, from the executors of Mr. Peter Digges La Touche (p. 123), was one of the distinguished Nisi Prius lawyers of his time.   He was the son of James Wallace, Esq., of Bristol, and was *b.* 1766.   He entered T.C.D. on July 7, 1789, taking first place at entrance.   He won a Scholarship in 1791, and graduated B.A. in 1793, and LL.B. and LL.D. in 1815. He was *c.* to the Bar in 1798, and was made a King's Counsel in 1816.   In 1827 he was returned to Parliament as member for Yarmouth, and continued to represent that borough until 1830.   He sat for Drogheda from 1831 to 1832, and was one of the members for the Co. Carlow from 1832 to 1835.   He *d.* at Belfield, Jan. 9, 1847.   He *m.* Katharine (*d.* May 20, 1857), dau. of John Chapman, Esq., of Castle Mitchel, Co. Kildare, and granddaughter of Sir Robert Waller, Bart., of Newport, and had issue—1. Thomas, B.A., T.C.D., *c.* to the Bar, subsequently took Holy Orders, and was some time Curate of St. Michan's and St. Thomas', and Incumbent of Kill, Diocese of Dublin, from 1865 to 1890, *m.* at Beaumaris, April 6, 1847, Sophia Mary (*d.* July 23, 1894), third dau. of the Rev. William Roberts, Rector of Llanfaelog, in

Anglesey, and granddaughter of the Ven. Thomas
Roberts, Archdeacon of Merioneth, and had issue
(*bapt.* T. C.)—i. Thomas William, *d.* Aug. 13, 1862;
ii. Robert Waller, in H. O., M.A.; iii. Norris
Edmund, B.A., Barrister-at-Law, *d.* at Capetown,
South Africa, May 19, 1883; iv. Charles John,
M.A.;* v. Sophia Elizabeth: vi. Edith Katharine
Maria, *d.* Jan. 7, 1859; 2. Martha, *m.*, T. C., Feb.
6, 1836, Thomas Higginbotham Thompson, Esq.,
of Clonskeagh Castle (p. 144).

Mr. Wallace was author of the following works:
Essay on the Manufactures of Ireland, Dub., 1798;
Variations of English Prose from the Revolution,
Trans., Irish Acad., 1796; *View of the Present State
of the Manufactures of Ireland*, Dub., 1800; *Observa-
tion on the Discourse of Natural Theology by Lord
Brougham*, Lon., 1834;† *Additional Observations*,
Dub., 1835; *Thoughts on the Elements of Civil
Government*, Lon., 1836.

Curran, in his *Sketches of the Irish Bar*, gives a
most interesting account, written by him in 1826, of
Mr. Wallace, then at the head of his profession.
He says (p. 334) that—

" He is distinguished for a solid and comprehensive judgment—for manly sagacity rather than captious subtilty in

* Author of *The Analogy of Existences and Christianity*,
Lon., 1892.

† Archbishop Whately, in one of his letters, says, refer-
ring to this book, that Mr. Wallace appears to be a much
sounder philosopher than Lord Brougham. (*Life of Richard
Whately*, by his daughter, Lon., 1868, p. 113.)

argument—for the talent (and here he peculiarly excels) of educing an orderly, lucid, and consistent statement out of a chaotic assemblage of intricate and conflicting facts—for his knowledge of human nature, both practical and metaphysical—and along with these for the sustained and authoritative force of his language and delivery, which operate as a kind of personal warranty for the soundness of every topic he advances."

Curran mentions (p. 329) that in the intercourse of private life Mr. Wallace was—

"Of the most frank and familiar manners, an extremely attractive companion, and a warm and constant friend."

CHAPTER IX.

SCHOOLS.

THE earliest record of the existence of a school in the parish is a license issued by Archbishop Fowler on May 7, 1790, appointing, on the nomination of Archdeacon Hastings, Henry Curran as Parish Clerk and "English Schoolmaster" of Taney ; and it is probable that a parochial school was first established in that year.

The next mention is to be found in the Vestry Book. At a Vestry held on Sept. 25, 1792, a vote of thanks was passed to the Rev. George Horan, A.M., "for his excellent sermon preached here last Sunday for the charity of the school of this parish," and immediately following the minutes of this Vestry are the proceedings at a meeting "of the Treasurer, Governors, and Subscribers to the Charity School of Taney," held on Oct. 7, 1792. The accounts from August, 1790, to September, 1792, were presented by the Treasurer, Sir Thomas Lighton, and showed receipts amounting to £145 16s. 9d., including a collection of £62 16s. after Mr. Horan's sermon, and an expenditure of only

£45 3s. 9d. Mr. Sweetman and Mr. Potts* were then appointed Governors, and the following expenditure approved of for the ensuing year:—

Master	... ...	£15	0 0
Mistress	... ,..	6	0 0
Coals, &c.	... ...	5	0 0
Books, &c.	... ...	2	10 0
For Clothes for any number under 80 Boys, sum not exceeding	... ...	22	15 0
For Food	... ...	15	0 0
Materials for Work	...	10	0 0
Sundries	... ...	8	0 0
		£79	0 0

The history of the schools from 1805 can be easily traced, as the book containing the accounts

* Mr. James Potts, of Roebuck (p. 138), and Mr. John Sweetman, of Churchtown. The appointment of the latter— a Roman Catholic—shows the liberal principles on which the schools were managed. He was afterwards concerned in the Rebellion of 1798, and the informer, John Hughes, of Belfast, in his evidence given before the Secret Committee of the Irish House of Commons, mentions that in April, 1798, Neilson, one of the leaders of the United Irishmen, called on him when in Dublin, and that they went to Sweetman's, near Judge Chamberlaine's, to breakfast. Sweetman was then in prison, but Neilson lived in the house. They drove subsequently in Sweetman's carriage to Mr. Grattan's, at Tinnehinch. A copy of the Report of the Committee is in Marsh's Library, and was presented to it in 1798 by Mr. James Crofton, of the Treasury (p. 105).

from that year until 1858 has been preserved. It was carefully kept, and shows that the necessary funds to support the schools were in the early years provided by an annual sermon, supplemented by some subscriptions. The offertories were large, as the following instances will show :—

1805	...	...	...	£90 16 10
1810	...	...	...	84 7 11
1815	...	...	...	112 19 5
1820	...	...	...	91 19 5
1825	...	...	...	81 4 8
1830	...	..	...	76 12 2
1835	...	...	...	63 3 10

From 1836 to 1858 two sermons were annually preached in aid of the charity ; but the revenue from that source declined, while the receipts from subscriptions increased.

The sermons were at first advertised in the Dublin Newspapers, and particulars about the schools are given in the advertisements. In 1808 42 boys and 42 girls were educated, 75 children were clothed, and 1,606 breakfasts were provided. In 1813 63 boys and 80 girls were educated, 75 received clothing, and 2,795 breakfasts were provided. In 1819 200 children were educated, and 80 were clothed.

It appears from the advertisements that the children were of all persuasions, and that they were instructed in the first principles of Christianity, in reading, writing, and arithmetic, and that the girls

were taught to sew and knit. In 1817 it was
mentioned that the male school would have to be
enlarged to accommodate the increasing number
under the new master, who was educated in the
school of Kildermo.

In the advertisement in 1814, in addition to the
school-work, it is stated that—

" The poor of the parish are constantly supplied with
money, and with clothes, blankets, fuels, and provisions at
a cheap rate, and a sum of money is lent on securities repaid by weekly instalments."

The schools were under the control of the clergy
and a treasurer, who sometimes were assisted by a
committee. As the Treasurer seems to have taken
a very leading part in the management, a list of
the parishioners who filled the office may not be
without interest :—

> 1790-1805—Sir Thomas Lighton.
> 1805-1819—Alderman Nathaniel Hone.
> 1819-1825—Joseph M'Dermott.
> 1825-1827—Henry Dawson.
> 1827-1830—Brindley Hone.
> 1830-1834—William M'Caskey.
> 1834-1850—Arthur Burgh Crofton.
> 1850-1853—John Lee Wharton.
> 1853-1858—Robert Orme.*

The schools were originally held in one of the

* With the exception of Mr. Brindley Hone, all the
Treasurers filled the office of Churchwarden, and are
mentioned in chapter vii.

houses under the graveyard; but D'Alton,* writing in 1838, says that the old church was then converted into a school attended by about thirty boys, and that at the foot of the burial ground was a female charity school attended by about thirty girls, and near it a repository for selling goods to the poor at moderate prices; so evidently the increased accommodation which was mentioned in the advertisement of 1817 as required, was obtained by annexing a portion of the old church for the use of the boys' school.

This arrangement continued until the present school-house, with the teacher's residence at Eglinton Terrace, was built by Lord Pembroke about the year 1859, of which he granted a lease in 1878 to the Representative Church Body for 150 years at 1s. per year. This lease contains a covenant that the school-house is to be used only as a parochial school under the Church of Ireland, and for no other purpose without the permission of the lessor.

The infant school was a separate institution, and it appears from a report for the year 1857 that it was established in 1829. It was under the management of a committee of ladies and the parochial clergy, and was supported by an annual collection in the church and subscriptions.

* *History of the County Dublin*, pp. 813-14.

APPLOTTERS AND APPRAISERS.

In addition to the Churchwardens, there were appointed each year, until the Church Rate ceased to be levied in 1862, two Applotters, whose duty it was to applot the assessments on the parishioners; and, until 1821, there were also appointed two Appraisers, who made any valuations which were required for the purpose of assessment.*

VESTRY CLERK AND PARISH CLERK.

These offices were held by the same person. In 1792 Henry Curran received a salary of £10 as Vestry Clerk, and of £2 5s. 6d. as Parish Clerk. In 1813 his salary as Vestry Clerk was £9 2s., and as Parish Clerk, £10. In 1823 John Sherlock had a salary of £6 16s. 6d. as Vestry Clerk, and of £10 as Parish Clerk, and in 1832 he had £12 as Vestry Clerk, and £10 as Parish Clerk. No assessment was made for the salary of the latter office after 1832, as it was paid by the Ecclesiastical Commissioners from that time. The duties of the Vestry Clerk were defined by Mr. Daniel Kinahan in 1836, and were "to receive instruction from the Clergymen and Churchwardens for serving notices of Vestries, to prepare same, and have them served by Beadle of the parish, to keep up the minutes of the Vestry, and to write out copies of the Parish and Grand Jury Cess." In 1843 James C. Kelly had a salary of £17 as Vestry Clerk, which in 1853 had risen to

* See *Assessments*, chapter xi.

£19 10s. In 1862 the office was held by John Kingston, at a salary of £21; but at the Easter Vestry, on April 22, the assessment for the amount was rejected, and the office ceased to exist.

PARISH CONSTABLE.

A Parish or Petty Constable was appointed each year until 1829, when the office became amalgamated with that of Beadle. Until 1806 the position was an honorary one, but in that year a sum of £2 5s. 6d. was assessed for his salary; this was afterwards increased, and in 1829 it was £6.

BEADLE.

In 1802 a Beadle was appointed at a salary of £2 5s. 6d., which rose to £4 in 1833, to £10 in 1843, and to £18 in 1853. In 1862 the assessment for his salary was rejected, and the office, like that of Vestry Clerk, ceased to exist.

SEXTON.

The Sexton's salary in 1792 was £4; in 1813, £6 16s. 6d.; and in 1832, £15; after which year it was paid, like the salary of the Parish Clerk, by the Ecclesiastical Commissioners.

COLLECTOR OF CESS.

There was also a Collector of the Church Rate, who was paid a salary which varied from time to time.

GLEBE HOUSE AND LAND.

The Glebe Land originally extended from the Graveyard to where the Glebe House now stands. Before the railway was made, it was intersected only by the road leading to Windy Arbour; but the Railway Company, under its compulsory powers of purchase, took the portion lying between that road and the road wall bounding the lawn of the Glebe House. Some further portions of the Glebe were alienated from the Church after the passing of the Irish Church Act, under which the tenants in occupation of Glebe Lands obtained a right of pre-emption of their holdings. By this means the field lying between the river and the road to Windy Arbour, together with the buildings standing upon it, passed to the occupiers.

The Glebe Land now consists of the field lying round two sides of the graveyard, and the plot of ground upon which the Glebe House stands, together with its lawn and garden. This land was purchased in 1873 from the Church Temporalities Commissioners, for the sum of £541 19s 1d., which was made up partly by £150 subscribed for the purpose by Mr. George Kinahan and Mr. Edward Hudson Kinahan; partly by the composition value of the Sexton's salary, and some rent of the Glebe placed to the credit of the parish by the Representative Body, and partly by money paid out of the Parochial funds in 1875.

The purchase-money paid by the Railway Company was about £800; it had been lodged in the Court of Chancery by the Company, and the income paid to the Rector for the time being.

In 1868 the Rector (the Rev. Alfred Hamilton) gave up his interest in the fund in Court, and consented to the capital being devoted to the building of the Glebe House; and a further sum of about £700 was subscribed by the parishioners, which enabled the house to be built.

In 1874 a loan of £200 was obtained from the Board of Works to build a stable; this loan is repayable by thirty-five annual instalments of £10 8s. each. The present Rector pays a rent for the Glebe House, which is placed to the credit of the parish, in part payment of the annual sum required to provide for the stipends of the future clergy. The next Rector will have the Glebe House free of rent.

CHAPTER X.

IN 1859 a cottage in the grounds of Seafield, Stillorgan Road, then the property of Mr. Thomas Crozier,* was opened for Sunday Evening Service, and continued to be used until 1873, when it was decided to build a church, the cottage having become too small for the congregation attending it.

The Earl of Pembroke granted a site at the corner of Mount Merrion Demesne, where Foster Avenue joins Stillorgan Road.

A committee was formed, consisting of Lord Viscount Gough,† the Archbishop of Dublin (Dr.

---

* Until his death Mr. Crozier took a deep interest in the services, and was a much valued supporter of this auxiliary place of worship. His good work has been carried on with respect to St. Thomas's by his daughter and her husband, Henry Malkin Barton, Esq., of Stonehouse, the adjoining place to Seafield, where the Barton family have resided for over sixty years.

† George Stephens, second Viscount Gough, who *d.* at his residence, St. Helen's, on May 31, 1895. Up to the close of his life he was a constant attendant at the services in the Chapel of Ease. St. Helen's is in the parish of Booterstown, but a small portion of the land, adjacent to Foster Avenue, is in the townland of Owenstown, and consequently in this

Trench), Thomas Crozier, Esq., John E. Vernon, Esq. (p. 181), and Henry Roe, Esq., junior (p. 141), and by the exertions of the Rector, the Rev. Alfred Hamilton, subscriptions, including £100 from Lord Pembroke, were raised, and in 1874 the church, which was built at an expense of £850, was opened free of debt.*

It was licensed by the Archbishop for the performance of, "according to the use of the Church of Ireland, Evening Prayer, and all rites and ceremonies of the said Church, which legally might or ought to be performed in a Chapel of Ease."

The building is in the form of a single aisle, with a suitable chancel at the east end; it is in the pointed style, in granite, with cut stone dressings to the door, windows, and coigns. The interior is fitted with pitch-pine pulpit, reading-desk, communion rails, and pews, and is supplied with a harmonium.

The chancel contains a painted window, representing Christ blessing little children, and two side-lights. A brass tablet upon the north wall bears the following inscription :—

"To the glory of God, and in loving memory of Thomas Crozier and Mary, his wife, of Seafield, County Dublin, these windows have been placed by their children, June, 1875."

---

parish. Blacker, in his *Sketches of Booterstown*, gives much information about the Gough family, and particularly about that distinguished officer, Field-Marshal Lord Gough, father of the second Viscount.

* The Opening Service was on Thursday, December 3rd, 1874; *vide Irish Ecclesiastical Gazette*, Dec. 23, 1874.

A marble tablet on the south wall was erected—

" In memory of Edward Perceval Westby, D.L., of Roebuck
Castle, Co. Dublin, and Co. Clare, who entered into rest,
April 23rd, 1893, aged 64.   The Lord always did lead him.
Deut. xxxii. 12.   The beloved of the Lord shall dwell in
safety.   Deut. xxxiii. 12."

And a similar tablet on the west wall was placed—

" To the praise of God and the hallowed memory of Eleanor,
dearly loved wife of Warren Wynne, Lieutenant, Royal
Engineers, and seventh daughter of James Turbett, Esq., and
Sophie, his wife, of Owenstown, Co. Dublin, who, at the age
of 24 years, was, by God's will, removed from the home she
so sweetened and adorned to one far sweeter and brighter,
she fell asleep on the Lord's Day, 14th December, 1873.   As
Jesus died and rose again, even so them also which sleep in
Jesus will God bring with him.   So shall we ever be with
the Lord."

CHAPTER XI.

Assessments.

THE Church Rate seems to have been levied in a very rough and ready manner until 1794, when, at a Vestry held on April 22, the Church-wardens were ordered "in future, to the best of their power, to procure an estimate of the number of acres respectively in the parish, and enter the same in the parish Applotment Book, for the purpose of making out an applotment."

The Vestry were called upon occasionally to applot rates other than those for the church, and on June 21, 1796, the sum of £438 16s. 11d. was applotted at the rate of 1½d. half-farthing per acre as barony cess, under warrant of the Treasurer of the Grand Jury.

Again, on June 12, 1804, the sum of £151 2s. 10d. was applotted as barony cess, and from time to time Vestries were held to applot assessments under warrants from the Treasurer of the Grand Jury.

The following minute appears in the proceedings at a Vestry held on April 16, 1805 :—

"Whereas it appears Mr. Mark Moran has been charged parish cess for forty-four acres, and it appearing that a

great part of the ground is rock and mountain, therefore
it was agreed in Vestry to reduce the acreable tax one-
fourth, leaving him liable to pay cesses for thirty-three
acres."

At the Vestry held on May 28, 1810, Messrs.
Verschoyle and Bourne, residing within the parish,
and occupying " respectively a house value for at
least £30 Irish currency," were appointed as valuators of houses under an Act of that session relating
to the making of Public Roads in the County of
Dublin, and on June 18, 1813, Alderman Hone and
Mr. Morris Hime were appointed in a similar
capacity.

Special Vestries were held on the 13th October
and 13th November, 1824, under the provisions of
an Act made in the fourth year of the reign of His
Majesty King George IV., entitled "An Act to
provide for the Establishing of Composition for
Tithes in Ireland for a limited time," when the
Archdeacon (Torrens) agreed to accept £450 per
annum as a composition for all tithes from November 1st, 1824, for a period of twenty-one years.

An autograph consent to this arrangement from
the Archbishop, as Bishop of the Diocese and
Patron of the Parish, is inserted in the Vestry
Book.

Mr. Richard Verschoyle, on the part of the
parish, and Mr. Daniel M'Kay, on the part of the
Archdeacon, were appointed Commissioners under
the Act, and were thanked for acting without
remuneration. They state in their certificate that

the average price of oats—being the corn principally grown in the county—for the period of seven years ending November 1st, 1821, was 15s. 2¼d. per barrel.

At a Vestry held on May 9, 1826, it was resolved that, in consequence of the great inequality in the value of land in the parish, a suitable gradation should be made in the applotment for parish cess, and that the model and basis be the applotment for carrying out the tithe composition. Twenty-eight acres were to be taken off Ticknock, being " the number assessable, equal with the number already paying tithe."

And at a Vestry held on April 24, 1848, it was resolved that Ticknock was not to be included for the future in applotments for parish cess, on account of the poverty of the occupiers, which was shown by the many years arrears they owed.

The Church cess ceased to be levied in the year 1862. (See p. 208.)

Coaches.

It was not until 1816 that regular communication with Dublin by a public conveyance was established. In the commencement of that year Mr. Robert Turbett (p. 148)* devised a scheme for

---

* It is an interesting coincidence that Mr. Robert Turbett's grandson, James Turbett, Esq., formerly of Oaklawn (p. 148), now of Field House, Chester, is a well-known "whip." He takes a great interest in the coaching world of the present day, and ran a coach between Dublin and Bray within recent years.

providing a service of coaches. He was supported
by a Committee consisting of all the leading inhabitants at the time, and the following plan was
printed :—

"PROSPECTUS of *A Plan for running Coaches between
Dublin, Dundrum, and Enniskerry*, With a Calculation
of Expences and Income, &c.

" One Coach to leave Dublin every Morning for Enniskerry
and return to Dublin from Enniskerry every Evening. Another Coach to leave Dundrum every Morning for Dublin,
and to leave Dublin for Dundrum at five o'Clock.

" It is supposed that the Coach to Enniskerry would be filled
by Persons going to see the County of Wicklow, the Dargle,
Waterfall, &c., and returning from them, and by Persons
going in the Morning to Dundrum to drink Goats' Whey.
The Dundrum Coach to Dublin in the Morning would be
filled by Persons living in Dundrum going to Dublin on
business, and by those who came out in the Enniskerry
Coach to drink Goats' Whey. The Dublin Coach to Dundrum would be filled at five o'Clock by Persons living at
Dundrum returning to Dinner, and Persons not living there,
but going to dine, who could return in the Evening by the
Enniskerry Coach returning to Dublin.

" The Enniskerry Coach to be drawn by four Horses with
two spare Horses. The Dundrum Coach to be drawn by
three Horses without a spare Horse. The Coaches to carry
six inside and ten outside Passengers, with Luggage and
Parcels.

Outfit ...	...	...	£700	0	0
Income'...	...	... £1,017	5	0
Yearly Expenditure	...	617	17	6
Profit ...	...	...	399	7	6

Should the Profit be only £300 per annum, it would leave
£42 per cent."

The result of Mr. Turbett's scheme was the establishment of two coaches, each carrying six inside and twelve outside passengers, to run between Enniskerry and Dublin. One coach left the Ram Hotel, Aungier Street (the starting-place was afterwards changed to Molesworth Street) at 7 a.m., arriving in Enniskerry at 9 a.m., and returning from Enniskerry at 8 p.m.; the other left Enniskerry at 8 a.m., arriving in Dublin at 9.55 a.m., and returning from Dublin at 4.30 p.m. The fare from Dundrum was 1s. 3d. inside and 10d. outside.

Derivation of Place Names.

Dr. Joyce says that Dundrum means a citadel on a low hill or ridge, and thinks the fort was situated where the present church stands. Ballinteer is the town of the builder or carpenter. Farranboley is land where cattle are fed or milked. Tiknock, or Tiknick, is the house of the hill; and Callary was the name of an Irish tribe. The derivation of Ballawley has been already given in a footnote (p. 14). Clonskeagh means the meadow of the white-thorn bushes. (See Joyce's *Irish Names of Places*, vol. i., pp. 277, 280, 524, 224, 347, 240, 882, 125, 519.)

Dispensary and Officers of Health.

In the year 1812, as appears from the Vestry Book, a meeting of the parishioners of Taney was held in the Parish Church on Sunday, Oct. 25, " for the purpose of taking into consideration the expediency and best mode of establishing a Dispensary in Dundrum to promote the comfort of the poor in that village and its vicinity." The following Committee was appointed, with directions to make their report on the next Sunday:—Right Hon. Lord Chief Justice Downes, Hon. Mr. Justice Mayne, Rev. Matthew Campbell, William Ridgeway and Richard Verschoyle, Churchwardens; Alderman N. Hone, Peter D. LaTouche, John Duffy, Thomas Sherlock, James Crofton, Daniel Beere, Solomon Richards, John Walsh, Edward Butler, Richard Corballis,* and Walter Bourne.

There is no record with regard to any further proceedings; but D'Alton† says that a dispensary was established in 1816.

In the *Freeman's Journal* of Oct. 24, 1818, there appears an advertisement of a charity sermon in aid of the " Taney Charitable Fund and Dundrum Dispensary," which states that " contributions will be received by the treasurer, Mr. Robert Turbett, or by the physician, Dr. Burke."

Before the Poor Law system was introduced, grants were made by the Grand Jury towards the expenses of the dispensaries which were organized

---

* Of Rosemount, Roebuck, where the Corballis family have resided for over ninety years. Mr. Richard Corballis, who *d.* 1847, was succeeded by his son, John Richard Corballis, Esq., LL.D., Q.C., who *d.* 1879, and he was succeeded by his son—the present owner—Richard John Corballis, Esq., M.A., J.P.

† *History of the County Dublin,* p. 812.

by voluntary effort; the first presentment for Dundrum was passed at Michaelmas Term, 1817, the
amount being £60, "to be applied, with £60 received by private subscriptions, in providing
medicines and medical or surgical aid for the poor
of Dundrum and its neighbourhood."

It appears from a map in the possession of the
Grand Jury that the dispensary was first established in a house at the corner of the road now
leading to the back of the railway station.

In 1831 cholera had appeared in England, and a
meeting of householders was held for the purpose
of appointing officers of health (under 59 Geo. III.,
chap. 41). The following were nominated :—A. B.
Crofton, R. Charles, T. M. Scully, W. M'Caskey,
and Capt. Whyte, R.N., and it was resolved that
"the assistance and advice of the medical gentlemen of the parish will be highly desirable and much
valued." Mr. M'Caskey was appointed treasurer,
with power to solicit and receive subscriptions.

At a Vestry held on Dec. 26, 1831, a parochial
rate equivalent to one half of the parish cess was
ordered to be levied on the parish under the same
Act, and a voluntary contribution of 1s. to 5s. each
was approved from the householders to provide
flannel and other necessary things to preserve the
health of the poor.

On April 19, 1832, the following were appointed
officers of health :—J. Duncan, J. A. Curran, P.
Magan, Daniel Kinahan, and Thomas Wright.

It appears from the proceedings at a Vestry held

on May 20, 1833, that an advance of £150 had
been made from the Consolidated Fund (under 2
Will. IV., chap. 9), and it was ordered to be
assessed on the parish. The accounts of the
officers of health were presented by the Treasurer,
Mr. Daniel Kinahan, which showed an expenditure
of £173 15s. 8d., and receipts amounting to £185
14s. 8d.; and it is evident from them that there
was a number of cases of cholera in the parish.

Officers of health were annually appointed from
this time until 1862, and minutes of their meetings
appear in the Vestry Book.

Distress.

In the minutes of the Vestry there are resolutions
showing that exceptional want existed in the parish
on more than one occasion.

At a meeting on April 15th, 1800, it was resolved
that—

" On account of Henry Curran's extraordinary trouble in
conducting the poor accompt, from the dearness of provisions,
and distributing meal to the poor of this parish, that we pay
said Curran for the last year the sum of £2 5s. 6d."

On Sunday, April 12, 1801, a Vestry was held—

" To consider who are the most proper poor persons to
receive three tons of potatoes ordered by the Lord Lieutenant for the express purpose of planting them."

In 1812 provisions were at a very high price, and
this gave rise to riots in various parts of the kingdom (*Annual Register*, 1812, p. 132); but our parish

retained its quiet character, and on March 31 it was resolved—

" That the loyal and peaceable conduct of our poor neigh-bours and fellow-parishioners in the Parish of Taney, entitles them to our affection and utmost assistance in this time of apprehended scarcity, and that the affluent parishioners be and are hereby called upon to subscribe to form a fund to furnish provisions at a moderate price to such persons inhabiting this parish as shall stand in need thereof.'

A committee was appointed consisting of Arch-deacon Fowler, President; Rev. Matthew Camp-bell, Vice-President and Treasurer; the Church-wardens, and every gentleman who subscribed three guineas; and a list of subscriptions, amounting to £184 11s. 6d., is given.

A circular was also prepared, stating that it was the duty of the more opulent classes effectually to cherish, relieve, and support the poor inhabitants under every distress, and that it was " true mercy that blesseth him who gives, and him who takes," which *Faulkner's Dublin Journal* (April 16, 1812) said manifested the true benevolence which should subsist between Irishmen.

On June 12, 1814, a meeting was held for the purpose of taking into consideration the state of the poor, and adopting such measures as might be best calculated to afford them permanent relief.

We also insert here a resolution passed on January 1, 1822, which records the good work of some kind ladies in the parish at that time—

" That the best thanks of this parish be presented to the Misses Drury for the unremitting attention which they have bestowed on every occasion to the Poor and Charitable Insti-tutions of this parish."

Effects of Disestablishment upon the Parochial Finances.

In the early part of the nineteenth century—from whence the parochial records afford us continuous information—we find that the sources of income for the requirements of the parish were as follows : —(1.) The Tithes, which were paid to the Archdeacon of Dublin as Rector, and out of which he paid the curate's stipend—in 1837 the Tithe composition was £415 7s. 8½d., and the curate's stipend £75.* (2.) The Marriage and Burial Fees, which went to the curate. (3.) The offertories and other collections in church, for the poor. (4.) The special collections made for the schools. (5.) The cess levied upon the parish for the expenses of Divine Service, and of repairing the church fabric, and for the payment of the parish officers, &c.

In 1851 the Archdeacon ceased to be Rector, after which the tithe rent charges and the marriage and burial fees were paid to the Rector (in 1868 the tithe rent charges amounted to £311), and the collections for the poor and schools were raised and applied as before.

In 1833 the Ecclesiastical Commissioners undertook the payment of the expenses of Divine Service, and of repairing the church fabric, and in the year 1862 the cess for the payment of parish officers, &c.,

* For some years the parishioners contributed to supplement Mr. Stanford's income—the last curate under the Archdeacon.

ceased to be levied, by reason of the opposition of some of the Roman Catholic parishioners. From the latter date, all expenses, except those provided by the Ecclesiastical Commissioners and the Poor Law Union, were raised by voluntary subscriptions.

For some years after the appointment of the rector in 1851, he continued to pay the curate out of his tithe rent charges, as the Archdeacon had done; but at length the parishioners relieved him of this burden, and thenceforward raised the curate's salary by voluntary subscriptions.

It will appear from this that the expenses connected with the church had gradually come to be more of a voluntary burden, so that when disestablishment and disendowment came in 1869, the parishioners were not wholly unaccustomed to support the parochial institutions themselves.

Were it not for the fact that it behoved the parish to make provision for the clergy who should succeed those in office in 1869, there would have been no additional expense thrown upon it during the tenure of the then clergy, because the rector retained his stipend for his life; and the curate, although he had received no stipend from the Establishment prior to 1869, was then able (with others in the like position) to make good a claim to receive a stipend of £120 a year out of the Church funds for his life, so that in his case there was a gain instead of a loss to the parish. Thus it will be seen that the provision for the future clergy was the only immediate burden thrown upon the parish by Disestablishment.

It is not necessary to explain here the principles of the financial plan of the diocese, whereby provision has been made for the future clergy; it is enough to say that by an annual payment of £192, commencing in 1871, the parish has secured stipends of £220 for the rector, and £110 for the curate of the future.

Goats' Milk.

Dundrum was at the beginning of the present century celebrated for its goats' milk, which was much ordered at that time by physicians for their patients; and no doubt the village of Goatstown derives its name from goats having been kept there.

Rutty, in his *Natural History of the County Dublin*, published in 1772, says (p. 272 *et seq.*)—

"Goats' milk has been observed to have affected some remarkable cures of consumption where the cows' and asses' milk had failed, and for this purpose it is sometimes sent from the neighbouring mountains to Dublin, and sold at 3d. per quart. Goats' whey deserves to be considered as a medicine, which, as goats abound on the mountainous parts of the country, our physicians have of late learned to order their chronical patients in the neighbourhood of Dublin, instead of dismissing them to the mountains of Mourne, and for this purpose good lodgings have been lately provided at Carrickmayne, and also the whey has been drank at Dundrum, a distance of only three miles from the city."

He then goes on to say that

"The goat kids in *March*, and consequently that month, or rather *April* and *May*, when the season is further advanced for supplying them with vegetables, is the proper season for drinking the whey. The use of it, indeed, is continued by many in *June* and *July ;* but even in *June* the milk thickens, for which reason they then mix four ounces of water with a quart of the milk before they turn it, and more water in *July*, the milk growing thick as the season advances, so that in *August* it is not to be drank ; but in *September* is a second Spring, and the milk becomes thinner again, and may be used medicinally, though not with equal advantage as in the former season."

This explains an advertisement which appears in the *Freeman's Journal* of Sept. 27, 1813—

" MEADOW BROOK BOARDING HOUSE, DUNDRUM.—The *Second Whey Season* having commenced, Ladies and Gentlemen are respectfully informed there are a few Vacancies in the House ; the Accommodation will be found agreeable, and terms very much reduced—respectable Society in the House."

Brewer, in his *Beauties of Ireland,* published in 1825, says (p. 215)—

" Dundrum is the fashionable resort of invalids for the purpose of drinking goats' whey. At early hours of the morning numerous jaunting-cars convey from the city large parties of visitors to partake of that sanative beverage, amidst the reviving scenery over which the animals have browsed."

Lay Patron and Nominators.

There is ancient precedent in the case of our parish for the office of nominator under the present constitution of the Church of Ireland ; and it is a fact worthy of note that the lay patron more than 300 years ago was a Lord Chancellor of Ireland, and that now in our own day one of the existing nominators should also have filled that high legal office.

We find that in the first year of the reign of
Edward VI. (1547) a lease, dated June 22, was
granted to Richard Rede, Knight, Lord Chancellor
of Ireland,* of the precinct of the house of the late
Chancellor of the Cathedral of St. Patrick, Dublin ;
the rectory or prebend of Tawney, lands in Tawney,
with tithes, &c ; the rectory or prebend of Raffernan, the house and lands belonging thereto, with
the tithes, &c., to hold for twenty-one years, at a
rent of £69 6s. 8d., finding fit chaplains for the
churches of Tawney and Raffernan. (See the 8th
Report of the Deputy Keeper of the Public Records
in Ireland, p. 29.)

The nominators since disestablishment have
been—

1876—. George Kinahan.†
1876-82. James Stirling.
1876-81. John Walsh.
1881-88. Robert Tilly.
1882-93. Edward Perceval Westby.
1888—. Right Hon. John Thomas Ball.†
1893-94. Everard Hamilton.
1894—. John C. Parkes.†

Militia and Yeomanry.

Amongst the numerous volunteer forces raised in
Ireland at the close of the last century, was a troop
of Yeomanry called the Rathdown Horse, to which
Dundrum seems to have contributed both officers

---

* See Burke's *Lord Chancellors of Ireland*, p. 43.
† Still in office.

and men. In Walker's *Hibernian Magazine* for January, 1797 (p. 92), the Rathdown Horse, commanded by Sir Thomas Lighton, is mentioned amongst the regiments tendering their service on the occasion of the apprehended invasion by the French, and in the same number of this periodical (p. 95) it is stated that the remains of Lord Trimleston were moved from Kildare Street to the County Meath, attended by a detachment of the Roebuck Cavalry.

There was also a corps of infantry raised in Dundrum at the beginning of the present century ; for in the same magazine for May, 1808 (p. 315), it is mentioned that on the previous Sunday the Dundrum Infantry and Harold's Cross Corps exercised together, and practised firing at a target for some hours on the strand of Rathfarnham, near Lord Ely's gate.*

In consequence of war being declared with France in 1803, several Acts of Parliament were passed with regard to the Militia, and under the provisions of this legislation, a Vestry was held on Aug. 15, 1803, to raise the quota of four men for the army of reserve. An assessment for this purpose, amounting to £35 17s. 6d., was ordered to be levied at 8½d. per acre.

On Nov. 18, 1807, a similar assessment of £60 was ordered to be levied at 7d. per acre, for a quota

* The gate of Rathfarnham Castle, now the residence of Edward Blackburne, Esq., Q.C. His father, the Right Hon. Francis Blackburne (see p. 155), left Roebuck Hall on purchasing the Castle from the Loftus family.

of four men, and on March 6, 1810, a sum of
£27 6s., at 3½d. per acre, for three men. On April
20, 1813, an assessment of £47 7s. 11d. was
ordered to be applotted at 5d. per acre, for a quota
of four men ; but at a meeting on June 8 the con-
firmation of the applotment was suspended, and it
never seems to have been levied.

In the accounts there is an allowance to the
collector of the Militia Cess, of 5d. each upon 72
dollars ; these coins were Spanish dollars, which
were re-stamped, with an inscription purporting
that they would circulate for 6s. each, and were
issued by the Bank of England at the beginning of
the present century, owing to a scarcity of silver
coinage. (Walker's *Hibernian Magazine*, 1804, p.
446.) No doubt, the allowance was to cover a
depreciation in their value.

The fact that Kilmacud, which is a townland in
the parish of Stillorgan, was included in Taney for
the Militia assessment, is not so easily explained,
and no reason for it has been ascertained.*

Ordination.

Taney was on one occasion selected as the church
in which an ordination should be held. In *Pue's
Occurrences* it is related that on Sunday, July 5,
1761, the Bishop of Limerick (Dr. James Leslie)†

---

* Also see under Giffard, John, p. 112.

† Dr. Leslie commenced his clerical life in the Dublin
Diocese. He was Curate of Swords, Vicar of Donabate, and
Perpetual Curate of St. Nicholas' Within. (See Cotton's *Fasti*,
&c., vol. i., p. 389 ; vol. v., p. 60 ; also the *Irish Builder* for
January 15, 1890, p. 24.)

held an ordination in Tawney, by licence from the Archbishop of Dublin, and that Edward Ledwich, John Bowden, A.M.; Beather King, George Hickes, and Matthew Browne, were ordained Priests ; and Josias Fleming, B.A. ; Stephen Baldwin, B.A. ; and James Ford, B.A., were admitted Deacons.*

Outrages.

In Walker's *Hibernian Magazine* for Feb., 1791 (p. 191), there appears the account of an occurrence which probably greatly excited the residents of Dundrum at the time—

" A night or two ago, at a very late hour, two persons, seemingly gentlemen, drove themselves out in a post-chaise to Churchtown, where there is a burial-place, with a dead body coffined up in the carriage. They rapped up the grave-digger, and told him that they had, under the disguise of

---

* Ledwich was a B.A. and LL.B. of T.C.D., and became Vicar of Aghaboe, Diocese of Ossory. He was a distinguished antiquary and Irish historian. His name has been already mentioned in the note on Mr. William Ridgeway (p. 140). (See Webb's *Compendium of Irish Biography*, p. 287, and *Dictionary of National Biography*, vol. xxxii., p. 340.) Bowden became a D.D. of T.C.D., and was Vicar of Santry and Chancellor of Lismore Cathedral. (See Adams's *History of Santry and Cloghran*, pp. 5, 15, 71.) King was a Sch. and LL.D. of T.C.D. He became Curate of Stillorgan, of St. Bride's, and of St. John's, Dublin, and was Vicar of Straffan, and Prebendary of Kilmacdonagh, Diocese of Cloyne. (See Hughes's *St. John's*, p. 74, and Brady's *Records of Cork*, vol. ii., pp. 271, 351.) Hickes, Browne, and Fleming were all Scholars and Graduates of T.C.D. Baldwin was a Scholar and B.A. of T.C.D., and became Curate of Murragh and of Holy Trinity, Cork. (See Brady's *Records of Cork*, vol. iii., p. 146.) Ford was also a Graduate of T.C.D.

night, brought out a corpse to be interred, which in the day
time they were apprehensive might be arrested for debt, and
for the burial of which he should have a guinea. The grave-
digger alleged he was unequal to the business himself ; upon
which these persons said they would give him half a guinea
for an assistant ; which was agreed to, and the corpse was
accordingly left with the grave-digger. The latter immediately called up an assistant ; but upon an agreement they
determined postponing the business until daylight. When
they arose in the morning, curiosity urged them to open the
coffin, which on so doing—O ! shocking to mention—they
found the body of a man in his clothes, with boots on, and
his throat cut in a most frightful manner. In his pockets
were found six guineas and a watch ; for the property of
which these two persons differed, or else the transaction
would probably never have come to light. The body remains
at the place to be owned, which as yet has not taken place,
nor has anything occurred which can lead to a discovery."

In the same periodical for Dec., 1798 (p. 898), it
is mentioned that—

" The house of one Ennis, a poor farmer at the foot of the
Three Rock Mountain, was lately robbed for the fourth time
since the rebellion broke out. The unfortunate farmer has
been completely dispossessed of his habitation by the last
attack, and forced to take refuge in the house of his land
lord at Dundrum."

At a Vestry held on April 16, 1816, Major
Broome produced a requisition from John Pasley,
Esq. (Coroner of the County of Dublin), that five
guineas should be paid to Doctor Thomas Hewson
for his attendance on an inquest, and opening the
body of Mrs. Browne, who had been murdered by
robbers in the house of Major Broome. The requisition was received, and inquiry was to be made
whether the parish was liable to the charge.

In the *Freeman's Journal* of Feb. 22, 1815, there is an account of the trial of four men—Thomas Markey, Thomas Giffin, Thomas Byrne, and Michael Collins—for the murder of Hannah Browne in the house of her master, William Broome, Esq., at Kilmacud, on the 12th December, 1814. The first three were convicted, and sentenced to be hung. Collins was acquitted.

At a Vestry held on May 27, 1817, Major Broome's claim was again adjourned, and there is no further record respecting it.

Parochial Accounts.

Some curious items appear in the accounts from time to time; and as they are interesting in showing the manners of our ancestors, they are given here.

1793-4	Holly and ivy £0	2	8½
	(This item appears for many years.)		
	Washing surplices 4 times 0	4	4
	Whitening the Church 1	0	0
1797-8	Framing and glazing 2 panes in Church		
	window for letting in air 0	5	5
1800-1	Church hangings and pulpit cushion ... 6	16	6
	Eliza Kennedy for 20 weeks assisting the		
	parish clerk 2	14	8½
1802-3	Eliza Kennedy for 20 Sundays singing		
	at 2s. 8½d. per 2	14	2
1805-6	Velvet pulpit cushion and hangings,		
	covering reading and clerk's desk ... 6	12	0½
1806-7	Anne Mann for her attention to the stove		
	and cleaning the church 2	5	6
	8 washings of surplices 0	8	8
	By making an additional surplice ... 0	6	6
1816-17	By 4 lb. candles to wake Murphy and		
	Wynn 0	4	0
	Washing surplices 14 times at 1s. 1d. ... 0	15	2

Pound.

In the accounts for 1792 the following item appears :—

Cash paid Mr. Ely in full for a pound   ...   £12 12 9

At the Easter Vestry, April 2, 1793, a pound-keeper was appointed.

In the year 1804 this extraordinary minute appears in the Vestry Book:—

"At a Vestry held on April 29, for the purpose of taking into consideration the enormity of cutting the pound gate on the night of the 24th April, and feloniously taking the cattle of —— Atkins, Donnybrook, that were impounded for trespass on the lands of Mt. Pleasant by some evil-minded person or persons, Now, in order to bring to condign punishment the perpetrator or perpetrators of the above outrage, We, the undersigned, do offer as a Reward the sums annexed to our respective names to any person or persons that will give information and prosecute to conviction the person or persons concerned in committing said outrage."

There are no sums or names annexed.

A pound-keeper was appointed annually at the Easter Vestry, from 1812 to 1822, and at a Vestry held on March 23, 1818, it was resolved that—

"Mr. Walsh be allowed to change the 'scite' for the parish pound, he undertaking to build a new one in all respects equal to the present pound."

At a Vestry held on Nov. 16, 1829, there was a contested election for the office of pound-keeper, and a ballot was taken. There were two candidates; one received 12 votes, and the other 8 votes.

Profanation of the Sabbath.

At a Vestry held on March 9, 1829, to appoint overseers to assist the churchwardens and civil officers in preventing the profanation of the Sabbath, fourteen leading parishioners were nominated under 55 Geo. III., chap. 19, and 100 copies of their nomination were ordered to be printed and served in all the public-houses, and also posted in the most conspicuous places, in the parish. A report of the houses where spirits were retailed was also ordered to be made to the Churchwardens every month, in order that they might see how they were conducted.

At a Vestry held on April 13, 1830, the Churchwardens were requested to put their powers in force in restraining the profanation of the Sabbath.

Railway.

The most important event which perhaps ever occurred in the history of the Parish, though probably its full significance was not realized at the time, was the establishment of railway communication with Dublin. The construction of a line which would touch Dundrum had been long in contemplation—originally by a company formed to promote a line called the Dundrum and Rathfarnham Railway, which was afterwards merged in the Dublin and Wicklow scheme—but had been delayed from various causes. Finally, however, the railway from Harcourt Street to Bray was opened on Monday, July 10, 1854. The *Dublin Evening Post* of July 11, in giving an account of a private inspection of the line, says—

"A rich treat was on Saturday afforded to the share-holders of the Dublin and Wicklow Railway and their friends, who through the medium of special trains were conveyed along the line to Bray, and thus enabled to witness the complete manner in which the works have been executed. . . . The trains started from the new terminus, Harcourt Road, at 12, 2, and 4 p.m., occupying about half-an-hour in running down to the other end of the line, and returned to town at 6 and 8 p.m. Each train conveyed upwards of 200 persons. . . . At the Dundrum station, although not yet entirely completed, the evidences of attention to the comfort of the public, as well as to the details of the building, are observable."

An advertisement in *Saunders' News-Letter* of July 15 gives information as to the train accommodation which was then provided—

"*Dublin and Wicklow Railway.*

"The above line is now open for Passenger Traffic between Dublin (Harcourt Road) and Bray. Trains calling at Dundrum, Stillorgan, Carrickmines, and Shankill will run as follows :—

From Bray at 7, 9, 11, 2, 4, and 7 o'clock.
From Dublin at 8, 10, 1, 3, 5, and 8 o'clock."

Roads.

At the end of the last century the approaches to Dundrum from Dublin were the same as those at the time of the Down Survey (p. 21), by a bridge at Clonskeagh, and by the bridge now known as Classon's* Bridge. The latter was probably the

---

* Mr. Classon is mentioned in the applotments from 1794 to 1796 as residing in the townland of Rathmines.

one principally used; the route to Powerscourt given in the *Post-Chaise Companion* of 1788 is by it and on through Churchtown. There was also a ford at Milltown, which appears, from the following paragraph taken from the *Hibernian Magazine* for 1782, p. 551, to have been a source of danger to incautious travellers :—

"In the heavy rain last night [Oct. 10], as Mr. Clarke, Steward to the House of Industry, was returning home on horseback, about 9 o'clock, from Dundrum, in crossing the river at Milltown, the flood was so violent that it threw him off his horse, and he was unfortunately drowned. It is somewhat remarkable that his daughter and only child was drowned in the same river about twelve months ago."

The records of the proceedings of the Grand Jury are extant from 1807, and there is also in their possession a fine map made on a very large scale *circa* 1820 ; from these it appears that the roads kept in order by the County in Taney Parish at the commencement of this century were nearly the same as at present—the Roebuck Road, with its two branches, Foster's Avenue, Mount Anville Hill Road, Drummartin Road, Taney Hill Road (then called Hag Lane, and ending at a point opposite the Churchtown Road, from whence it was diverted at the time of the construction of the railway), Kilmacud Road, the Main Road,* Birds' Avenue, Ballinteer Road (the bridges on which were called the Rock Tavern Bridge and Towers'† Bridge), and

* This road then branched off at a point below Windy Arbour to Classon's Bridge.

† Mr. James Towers is mentioned in the applotments from 1794 to 1801 as residing in Dundrum.

the Churchtown Road. They were then, however, in a very unsafe condition, and there are frequent presentments to take down hills " to make it easy and safe for passengers to pass over same," and to build walls " to prevent carriages and passengers falling into dangerous precipices."

At Easter Term, 1807, a presentment was made to build a new bridge at Clonskeagh at a cost of £535 19s. 6d.; and at Michaelmas Term, 1816, a presentment was passed to build the present bridge at Milltown at a cost of £1,662 6s.

Seats in the Parish at the beginning of the century.

The parish has undergone great alterations during the last hundred years. At the end of the eighteenth century it was only emerging from what may be called its prairie condition, and farms were gradually being changed into the well-kept places surrounded by high walls and trees which are now so remarkable a characteristic of the neighbourhood.*

It appears from the Registry of Trees, kept by the Clerk of the Peace, under the provision of an

* Archbishop Whately's friend, Mr. Senior, writing in 1852 of the drive from Dublin to Redesdale, in the parish of Stillorgan, said : " Nature meant the road to be an open terrace between the sea and the mountain. Man has made it a dirty lane, twisting between high walls. Almost all the country near Dublin is cut into squares, each with its wall without and its fringe of trees within ; merely ugly in summer, but damp and unwholesome in winter."—*Life of Richard Whately*, p. 267.

Act passed in 1765,* that vast plantations of beech, ash, elm, sycamore, oak, and other trees were made by the residents about the beginning of this century. Amongst those who registered trees we find—in Dundrum, Alderman Hutton (4,182), Mr. Randle MacDonnell (24,707), and Mr. John Walsh (3,400) ; in Ballinteer, Mr. Richard Johnston (10,596), and Mr. Valentine Dunn ; in Ballaly, Mr. James Towers (909) and Mr. Robert Turbett; in Roebuck, Mr. Thomas Leland; in Friarsland, Mr. Thomas Wilson ; in Churchtown, Mr. Townsend Sinnett, and Mr. William Corbett; and in Drummartin, Mr. William Scott.†

There were then very few places which presented any feature worthy of notice; much information about the seats in the County Dublin at that time is to be found in Archer's *Survey of the County Dublin* (Dub., 1801), and in Dutton's *Observations on Mr. Archer's Survey* (Dub., 1802), but only five places in our parish are mentioned.

Merville is described by Archer as a well laid out demesne, with some timber trees, in good order, and highly cultivated. The gardens were then remarkable for their extensive glass. Dutton, who was a landscape gardener, carried out various improve-

---

* This Act (5 Geo. III., c. 17) enables tenants to claim, at the expiration of the term of their lease, compensation for trees planted and duly registered by them.

† The only entry in our own day is the registration by the Right Hon. Christopher Palles, Lord Chief Baron of the Exchequer, of a plantation in the grounds of Mount Anville Park.

ments for Sir Thomas Lighton, "who was ever ready to try experiments with great public spirit," and gives a curious account of breaking up an avenue by means of a plough drawn by four mules. He mentions that Sir Thomas had erected a comfortable and highly ornamental range of cottages for his workmen, but observes that they were usually kept in a very filthy state.

Mount Merrion is described as an excellent house, with a well-wooded demesne and handsome gardens.

Roebuck Castle, then recently purchased by Mr. James Crofton (see p. 183), is mentioned as a fine old castle, with a small demesne and good gardens.

Belfield, Stillorgan Road, had just been built by a Mr. Ambrose Moore. Archer says that it promises to be a handsome seat; but Dutton does not join in this commendation, and says that there is no space left for planting out the garden wall—in which time has shown he was mistaken—and complains of the "steep zigzag turn" on the avenue. Probably these remarks would not have been necessary if Dutton's services had been retained by Mr. Moore.

Milltown, the seat of Judge Chamberlain, is described as a capital house, pleasantly situated, with a beautiful small demesne and good gardens.

Services.

Some seventy years ago service seems to have depended on fine weather, for it is noted in the Vestry Book, in connection with giving notices of Vestries, that on Jan. 10, 1819, there was "no service ; wet day," and also on Feb. 21 in the same year a similar entry was made.

Stocks.

At a Vestry held on May 17, 1796, the Churchwardens were empowered and authorized to provide and erect a pair of stocks for punishment of offenders, to be charged to the " parish accompts," and to be erected in the most suitable position.

In the accounts for 1796-7 the following items appear :—

Paid sundries for Stocks—

B. M'Clune for Timber ... £1 17 3		
L. Kearney for Smith's Work ... 0 4 4		
Carriage of Timber 0 2 2		
Padlock and 3 Keys 0 7 0½		
Carpenter's Work and Painting 1 14 1½		
———4 4 11		
John Wright for Masonry ... 1 0 0		
£5 4 11		

Vestry Books.

The custody of these books seems to have been a disputed point in 1818, in consequence of the proceedings at the meeting about the Window Tax (*q. v.*), and Dr. Radcliff, the Vicar-General, was consulted as to who had a right to keep them. His opinion, which cost the parish £1 19s. 3d., was to the following effect :—

" If there be a Vestry Clerk, he has a right to the custody of the Vestry Books; if there be not, the Churchwardens, in whom all the personal goods of the Parish are vested, have a right to the custody until the Vestry Clerk shall be appointed.

" J. RADCLIFF.

" *March* 28, 1818."

Window Tax.

Meetings for the purpose of securing a repeal of this tax, which was assessed according to the number and size of the windows in the house, and which had been imposed by an Act of the Irish Parliament in 1799 (which was not finally repealed until 1879), were held in the various Dublin parishes during the years 1817-18. In moving a motion on the subject, which was defeated, in the House of Commons on April 21, 1818, Mr. Robert Shaw, Member for Dublin, said that the tax was obnoxious to the citizens of Dublin for its unequal pressure, the inquisitorial nature of its levy, and the ruinous consequences resulting to the health of the City.—*Annual Register*, vol. lx., p. 119. In Taney the question arose in connection with the appointment of valuators, and seems to have given rise to some difference of opinion at the Vestry. The proceedings are thus recorded in the minutes :—

" At a meeting held on Monday, October 6, 1817, for the purpose of appointing valuators according to the request of the Chief Commissioner of Excise, it was resolved :—

" That the Window Tax having been originally proposed to Parliament by the Minister of the Crown as a war tax, to subsist during the war and no longer, we claim it as a right from the Crown, now that the war is happily and honorably terminated, to redeem its pledge so solemnly given to the Irish Parliament, under the faith of which we have hitherto patiently borne a heavy and oppressive tax.

" That relying on the justice of the Crown, and the wisdom of Parliament to keep faith with the people, we do reject the proposed commutation, preferring even to bear those ills we have than to fly to others that we know not of.

"That these resolutions be respectfully communicated to Mr. Hawthorne as our opinion upon his letter, and that they be also published in the *Freeman's Journal* and the *Correspondent* papers.

"(Signed)   RICHARD RYAN, L. Curate."

The following proceedings are recorded on a sheet of paper fastened into the minute book :—

"The Rev. Mr. Ryan having left the chair, and the Churchwarden being called thereto—

"Resolved—That the thanks of this meeting be given to the Rev. Mr. Ryan for his upright and independent conduct in the chair.

"Resolved—That the following gentlemen be appointed a committee for this parish to communicate and co-operate with our fellow-citizens of the metropolis in petitioning Parliament for a Repeal of the Window Tax—viz., Mr. Hime, Mr. Dillon, Mr. Turbett, Mr. Minchin, Mr. John Power, and Mr. M'Dermott, and that these resolutions be published along with the other resolutions of this parish.

"(Signed)   GEO. THOMPSON.

"Resolved—That the thanks of this meeting be given to Mr. Thompson, our Churchwarden, for his spirited and proper conduct in the chair.

H. MINCHIN.

"Note.—The proceedings mentioned above were not passed at a Vestry, and were inserted thus in this book without my knowledge several days after.

"(Signed)   RICHARD RYAN, L. Curate."

At a meeting on October 13, 1817, it was resolved unanimously—

"That the thanks of this parish are justly due and are hereby given to Charles Stewart Hawthorne, Esq., first Commissioner of Ireland's Excise and Taxes, for the manly,

candid, and constitutional manner in which he sought th
free and unbias'd opinion of the People of Ireland on th
proposition for commuting a proportion of the Window Ta
for a Rent or House tax, and also for his polite and gentle
manlike attention to our application to him for explanatio:
on the subject, and that this resolution be communicated t
Mr. Hawthorne by our Churchwardens in the most respect
ful manner.

"That the anonymous publication in the *Hibernia:*
Journal of the 10th instant (and since republished in othe
newspapers), purporting to be a statement of the proceeding
of our Vestry on Monday last on the subject of the sai
commutation, is an insidious and malignant misrepresenta
tion of the proceedings of this parish on that occasion
calculated to deceive His Majesty's Minister in his endeavou:
to collect the unbiased sense of the people.

"That the ancient mode of summoning Vestries in thi
parish has been by written notice delivered at the houses o
the resident landholders, in addition to the usual notice i:
church, and that the same be from henceforth continued.

(Note.—This not to be published in the newspapers.)

"That the foregoing resolution, together with the resolu
tion of Monday last, be published in the *Correspondent* and
Freeman's Journal.

"(Signed)   RICHARD RYAN, L. Curate."

The volume of the *Hibernian Journal* for 1817 is
in the National Library. The report of the meeting
on Oct. 6 is very full, and extends to several
columns.

APPENDIX A.

ORDER OF THE PRIVY COUNCIL SEVERING TANEY AND
RATHFARNHAM FROM THE CORPS OF THE ARCHDEACON
OF DUBLIN.

By the Lord Lieutenant and Council of Ireland.

CLARENDON,

WHEREAS the Archdeaconry of Dublin being now vacant,
it is expedient that the Parishes of Taney and Rathfarnham, part of the corps of the Archdeaconry, should be
disappropriated and disunited therefrom:

Now we, the Lord Lieutenant and Council, by virtue of the
powers vested in us by the statutes in that case made and
provided, do order and direct that the said Parishes or
Vicarages of Taney and Rathfarnham be, and the same are,
hereby severally disappropriated, disunited, and divested
from and out of the said Archdeaconry, and that the said
Parishes or Vicarages respectively shall be and become
separate and distinct Parishes for ever, with all Parochial
rights, and that the residue of the corps of the said Archdeaconry as heretofore constituted shall henceforward form
and constitute the new corps of the said Archdeaconry for
ever.

Given at the Council Chamber in
Dublin, the 5th day of July,
1851.

MAZIERE BRADY, C.
THOS. MEATH.
CLONCURRY.
F. BLACKBURNE.
E. BLAKENEY.
K. KEATINGE.
RICHD. W. GREENE.

APPENDIX B.

CHURCH PLATE, REGISTERS, &c.

Church Plate.

The Plate consists of two Chalices, two Patens, and a Flagon. The following are the inscriptions :—

Chalice (1.)—

DEO OPT. MAX.
TRI-UNI
in usum S. CŒNÆ DOM. Sacramenti
in Ecclesiâ Parochiali TACHNENSI
nunc denuo sumptibus pub. extructâ
participum
D.D.D.
ISAACUS MANN
Archidiac. Dubl.
MDCCLX.

Chalice (2.)*—
The gift of Henry Dawson, Esq.—Taney Parish, 1825.

Paten (1.)—

DEO OPT. MAX.
TRI-UNI
D.D.D.
ISAACUS MANN
Archidiac. Dubl.
MDCCLX.

Paten (2.)—
Tawney Church, 1835.
Flagon—Modern, and bears no inscription.

* At a Vestry on May 10, 1826, a vote of thanks was passed to H. Dawson, Esq., for his very liberal donation of a silver cup for the use of the Parish.

Registers.

Book 1*—Baptisms	...	...	1791 to 1835.
„ Marriages	...	...	1795 to 1835.
„ Burials	...	...	1814 to 1835.
„ 2 — Baptisms	...	...	1835 to 1867.
„ Marriages	...	...	1835 to 1845.
„ Burials	...	...	1835 to 1857.
„ 3 — Baptisms	...	...	1867 to 1895.
„ 4 — Marriages	...	...	1845 to 1875.
„ 5 — „	...	...	1875 to 1890.
„ 6 — „	...	...	1890 to 1895.
„ 7 — Burials	...	...	1857 to 1866.
„ 8 — „	...	...	1866 to 1883.
„ 9 — „	...	...	1883 to 1895.

Vestry Books.

Book 1	...	...	...	1792 to 1813.
„ 2	...	...	...	1813 to 1830.
„ 3	...	...	...	1830 to 1847.
„ 4	...	...	...	1847 to 1861.
„ 5	...	...	...	1861 to 1895.

* The Parochial Returns for Taney, which were furnished to the Archbishop at the annual Visitation, are in the Public Record Office, and contain a complete list of the Births, Marriages, and Burials from the year 1788.

APPENDIX C.

TABLE OF FEES
TANEY PARISH.
(In the Archdeaconry of Dublin.)
A TABLE OF FEES FOR 1814, &c., &c., &c.

	£	s.	d.
Marriages by License—			
To the Minister...	0	10	0
To the Clerk ...	0	5	0
To the Sexton ...	0	1	0
Marriages by Publication—			
To the Minister ...	0	5	0
To the Clerk ...	0	2	6
To ditto for publication ...	0	1	0
To the Sexton ...	0	1	0
Churching of Women—			
To the Minister...	0	2	6
To the Clerk ...	0	1	3
To the Sexton ...	0	0	6
Burials in the Chancel—			
To the Church-			
wardens for the			
use of the parish	10	0	0
To the Minister for			
vault ...	5	0	0
To ditto for interring	0	6	0
To the Clerk ...	0	5	0
To the Sexton ...	0	5	0
Burials in Tombs or Vaults—			
To the Minister ...	5	0	0
To the Clerk ...	0	2	6
To the Sexton ...	0	3	4

	£	s.	d.
Burials in the Church—			
To the Church-			
wardens for the			
use of the parish	10	0	0
To the Minister...	0	6	0
To the Clerk ...	0	5	0
To the Sexton ...	0	6	0
Burials of Parishioners in the Churchyard—			
To the Minister...	0	2	6
To the Clerk ...	0	1	3
To the Sexton ...	0	1	0
Burials of those who live out of the parish—			
To the Minister ...	0	6	0
To the Church-			
wardens for the			
use of the parish	0	3	4
To the Clerk ...	0	2	6
To the Sexton ...	0	1	6
Funerals going out of the parish—			
To the Minister...	0	2	6
To the Clerk ...	0	1	3
To the Sexton ...	0	1	0
To ditto for passing bell ...	0	1	0

Palls—
To the Minister
for a velvet pall 0 13 4
To ditto for a
child's do. ... 0 6 8
Cloth or Plush
Pall ... 0 6 8

Monuments in the
Church—
To the Minister
for erecting a
Monument in
the Church ...10 0 0
To the Parish
Clerk ... 3 0 0
To the ditto Sexton 1 14 1½

Tombs, Vaults, or
Monuments in
the Churchyard—
To the Minister
for erecting a
Tomb, Vault, or
Monument of
the ordinary
dimensions ... 5 0 0
To the Parish
Clerk ... 2 10 0
To the ditto Sexton 1 2 9

Flat Stone—
To the Minister... 5 0 0
To the Clerk ... 0 10 10
To the Sexton ... 0 4 4

Head Stone—
To the Minister... 1 3 0
To the Clerk ... 0 5 5
To the Sexton ... 0 4 4

Funeral Desk Prayers in
the Church—
To the Minister
for a velvet pall
on the desk or
pulpit, in addition to the fee
for a pall in
parish ... 0 10 0
To the Minister
for desk prayers
in addition to
the Burial Fees 0 6 6
To the Parish
Clerk ... 0 5 5
To the Organist... 0 5 5
To the Sexton ... 0 2 6

Registry—
To the Vestry Clerk
for searching the
Registry Book 0 2 8½
To ditto for a Certificate ... 0 5 5
To ditto for Registering Seats
or Pews in the
Church Books 0 10 10
To the Parish
Clerk for Easter
Dues, ninepence
per house ... 0 0 9
To the Beadle for
attending Funerals out of the
parish ... 0 2 2
To ditto in the
parish ... 0 1 1
To the Sexton for
a passing bell... 0 1 0

(Signed)

WM. RIDGEWAY. } Church-
GEO. THOMPSON. } wardens.

APPENDIX D.

PURCHASERS OF PEW SITES, &C.

No. of Pew.	Purchasers at the Auction held on October 24th, 1816.	Price of Site.			Expense of Carpenters' Work.		
		£	s.	d.	£	s.	d.
1	Reserved for Chief Justice Downes		...		41	8	6
2	Reserved for Alderman Hone		...		19	9	2
3	John Busby	14	0	0	19	9	2
4	Daniel Kinahan	20	5	0	19	9	2
5	Robert Turbett	18	5	0	19	1	10
6	James Lyne	13	15	0	19	3	7
7	Reserved for Parish ...	—			—		
8	,, ,, ...	—			—		
9	,, for Rector and Church-wardens	—			—		
10	George Thompson	17	5	0	19	9	2
11	Solomon Richards	17	5	0	19	9	2
12	John White	17	5	0	19	9	2
13	Samuel Scott	15	0	0	19	3	7
14	Joseph M'Dermott	10	0	0	19	3	7
15	Reserved for Parish ...	—			—		
16	,, ,, ...	—			—		
17		—			19	14	7
18	William Scott	5	0	0	18	4	10½
19	Daniel Beere	10	5	0	18	4	10½
20	James Crofton	17	5	0	23	8	6
21	Richard Verschoyle ...	11	15	0	23	5	4
22	Reserved for Parish ...	—			—		
23	,, ,, ...	—			—		
24	,, ,, ...	—			—		
25							
26	Humphrey Minchin ..	6	10	0	19	8	6
27	William Ridgeway	9	0	0	19	5	0
28	Robert Blake	11	15	0	24	14	6½
29	William Wood	10	10	0	25	8	6
30	Reserved for John Giffard ..	—			19	12	5
31	Richard Ryan, passed to Alderman Exshaw	8	10	0	19	17	6½
32					18	12	1

No. of Pew.	Purchasers at the Auction held on October 24th, 1816.	Price of Site.			Expense of Carpenters' Work.		
		£	s.	d.	£	s.	d.
	GALLERY (North).						
1	James Lafarelle	24	10	0	34	15	1½
2	Humphrey Minchin ...	10	0	0	23	2	3
3	John M'Kay	20	0	0	32	16	7½
4	Walter Bourne	20	5	0	32	18	0½
5	William Ball	20	15	0	32	18	0½
6	Thomas Cusack	23	5	0	32	16	7½
7	Charles Philip Moore ...	9	0	0	23	2	3
8	George Thompson	23	5	0	34	15	1½
		384	10	0	731	16	11
	SOUTH GALLERY. Erected in 1833.	Subscription.					
1	Judge Burton	40	0	0	—		
2	Mr. Deane	20	0	0	—		
3	Free Sittings	—			—		
4	„	—			—		
5	„	—			—		
6⎱ 7⎰	Lady Harty	40	0	0	—		
	„	—			—		
8	Free Sittings	—			—		
9⎱ 10⎰	H. Williams	40	0	0	—		
	„	—			—		
11	Thomas Leland	40	0	0	—		
12	Mr. M'Caskey	15	0	0	—		
13	Free Sittings	—			—		
14	„	—			—		
	Additional subscriptions and interest	10	9	3	—		
		205	9	3			

APPENDIX E.

ESTIMATE FOR BUILDING TANEY CHURCH.

CHURCH.

	£	s.	d.	£	s.	d.
Mason Work	2,350	15	1			
Carpenters' Work	2,138	14	5			
Plaisterers' Work	298	4	0			
Stone-Cutters' Work	238	14	0			
Glaziers' and Painters' Work ...	80	0	0			
Carvers' Work	28	10	11			
Slaters' Work	136	6	10			
Plumbers' Work	23	11	3			
Ironmongers' Work	31	19	10			
Erecting Stoves	60	0	0			
Incidentals	100	0	0			
Architect's charge	274	16	0			
				5,761	12	4

SPIRE.

	£	s.	d.	£	s.	d.
A Bath Stone Spire, 64 feet high, 6 inches thick	320	0	0			
Ornament at top	25	0	0			
Architect's charge	17	5	0			
				362	5	0
One large and one small Bell, including wheels, mounting, &c.				136	0	0
A large Clock, Dials, &c.				110	0	0
Surrounding Walls				190	0	0
Gate Entrance and Iron Railing ...				300	0	0
Forming and Gravelling Ground ...				100	0	0
Cash paid by Architect for Advertising ...				10	12	5
				£6,970	9	9

SUPPLEMENTAL NOTES.

THE PALE (p. 8).

D R. STOKES has kindly supplemented the description of the Pale by the following additional particulars and graphic sketch of an invasion by the Irish :—

"The Pale was a fence or bank, such as is commonly called a double ditch, ten or twelve feet high, made of earth and stone faced externally with a thick fence of bushes, and broad enough on the top for two persons to walk thereon. From Clongowes Wood College to the village of Clane a pathway is still carried along a portion of the original Pale there remaining. This double ditch did not entirely surround the four Pale counties—Dublin, Kildare, Meath, and Louth—as the makers of it availed themselves of every natural object—a river, lake, or wood—which served the same purpose; for we must ever remember that the Pale was not to keep the wild Irish out—a fence ten feet high could scarcely avail much in that way with bare-footed and bare-legged Celtic outlaws accustomed to climb like monkeys—but rather to keep the cattle of the Pale inside that boundary, and stop them for a little, so as to give the attacked and alarmed inhabitants time to collect their retainers and pursue the invaders. Let us throw ourselves back mentally to the year 1500, and imagine an invasion of the O'Byrnes or O'Tooles in a dark November night. They have swept down from the neighbourhood of Lough Bray, and have spread far and wide over the fields from Dolphin's Barn to Clondalkin, gathering as quietly and quickly as they can all the cattle there feeding. Suddenly a warder on Tallaght Castle gives the signal announcing that the Irish enemy are inside the Pale, and lights his beacon,

which is repeated from Tymon, Drimnagh, Baggotrath,
Rathmines, and dozens of other castles. All the English
assemble with their retainers at the indicated points of
attack, and follow the flying foe, who drive their prey before
them as quickly as they can. But then, flying to their native
haunts, they come straight up against this double ditch,
which the cattle refuse to mount. Meanwhile the pitiless
foe are behind, growing in numbers as they advance; and
knowing well the long rope and short shrift which await
him, the Irishman makes his escape across the ditch, leaving
the cattle behind. And thus the Pale served its purpose."

ANCIENT DEEDS (p. 12).

Among the deeds in the *Liber Niger* is one from Walter
the Miller confirming to William of Winchester the lands of
Tirknoc (Tiknock) near the Dodder (fol. 26), the rent to be
a pair of white gloves; and there is also a memorandum of
eighty-five acres of land at Taney, granted by Archbishop
Alexander de Bicknor (1317-49) to Edmund Hacket (fol. 27).
This land was in the manor of St. Sepulchre; sixty acres lay
between Roebuck and the king's highway, and extended from
Dundrum to Bolie (Farranboley); and twenty-five acres extended into the lands of Galfridi de Bret of Rathfarnham.
In 1325, at an inquiry held on the request of John Hacket,
it was proved that three acres of land near "Renville Parkes"
did not belong to the Archbishop of Dublin, but were part
of the holding given by Edmund Hacket to the said John
Hacket. In a subsequent note it appears that in 1317 this
land was in the occupation of Thomas Fitzwilliam, who had
succeeded William Runncoile (fol. 571).

WILLIAM POWER (p. 13).

His pension, in lieu of all his endowments, was £40 per
annum (8th Report of Deputy Keeper of Records in Ireland,

Fiant No. 94), which would be equal to about £400 a year of our money.

ARCHBOLDS (pp. 17, 18, 27, 28).

Amongst the Fiants of Elizabeth is a pardon granted in 1584 to "Piers, son of Rich. Archbold of Kilmacod, gent." (Fiant 4,405). The family was one of the oldest in the Co. Dublin, and the name appears frequently in the Fiants and Close Rolls. The earliest mention of the name which we have found is in Gilbert's *Chartularies of St. Mary's Abbey* (vol. i., preface xxviii., and pp. 279, 333), which shows that the Archbolds were living at Rochestown about the year 1300. In 1408 John Archbold was examined as to the boundaries of the holding of the Abbey at Kilternan, and stated that he was born at Rochestown, and was then eighty years of age. In the reign of Henry VIII. we find Archbolds of Moche Bree and Lytle Bree ; in the reign of Edward VI., Archbolds of Glasmokrey, Kylbarroke, and Loughanston ; in the reign of Philip and Mary, Archbolds of Ballynloghan and Carrickmayne ; and in the reign of Elizabeth, Archbolds of Tymolenbeg, Kynleston, Ballerahin, and many other places. (See Reports of Deputy Keeper of Records in Ireland and Calendar of Patent and Close Rolls of Chancery in Ireland.)

In B. L. G., 1846, under Archbold of Davidstown, it is mentioned that Richard Archbold of Eadestown *m.* Mary, dau. of Matthew Ball, grandson of Nicholas Ball, Mayor of Dublin in 1582. Burke says he had a son "Garret;" so probably in Tomb II. we should have supplied "mother" instead of "wife."

HOUSEHOLDERS IN 1664 (p. 22).

The Hearth Money Returns are in the Public Record Office. The number of inhabitants in the parish about that time can, however, be obtained with more accuracy in a census

of 1659—a copy of which is preserved in the Royal Irish
Academy. It gives the numbers as follows:—

			No. of People.	English.	Irish.
Dondrom	...	...	47	14	33
Titnocke	...	...	15	—	15
Churchtowne	...	...	7	2	5
Moltyanstowne	...	...	18	7	11
Rabucke and Owenstowne	...		30	5	25
Rabucke	...	...	19	2	17
Kilmacudd	...	...	13	11	2
Balacoly	...	...	18	7	11
			167	48	119

JOHN DUNTON (p. 22).

In that most comprehensive of modern works, the *Dictionary of National Biography* (vol. xvi., p. 236), there is a biography of Dunton by the editor, Leslie Stephen, Esq.

DUNDRUM CASTLE (p. 23).

Through the kindness of Austin Damer Cooper, Esq., J.P., of Drumnigh, Co. Dublin, we have had an opportunity of examining the MS. notes made by his grandfather, Austin Cooper, Esq., who was an antiquary and patron of art in the last century, of various places of interest in the Co. Dublin. He thus describes Dundrum Castle, the date of his visit being April 16, 1780:—"The Castle of Dundrum, three miles S. of Dublin, is inhabited, and in excellent repair; at the N.E. end of it are the remains of a much older building than the present castle, which is visibly a modern addition in comparison to the old mansion. There is but very little of this ancient part remaining; some of the walls are six feet thick; about the castle are several traces of old walls, avenues, &c., proving it to have been once a very complete habitation. The whole is on the summit of a small hill, surrounded with ash trees, with a handsome rivulet running at its foot, but this shelter will soon be removed, as they are cutting away the trees."

Gabriel Beranger, a well-known artist in Dublin at the close of the last century, made three sketches of the castle, and describes it as very picturesque. He says the principal entrance was from the courtyard by a stone stairs. (See Appendix to Sir William Wilde's *Memoirs of Gabriel Beranger.*)

JAMES II. (p. 24).

In September, 1892, there was a very large find of brass money of this monarch's reign on the land of James Sheill, Esq., in the townland of Kingstown. (See *Journal of the Royal Society of Antiquaries of Ireland,* 1893, p. 164.)

WILLIAM BALL (p. 29).

Mr. Ball was one of the sub-commissioners employed in collating the records of Ireland, and prepared an authentic edition of the Irish Statutes. (See 2nd Report of the Commissioners of Records of Ireland, 1810-15.) Amongst his father's pupils were Henry Grattan and John FitzGibbon, afterwards Earl of Clare. (See *Irish Builder,* August 15, 1895, p. 194.)

MONKSTOWN CHURCH (p. 54).

In the paragraph in which this church is mentioned "1844" should read "1814." The present church was not built until 1832, and from a view of Old Monkstown Church in the *Journal of the Royal Society of Antiquaries of Ireland* for March, 1895, it will be seen that its design was similar to that of Taney Church as originally erected.

SIR THOMAS LIGHTON (p. 125).

In a series of articles on the Old Dublin Bankers, by C. M. Tenison, Esq., M.R.I.A., which has recently appeared in the

R

Journal of the Cork Historical and Archæological Society,
there is a short account of Lighton and Shaw's Bank (Feb.,
1895, p. 72). In its earliest years it had the largest circula-
tion of any of the Dublin banks; and in 1836 it wás merged
into the Royal Bank of Ireland, which now occupies its offices.
Sir Thomas Lighton was amongst those who voted against
the Union. His daus. Anne and Charlotte were *bapt.* in T.C.

ISAAC WILLIAM USHER (p. 149).

The following announcement appeared in the Dublin papers
in July, 1895 :—" On the 6th July, by special licence, at
Laurel Lodge, Dundrum, by the Rev. Edward Carroll, Isaac
William Usher, Surgeon, Tudor House, Dundrum, to Rosie,
youngest daughter of the late Captain Meyler, Dundrum
House."

RIGHT HON. WILLIAM BROOKE (pp. 159, 160).

Owing to an accidental transposition of the type the date
of the death of Master Brooke's first wife has been placed
after her mother's name.

Mrs. Bradford, mother of Master Brooke's second wife,
edited the *Memoirs of the Princess Daschkaw* (published by
Colburn in 1840), from whom Mrs. Brooke got the name.
The Princess Daschkaw was lady-in-waiting to Catherine II.
of Russia; she travelled with her son throughout Europe,
and came to Dublin. She was the lion of Dublin society in
1779, when she composed the music for a hymn sung at the
Magdalen Chapel in aid of a collection for that charity. She
was a great friend of Lady Arabella Denny, who then resided
at Lisaniskea, Blackrock, where the Princess planted two
ilex trees, which still flourish there. On this visit she be
came acquainted with Mr. Wilmot, and subsequently invited
his daughter to pay her a visit on her Russian estate; there
Miss Wilmot remained several years. On her return she
married the Rev. Mr. Bradford, the father-in-law of Mastei
Brooke.

RIGHT HON. ANTHONY FOSTER (pp. 168, 169, 170).

His great-great-grandson, James Foster Vesey Fitzgerald, Esq., supplies the following additional information:—"There can be no doubt that Merville was built by Chief Baron Foster. It was built to gratify his second wife, a very witty and capricious lady, which were family characteristics of the Burgh ladies. The country round Merville was quite wild and open at that time; and one day, while she was out driving, she stopped where Merville now stands, and declared she would have her house built there. The Chief Baron intended building a house at Collon; but in obedience to his wife, he built Merville instead. He was one of the founders of the Royal Dublin Society. He was distinguished for his impartial administration of the law, and steadily refused to admit Francis Higgins, the Sham Squire, to practise as an attorney in his court, characterizing his repeated attempts as 'impudence,' and threatening a committal to Newgate if repeated." (Fitzpatrick's *Sham Squire*, p. 21.)

ROEBUCK CASTLE (p. 183).

Mr. Austin Cooper (see p. 240) thus describes the castle on March 25, 1781:—"At Rawbuck near Merrion stands a large castle in the shape of an L. Part of it has a slated roof, and is used for sundry purposes by a farmer who has a snug house there. I could not see the inside. In the window over the gate, N. W. angle, is a stone whereon are the arms of the Trimblestown family, who are owners hereof and a large estate thereabouts. I suppose it was built by some of their ancestors. On it are the letters R. B. A. F., and on one side Robart."

ROADS (p. 220).

In the Royal Irish Academy there is a most interesting map, on a large scale, of the County Dublin, dated 1799.

TIPPERSTOWN AND MULCHANSTOWN (p. 19).

These townlands are now in the Parish of Kill, and not in the Parish of Stillorgan.

INDEX.

C. W. Gibbs, Printer, Dublin.